NOLO *and* USA TODAY

For more than 40 years, Nolo has been helping ordinary folks who want to answer their legal questions, create their own documents, or work with a lawyer more efficiently. Nolo.com provides quick information about wills, house buying, credit repair, starting a business—and just about anything else that's affected by the law. It's packed with free articles, legal updates, resources, and a complete catalog of Nolo books and software.

To find out about any important legal changes to this book's contents, go to this book's online companion page at:

www.nolo.com/back-of-book/USFTL.com

USA TODAY
The Nation's Newspaper

USA TODAY, the nation's largest circulation newspaper, was founded in 1982. It has nearly 3.9 million readers daily, making it the most widely read newspaper in the country.

The website usatoday.com adds blogs, interactive graphics, games, travel resources, and trailblazing network journalism, allowing readers to comment on every story.

3RD EDITION

First-Time Landlord

Your Guide to Renting Out a Single-Family Home

Attorney Janet Portman
Ilona Bray, J.D. &
Marcia Stewart

Third Edition	SEPTEMBER 2014
Cover Design	JALEH DOANE
Book Design	SUSAN PUTNEY
Editor	ILONA BRAY
Proofreading	SUSAN CARLSON GREENE
Index	MEDEA MINNICH
Printing	BANG PRINTING

Portman, Janet.
  First-time landlord : your guide to renting out a single-family home / by Attorney Janet Portman, Ilona Bray, J.D., and Marcia Stewart. -- Third edition.
      pages cm
  Includes bibliographical references and index.
  ISBN 978-1-4133-2065-7 (pbk) -- ISBN 978-1-4133-2066-4 (epub ebook)
  1. Real estate management--United States. 2. Rental housing--United States--Management. 3. Landlord and tenant--United States. I. Bray, Ilona M., 1962- II. Stewart, Marcia. III. Title.
  HD1394.5.U6P67 2014
  333.33'8--dc23
                          2014013203

For information on bulk purchases or corporate premium sales, please contact Nolo's Special Sales Department. For academic sales or textbook adoptions, ask for Academic Sales. Call 800-955-4775 or write to Nolo, 950 Parker Street, Berkeley, CA 94710.

Acknowledgments

We couldn't have written this book without the help of many people. Former Nolo legal editor Alayna Schroeder was particularly invaluable.

Also integral were the many first-time or accidental landlords who provided stories from around the country, including Amy Benton, Catherine Berryessa, Danielle Bray, Phil Cunliffe, Dennis Deen, Kathy Eldridge, Lisa Guerin, Stuart Jacobson, Darren Johnston, John Lindenmeyer, Laura Macht, Dan Nguyen, Sergio Raddavero, Amy Shelf, Kyung Yu, Sharon Vallejo, Gordon and Connie Finwall, and others who wished not to be named.

Thanks also go to Nolo authors and editors Steve Fishman and Diana Fitzpatrick for their help regarding the tax deductions associated with owning rental property, Richard Stim for contributions regarding the small business aspects of being a landlord, Mary Randolph and Emily Doskow for their advice on taking title and co-owning rental property, Matt Larson for information on investment considerations when buying rental property, Amy Loftsgordon for legal insights on buying properties undergoing foreclosure, and Stan Jacobsen for research help.

Finally, thanks to the ever-helpful Mike Mansel, certified insurance counselor (see www.publiability.com), for providing tips on converting homeowners' insurance when a home is converted to rental use; and to Michael Molinski, a co-author on the first edition.

None of this information would help anyone if it weren't laid out attractively, so hats off to Nolo's production team for their fine efforts and patience, including Jaleh Doane, Susan Putney, Emily Dunn, and Colleen Cain.

About the Authors

Janet Portman is an attorney and a nationally recognized expert on residential and commercial landlord-tenant law, including legal issues related to courts, landlords and tenants, and neighbor disputes. Portman is the author or co-author of *Every Landlord's Legal Guide, Every Landlord's Guide to Finding Great Tenants, Every Tenant's Legal Guide, Renters' Rights, Negotiate the Best Lease for Your Business, Leases & Rental Agreements, The California Landlord's Law Book: Rights & Responsibilities*, and *California Tenants' Rights*.

Marcia Stewart writes and edits books on landlord-tenant law, real estate, and other consumer issues. She is the co-author of *Nolo's Essential Guide to Buying Your First Home, Every Landlord's Legal Guide, Every Tenant's Legal Guide, Leases & Rental Agreements, Renters' Rights,* and *The Legal Answer Book for Families*.

Ilona Bray is a former attorney turned Nolo author and editor. Among her many popular titles (authored or co-authored) are *Nolo's Essential Guide to Buying Your First Home, Nolo's Essential Guide to Selling Your Home*, and *The Essential Guide for First-Time Homeowners*. Check out her blog on Real Estate Tips for Home Buyers & Sellers at blog.nolo.com/realestate.

Table of Contents

Introduction

1 Will Landlording Bring You Money and Happiness?_____7

2 So Happy Together: Landlording With Family or Friends_____55

3 Preparing and Marketing Your Rental Property_____73

Your First-Time Landlord's Companion

This book is for the millions of people who rent out (or want to rent out) a single-family house or condo, and who might want to do much of the work themselves. You may not consider yourself a "real" landlord—you may not even like the term. Yet you no doubt want to make money and avoid legal hassles.

If you're balancing a day job and a family, taking on the tasks of being a landlord can actually seem overwhelming, especially if it's not a role you actively chose. An increasing number of landlords are the "accidental" sort, having come into their rental property in one of the following ways:

- **Inheritance.** Many people become accidental landlords by inheriting a property (usually a single-family home) from a family member or friend. You may be deciding whether to sell or keep the place.

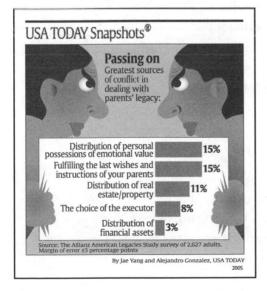

USA TODAY Snapshots®

Passing on
Greatest sources of conflict in dealing with parents' legacy:

Distribution of personal possessions of emotional value	15%
Fulfilling the last wishes and instructions of your parents	15%
Distribution of real estate/property	11%
The choice of the executor	8%
Distribution of financial assets	3%

Source: The Allianz American Legacies Study survey of 2,627 adults. Margin of error ±3 percentage points

By Jae Yang and Alejandro Gonzalez, USA TODAY 2005

- **Divorce.** When couples separate, they often agree—or a court decides—that one or the other gets to keep a property, whether a family home or investment or vacation property. And if two divorcing parties decide to share a property, renting it out can actually help them recover from the financial difficulties of the split, or at least put off selling until the market improves.

- **Trading up or moving out of the area.** Perhaps you need more space or are moving to a new location, but aren't prepared to sell your current home, maybe because the housing market is soft or you're thinking you might move back someday.

- **Trading down or fighting foreclosure.** You may be having trouble paying the mortgage on your current home—but reluctant to sell if prices are down. Renting out your home, while you live somewhere less expensive, can provide the cushion you need until you're ready to move back or sell.

- **Having extra space.** Perhaps your kids have graduated from college or you've divorced and the extra living space within your home could be rented out. Or you might own a duplex or a house with an in-law unit. If there's room for a tenant, you might be looking at a handy way to raise extra cash without much change to your fixed expenses.

- **Caring for a loved one's property.** A close relative or friend may need help renting out a property, for example, because he or she has moved to a nursing home.

- **Temporary move.** If you're taking an overseas sabbatical, serving in the military, or making some other temporary move, you probably don't want your house sitting empty. You can prevent this, and make money, by renting it out.

In any of these situations, you may be wondering whether to sell the property immediately, rent it out temporarily before selling, or turn it into a long-term investment property. This book will start by helping you make that decision, then orient you to all the financial, legal, and practical rules every landlord needs to know. It will also help you if you're thinking of going out to buy real estate for use as a rental (not to "flip" and sell quickly).

We provide nuts-and-bolts information on how to:

- find and choose good tenants (the number one key to your success)—from low-cost ideas for sprucing up a property to writing ads to checking prospective tenants' credit and references

- prepare a solid lease or rental agreement, which will help ensure that tenants pay rent on time, respect your property, and cause you little hassle
- make the most of landlord tax deductions, and manage financial record keeping
- handle repairs and maintenance legally and efficiently—without driving yourself crazy or going broke
- use careful landlord practices and a good insurance policy to stay out of legal trouble (and limit your liability) when it comes to tenant health and safety, discrimination, and crime on the property
- maintain a good relationship with your tenant, or deal with a tenant who's skipping out on the rent, damaging your property, or otherwise causing you sleepless nights
- manage rental property from a distance
- hire a property manager and other professionals as needed
- share the work (and ownership and tax benefits of landlording) with a spouse, relative, or friend—while maintaining your personal relationship
- take over a rental house with tenants in place, and
- get out of the landlording business while maximizing profit and minimizing taxes.

We've tried to concentrate on the things that every first-timer needs to know as well as some tips for people who are in unique situations (for example, if your rental property was recently in foreclosure).

We also include lots of hands-on practical anecdotes and advice from real landlords who've come before you—people like Catherine, who rents out a cottage behind her own house, or Laura, who lives in Washington but rents out properties in three states.

We hope this book provides a valuable companion on your path to being a successful and satisfied rental property owner.

Helpful Nolo Resources for Landlords

For many readers, this book will provide all the information needed to become a first-time landlord. But if you want specific legal forms or detailed legal information for your state, you'll want to check out other Nolo resources.

Let's start with what's available from Nolo for free: Nolo.com offers lots of relevant information, on topics such as property management, fair housing rules, occupancy standards, evictions, landlord liability for crimes and tenant injuries, and real estate investment. Check out Landlords under the Get Informed tab. Here, you'll also find charts with your state laws, including state security deposit limits, required landlord disclosures, tenant privacy, small claims rules, repair responsibilities, termination rules, and much more. Throughout this book, we'll refer to the state-specific information available on Nolo.com.

Nolo also publishes a comprehensive library of books (hard copy and electronic versions) for landlords and rental property owners. Two of Nolo's most popular titles are *Every Landlord's Legal Guide* and *Every Landlord's Tax Deduction Guide*. Nolo's many other books for landlords include California-specific titles, such as *The California Landlord's Law Book: Rights and Responsibilities*. Look to these books for state-by-state legal information, legal forms, checklists, and letters, including a lease and rental agreement, rental application, tenant repair request form, property manager agreement, security deposit itemization, and more.

Nolo also has many single-copy interactive online forms, such as state-specific leases and rental agreements.

For Nolo's full library, see the Landlord-Tenant and Leases & Rental Agreements sections of the Nolo store on www.nolo.com, or call Nolo at 800-728-3555.

Finally, be sure to see the legal updates on this book's companion page (described below).

Get Updates and More at This Book's Companion Page on Nolo.com

When there are important changes to the information in this book, we'll post updates on a dedicated web page:

www.nolo.com/back-of-book/USFTL.html

We call this the book's "companion page." You'll find other useful information on this page, too, such as author blogs.

Will Landlording Bring You Money and Happiness?

Being a landlord may sound appealing in theory—you find a decent tenant, collect a monthly rent check, and celebrate your good fortune. If only it were that simple. Before you start fantasizing about a multiunit building on Park Place, let's look at what it takes to own and manage rental property, and how to decide whether a particular property is actually going to make you money. Along the way, we'll share some helpful advice from other first-time landlords.

Great Things About Being a Landlord

Owning rental property offers both financial and lifestyle benefits. As Laura, a landlord with properties in Washington, Nevada, and Florida, says, "I like people and the feeling that I'm doing a good job. In fact, I have to be careful not to get too friendly—I have tenants in Florida with adorable kids, and I'm often tempted to volunteer to babysit, but have to remind myself to keep it all business. Of course, it's also nice to earn money through my efforts, and to be able to take tax-deductible trips. I remember the first time I sold one of my rental properties, and made a nice profit on the sale; it made me very happy."

Below is an overview of the various benefits that Laura and other landlords enjoy. Try to remember these later, when you're cursing the latest plumbing problem or fretting over how to fill a vacancy.

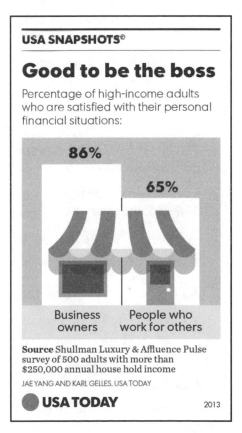

USA SNAPSHOTS®

Good to be the boss

Percentage of high-income adults who are satisfied with their personal financial situations:

86% Business owners

65% People who work for others

Source Shullman Luxury & Affluence Pulse survey of 500 adults with more than $250,000 annual house hold income

JAE YANG AND KARL GELLES, USA TODAY

USA TODAY

2013

Appreciation and wealth building

If you hold onto your property long enough, it will almost certainly go up ("appreciate") in value—eventually. Since World War II, real estate prices in America have risen an average of around 5% a year (with some nerve-wracking ups and downs in between). And even if the house's value isn't rising, renting it may allow you to build equity until you own it outright. Owning investment property is a great way to increase your net worth.

Income

A well-managed investment property, with tenants who pay the rent on time and monthly expenses that are less than the rent, can bring you a steady stream of income. Most landlords owning single-family homes buy with this purpose in mind.

Diversification of income

You never know what life is going to throw at you. If you're laid off from your job, or your health takes a turn for the worse, your primary source of income—presumably your salary—could be jeopardized. Owning an investment property diversifies your income stream and can give you somewhat of a cushion.

Low-risk investment

Unlike more volatile investments, the returns on real estate are fairly steady. While stock values can fall or even disintegrate entirely, land and property won't disappear on you. And history shows us that they almost always hold their value—or at least bounce back after a tumble.

And even when property values are down, people need places to live —a fact that kept rents relatively high even during the recent recession.

Investment diversification

Owning property also diversifies your investment portfolio, a cardinal rule of investing. And it's pretty easy to understand, if you get the idea of not putting all your eggs in one basket. Should something unforeseeable happen to your riskier investments, such as stocks, you'll have the backup of a tangible, relatively low-risk asset. As you approach retirement, it's good to start shifting into lower-risk investments, to ensure the cash you need doesn't disappear when you're relying on it.

Leverage

Unlike other investments, a little bit of cash will buy a lot of real estate: A down payment of 20%—or in some cases, as low as 10% of the value of the property—is usually enough to get you started. You could, for example, buy a $400,000 property with a $40,000 down payment, while that same amount will buy you only $40,000 worth of stock. And if the value of that stock were to increase by 10%, you'd have a $4,000 profit, whereas if the value of the property increased 10%, you'd have a $40,000 profit. (These are, of course, rough figures, in that they do not account for sales commissions, depreciation, capital gains taxes, and so forth.)

USA SNAPSHOTS©

How many hours do you usually work per week?

More than 40 hours **37%**

Less than 40 hours **33%**

40 hours **30%**

Source Jive/Harris survey of 1,192 workers

JAE YANG AND PAUL TRAP, USA TODAY

USA TODAY   2013

This is called being highly "leveraged"—in one sense, deeply in debt, but in another sense, poised to gain high returns based on a relatively small up-front investment. Leveraging your investment allows you to trade up to more profitable properties.

Short-term tax advantages

While the rental income from your property is taxable, you can deduct most of the expenses related to owning and maintaining the property. Among these are mortgage interest, insurance, repairs, and upkeep. They also include your business expenses, such as phone calls, office supplies, professional fees (for example, to the accountant who helps you figure out your business taxes), and more.

Does Owning Real Estate Create Millionaires?

Catherine McBreen and George Walper, authors of *Get Rich, Stay Rich, Pass It On*, are managing director and president, respectively, of Spectrem Group, a research and consulting company that has been studying the affluent since 1991.

Each year, the firm surveys more than 5,000 millionaire and megamillionaire (more than $5 million in assets, not including primary residence) households. While there are many ways to get rich, the authors identified two definitive ways to ensure lasting wealth: owning incoming-producing real estate and investing in an innovative company, product, or service.

In this model for getting rich, just below half of the typical megamillionaire portfolio is invested in marketable assets: stocks, bonds, mutual funds, and other securities. The rest of the assets are not so liquid.

If you dream of being really rich, you will need to actively invest in real estate, they write. "Building up a nest egg with the equity in your home is a fine thing. But what distinguishes the model for getting rich, staying rich, and passing it on is its emphasis on investing in current and future income-producing real estate." Look for opportunities initially in areas you know, they advise.

On average, 23% to 29% of your wealth should be allocated to real estate. Here's how it breaks down: 11%–13% of your real estate investments should be equity in your principal home, 3%–6% should be income-producing property, 5%–7% a second home, 3%–5% other real estate holdings such as REITS, 2%–4% undeveloped land, and 2%–4% third or additional homes.

There are a slew of caveats, of course, on top of the myriad decisions that go into selecting the right properties. And yet, for those willing and eager to go the distance, consider the book's parting thought: "Keep in mind that all this is doable."

USA TODAY "Path to wealth is through real estate holdings," by Kerry Hannon, January 28, 2008.

Another major tax advantage is the ability to "depreciate" your property—to take an annual deduction that reflects the decreased value of the property caused by wear and tear. (In the most literal sense, depreciation may turn out to be a fiction if the value of the property goes up a lot—but it can be a wonderful fiction for tax purposes.) Chapter 6 of this book discusses tax issues in detail.

Long-term tax advantages

Even if your property skyrockets in value on paper, the IRS won't expect you to pay taxes on that increased value until you sell. (Your state and local property taxes may be another matter, however, rising steadily to catch up with the property's value.) Unfortunately, when you do sell, you may lose the advantage of the capital gains tax exclusion ($250,000 per owner), if you haven't lived in the place for two out of the previous five years. However, there are several strategies you can use to decrease your tax liability. We'll discuss those in Chapter 11.

Part-time commitment

If you own just one property, and it's not too far from where you live, you can probably handle its management in your spare time, while still working a full-time job. A little job flexibility will help, of course. Although weeks may go by when the property needs little or no attention, there will be times when it will need hours from you, for example, when you're getting the place painted while dealing with the departure of the old tenant and interviewing prospective new tenants.

Your time commitment will be even less if you hire a property management company—though your profits will decrease as well. We discuss the pros and cons of hiring property managers in Chapter 10.

Professional development

Being a landlord and owning property can give you a sense of accomplishment (and some stories to tell at parties). It shows that you've broken out of the mold of the average working stiff, and are willing to take risks and accept major responsibilities. You're learning new skills involving finances, dealing with people, and maybe even home repair, which may help you in other areas of life.

Personal satisfaction

Being a competent and conscientious landlord will pay dividends in other respects, too—you're going to feel pleased about the way you're doing business. As Amy, who lives in Berkeley, California, and rents out her former home in Austin, Texas, puts it: "I've rented from a few crummy landlords myself, so it's very satisfying to be able to give my tenants a positive experience, for example, quickly taking care of repairs if something goes wrong."

Tough Parts of Being a Landlord

Landlording is not for everybody, and not every property is worth keeping or buying as an investment. The main reasons that people tend to give up on landlording are the time required to manage a property effectively, the risks involved (such as problem tenants, long vacancies, and legal risks), and the cost. Here's a quick overview of these issues. Later chapters in this book provide detailed advice on minimizing and dealing with problems.

Time

Even though landlording isn't a full-time job, it will take more than an hour or two of your time every few weeks. For one thing, you'll need to be reachable and available nearly around the clock, to respond to calls from tenants when the plumbing backs up or the neighbor's dog is barking all night. Occasionally, you'll need to put in large chunks of time, for tasks like listing and showing the property during a vacancy, screening and approving tenants, and handling rent checks and deposits, to name a few.

In this book, we'll help you strategize ways to cut down on the time you spend landlording. For example, Chapters 3 and 4 will give you tips on how to market your property, attract and choose the right tenants (who will hopefully stick around for awhile), and list the property so as to fill vacancies quickly and efficiently.

Problem tenants

One of the pitfalls of owning rental property is the possibility that you're going to get that rare "tenant from hell"—someone who doesn't pay the rent on time, trashes the property, or constantly bugs you about every little thing that goes wrong—all of which can be expensive to remedy. Catherine, who rents out a cottage behind her house in Berkeley, describes often feeling "vulnerable" because someone else has day-to-day control of property she owns and cares about.

It's more likely that your tenants will be perfectly decent, responsible people. Good screening procedures (as described in Chapter 4) will help assure this. Nevertheless, people can change. Catherine's low point as a landlord came, she says, when "one of my tenants, who six months before had a nice job and drove a BMW, developed a crack addiction. The neighbors formed a watch group around my house, and I'd see drug deals going on and find vials in the backyard."

A properly structured lease or rental agreement (as covered in Chapter 5) will help deal with difficult situations like this and reduce many of the risks associated with problem tenants. And knowing how to deal with bad tenants (Chapter 9) will also help you do damage control when needed.

Difficulty renting

There may be times when the market is soft and it will be difficult to rent your place out. Vacancies are a reality of life for most landlords, but can be made worse by local economic conditions, the need for major repairs in your property, or just sheer bad luck. That's why we'll make sure you factor expected vacancies into your analysis of potential profits on the property.

Legal risks

If you really want to talk worst-case scenario, you could worry about the legal risks that come with owning rental property—that is, the possibility

Landlording Duties

- [ ] Research and set rental price.
- [ ] Establish a bookkeeping system for tracking income and expenses.
- [ ] Participate in a local landlords' association (optional).
- [ ] Learn the key laws and ordinances that cover residential renting in your state and city.
- [ ] Advertise property for rent.
- [ ] Respond to people interested in renting the property.
- [ ] Clean property in preparation for tenants.
- [ ] Show property to prospective tenants.
- [ ] Review tenant applications, obtain credit reports, and conduct reference checks.
- [ ] Draft and negotiate lease or rental agreement.
- [ ] Supervise tenant move-in.
- [ ] Collect and manage security deposit.
- [ ] Respond to tenant problems or inquiries.
- [ ] Collect rent.
- [ ] Respond to late rent and other violations of the rental agreement.
- [ ] Pay mortgage, utilities, insurance, etc.
- [ ] Prepare annual tax paperwork.
- [ ] Evaluate and fix problems and contact maintenance repair people.
- [ ] Supervise tenant move-out.
- [ ] Evaluate the condition of the vacated rental and return tenant security deposit.
- [ ] Handle disputes among tenants (multifamily rentals) or disputes or complaints from neighbors.

that a tenant, prospective tenant, or someone else on your property will sue you over a health, safety, environmental, discrimination or other legal matter. You could even face legal trouble from third parties, stemming from misbehavior of your tenant. For example, if a tenant's drug dealing results in injury to a neighbor, you might be liable if the neighbor can prove that you knew what was going on but failed to take action.

Knowing your own responsibilities and potential liabilities (which we'll describe in Chapter 8) and acting to reduce the risk of problems occurring will limit the chances that you'll face serious legal situations.

Costs

The costs of owning an investment property go well beyond the mortgage. They include property taxes, insurance, utilities, upkeep, repairs, property management costs (if you choose), wages for a handyperson, legal costs when needed, and much more. It all adds up to more than you probably spent on the home if and when you lived there.

As Dennis, a landlord since 1982, describes it, "We haven't had much of a negative cash flow on our properties, but we have sometimes. From a financial point of view, if people are really tight, they shouldn't get into the landlord business. There's always the unexpected plumbing problem, or an appliance that wears out."

Reducing costs is one of the keys to being a successful landlord. We'll advise you on how to assess the cost side of your property in Chapter 6.

Location, Price, and More: Features of the Ideal Rental Property

Whether you're planning to buy a rental property or deciding whether to keep a property you already own, one of your first considerations should be whether the place is actually suited for renting. Look especially hard at features of the property that can't be changed, like its location and whether it has a yard. Let's consider its suitability from both the tenant's vantage point and yours.

What gives a property "tenant appeal"?

Here are the most important, primarily physical characteristics of a house that will appeal to a wide range of tenants:

- **Size.** This depends on the local population. For example, a house with several bedrooms will be attractive to large families.

- **Location.** Nearby transportation access—particularly public transport, with gas prices regularly setting new highs—is a big plus. So is proximity to shopping and commercial areas.

- **Security.** No one likes to live in a high-crime area—and making sure the property is secure enough for your tenants can add to your to-do list as a landlord, too.

- **Good nearby public schools.** A family that wants to make sure their children go to the best schools and finds a good home nearby to rent may settle there for years. But even short-term renters appreciate a good school and the corresponding community spirit.

- **Affordability.** With rare exceptions, it's difficult to find tenants for large, luxury houses. Any prospective tenant who has the money to afford the monthly rent can probably also afford to buy a house.

- **In good repair.** Even if it's otherwise in good shape, a house with ongoing maintenance issues—perhaps having a nearby creek that often floods, or being so old that everything is falling apart—may put off tenants who don't want to be dealing with inconveniences or calling you with numerous repair requests.

- **Layout.** Like everyone, rental tenants want a place that's well de-signed. Don't assume, for example, that a renter will be content with a tiny kitchen. And if the house is likely to be shared among roommates, each bedroom should be reasonably private and have bathroom access that doesn't involve invading someone else's room.

- **Charm and aesthetics.** Like home buyers, renters will be drawn to a place that looks nice. But you can't know every prospective tenant's taste. That's why a house with broad appeal rather than quirky features is your best bet.

Of course, tenants will also be concerned with certain nonphysical parts of the property, like how much rent you charge and whether you allow dogs. However, such policies are largely within your control, and don't affect whether you'll buy or keep the house in the first place, so we'll discuss them in Chapter 3.

When Cheap Houses Make Good Rentals

Most real estate investors would jump at the chance to buy a condo with water views along Florida's Gulf Coast, or a leafy estate in Greenwich, Connecticut.

Not Jonas Lee, managing partner of Redbrick Partners, a firm that runs the only U.S. investment fund dedicated to single-family housing. The 1993 Harvard Business School grad prefers to invest in humble row houses located in working-class neighborhoods in gritty Northeast cities, such as Philadelphia, Baltimore, and Trenton, New Jersey.

"It's all about the numbers," Lee said on a recent rainy day while inspecting the electric and heating systems in the wet basement of one of the 99 row houses he's contracted to buy for $5.4 million in the Kensington section of Philadelphia. "You have to keep your emotions out of it. It's not like I drive up to a home and say, 'I love the bricks; they are so red.'"

Real estate investing isn't as easy as it sounds on those late-night infomercials. Redbrick says residential landlords overestimate how much they will make off rental properties. The "Redbrick Rule" assumes 50% of rental income will get eaten up by expenses, such as vacancies, taxes, fixing leaky faucets, and replacing roofs and furnaces.

So why does Redbrick prefer buying homes in aging industrial towns rather than more desirable locations? The answer: Rental yields, which is how much you actually pocket from rent each year as a percentage of your purchase price. Redbrick uses a simple equation to calculate yield: It takes 50% of annual rental income and divides that by the property's purchase price.

When Cheap Houses Make Good Rentals (cont'd)

For example, a $1 million home that rents for $6,000 a month, or $72,000 a year, nets a rental yield of 3.6%. In contrast, a $75,000 home that rents for $1,100 a month, or $13,200 annually, delivers a heftier yield of 8.8%.

Most homes yield about 4% but can go as low as 2% and as high as 9%, depending on the market. Redbrick prefers yields at the high end of the range. The most expensive properties do not always translate into the best rental investments. If you strip out potential price appreciation, rents that fail to cover costs result in negative cash flow.

USA TODAY "Renting out a home 'all about numbers'; Cheaper house might provide better return," by Adam Shell, July 15, 2005.

What makes a good rental from the landlord's point of view?

After thinking about whether your property has sufficient tenant appeal, turn your attention to whether the house you're considering is appropriate for you, given your available time, skills, and interest. In most cases, this is a house that:

- **Requires little fixing up and maintenance.** For example, a house that's relatively new isn't likely to need new plumbing or wiring anytime soon. But this doesn't mean a newly built house is necessarily the best. A place that's well constructed but isn't on the verge of becoming "historic" is your best bet.

- **Is close to your own home or work.** Who wants to drive for an hour—or get onto an airplane—to interview new tenants or see to a maintenance problem? And even if you hire a property management company, it's good to be able to check on the property yourself from time to time.

CAUTION
Dealing with maintenance gets a lot harder at a distance.
As Kyung, who formerly rented out her triplex home in New Haven, Connecticut, explains, "For the ten years we lived in the unit above the rental, we had practically no maintenance problems. But wouldn't you know it, as soon as we moved to Pennsylvania, things started to fail. The tenants were calling in the middle of the night, and I'd have to call some 24-hour service and pay a premium to get the repairs made."

- **Isn't in a heavily regulated city or area.** If your property is in an area with rent control or other restrictions on landlords, take a careful look before you leap. Read the regulations and talk to other local landlords about their experiences. If you'll be buying a property with existing, long-term tenants who show signs of planning to stay there forever, you'll have to make do with below-market rent well into the future. In situations like this, your investment may be a losing proposition.

- **Will attract long-term renters.** For example, a house near a vacation resort or a college might not be optimal if you're hoping for year-round tenants. (Students tend to leave at the summer break and often switch housing every year, which means regular turnover and repairs.) If there's high turnover, you'll at least want correspondingly low vacancy rates and high rents.

- **Doesn't require evicting long-term tenants.** See "Evaluating Resident Tenants" in the discussion of buying foreclosed property, below.

- **Is convenient to commercial supply sources and repair people.** In other words, avoid houses in remote locations where you'll have to struggle to get to a hardware store or find high-quality help for maintaining or improving the property.

- **Is in a strong rental market.** Ideally, you're looking for a property that's cheaper to buy than to rent, so you can bring in income. But you're also looking for a market with lots of would-be renters: Otherwise, you'll find profits eaten up by vacancy periods.

Special concerns when renting out a condo or co-op

Whether you already own a condominium or another home in a common-interest development (CID) or are thinking of buying one, you need to be aware of how the property's unique features impact its suitability as a rental property.

Condos and townhomes are the most common types of homes in CIDs. Renting them offers special advantages, including:

- **Less maintenance responsibility.** The homeowners' association (HOA) will take care of common areas, freeing you from hands-on responsibilities like tending the garden or (in most cases) repairing the roof. (Of course, you pay to get these things done via your monthly HOA dues.)

- **Affordability.** A condo or townhouse is usually cheaper than a single family home, because you own less—you own your particular unit, and own common areas jointly. And the maintenance can be less expensive too, because costs that might otherwise be individually paid—like landscaping and insurance—are instead shared.

- **Amenities to attract tenants.** Without having to buy a whole apartment building, you may be able to offer your tenants access to a pool or other recreational or meeting spaces.

But let's not forget the disadvantages:

- **Community rules and regulations.** In a CID, residents typically must agree to live by a set of rules. These may govern everything from the size of residents' dogs to whether they can hang clothes on the line, add a spare room, smoke in the unit, change the color of the curtains, or change the color of the outside paint. Getting your tenants to read and abide by these rules, when they don't have a long-term stake in the community, can be challenging.

- **Restrictions on renting.** Possibly the most significant rule in a CID is a restriction on renting. Some CIDs place numerical limits on how many units can be rented, or ban renting altogether. Although the association is unlikely to weigh in on your choice of tenants (which would expose it to liability for discrimination and the like), it may insist that you put certain clauses in your lease (for example, committing the tenant to abide by community rules), or exert other oversight.

- **Community fees and costs.** Every CID charges a monthly fee for maintenance and shared costs, and the rules typically also allow special assessments for major expenses like a new roof on the property or dealing with a flood or other emergency. These can run into the hundreds, even thousands of dollars per month, which you'll need to figure into your budget. (The landlord is normally responsible for making these payments, not the tenant.)
- **Slow property appreciation.** Historically, condos and townhomes have appreciated in value at a slower rate than single-family homes.

We've given a broad description of CIDs, which can vary immensely in physical features and character. Your job, before deciding to buy or rent out one of these properties, will be to fully research its costs, rules (often in a document called Covenants, Conditions, and Restrictions, or CC&Rs), and current community concerns. Read the CC&Rs and recent meeting minutes thoroughly, talk to neighbors, and investigate the reputation and financial strength of the property's builder or owner.

Is Airbnb or VRBO for you?

Many people who own rental property in popular tourist destinations, such as San Francisco, or in college towns, such as Ithaca, New York, choose to rent their homes through Airbnb or another short-term hosting or rental service.

This book focuses on more traditional rental situations, where you sign a fixed-term lease or month-to-month rental agreement with one or more tenants. You will have screened these longer-term tenants by running a credit report and checking references.

Renting through Airbnb or a similar service involves a separate set of legal and practical issues concerning taxes, insurance coverage, liability for guest injuries, and so forth. Having different people come in and out of your rental house can cause major headaches for neighbors and may even violate municipal restrictions (some of which were under discussion as this book went to print).

While you may end up bringing in more money each month by renting your house through VRBO or a similar service, carefully consider all the relevant issues, including how much time you'll need to spend screening guests or arranging for cleaning in between visitors. To get further informed, see the Short-Term Rentals of Your Home area in the Real Estate section of Nolo.com. You'll find articles on insurance, taxes, screening renters, legal restrictions, and neighbor concerns. Also, to prevent your tenants from renting a room or space within their rental via Airbnb, make sure your lease or rental agreement prohibits sublets, as recommended in Chapter 5.

Is sharing your home with a lodger for you?

Some homeowners decide (either for financial or social reasons) to stay in their homes and rent out a room in their house to a lodger. Because this is different than the typical landlord-tenant relationship, we've devoted a special chapter to the subject. See Chapter 12 for details.

Thinking About Buying an Investment Property?

Not all landlords are accidental landlords. You may be thinking about buying a property so that you can rent it out. (If not, and you already own a property, skip down to the next section, "What Will Your Monthly Profit Be?") In fact, a survey by the National Association of Realtors® showed that 1.1 million second homes, or 20% of all new home sales in 2013, were for investment purposes.

Where are people buying investment properties?

In 2013, 18% of properties purchased were in the Northeast, 19% in the Midwest, 38% in the South, and 25% in the West. (Source: National Association of Realtors®)

Before you make that decision, you'll want to do a careful analysis of the costs and potential returns of your investment. Keep in mind that real estate is not a get-rich-quick business. You'll have to invest some significant cash up front. And while your rental income may be a source of ongoing profit (we'll help you calculate how much below), a large portion of the financial gain will come about as time passes and the value of the property increases. And you won't actually realize that benefit until you sell (though you could use your increased equity as collateral for a loan).

While some people have gotten rich in real estate, you've probably seen the headlines about the many who've been disappointed—the would-be house "flippers" who, during the recent real estate downturn, found they couldn't buy and sell property for quick profits as they'd planned, and ended up in foreclosure or bankruptcy. For many of them, turning their house into a rental

USA TODAY Snapshots®

Home buyers thinking smaller
Median square footage of new single-family homes sold:

2008 **2,234**

2009 **2,202**

Source: Census Bureau, June 2010

By Anne R. Carey and Sam Ward, USA TODAY 2010

property wasn't an option—their carrying costs were too high compared to the rents they could charge, and they faced a long road of losses ahead.

We're going to assume you don't have aspirations toward house flipping, but are looking to invest in rental property over the long term, and ride out the inevitable ups and downs of the market. Or perhaps your ultimate goal isn't to sell, but to live in the home yourself, after you've retired. Let's evaluate your budget and how buying a rental property will fit in, both as a short- and long-term investment.

> **RESOURCE**
> **This book doesn't attempt to present a complete guide to choosing a house to buy or financing investment property.** Some good resources for that include:
> • *Real Estate Investing for Dummies,* by Eric Tyson and Robert S. Griswold (Wiley Publishing, Inc.)

• *Nolo's Essential Guide to Buying Your First Home,* by Ilona Bray, Alayna Schroeder, and Marcia Stewart, and

• the Real Estate section of Nolo.com, which includes hundreds of useful articles on buying, owning, and selling real estate, including investment property.

How much cash you can put down

To determine whether buying an investment property is even a financial possibility for you, let's start with a simple calculation: How much cash can you free up for a down payment, and how much house will that buy? Most lenders require 20% down, especially on an investment property. (The days of zero down payments are gone, victims of the bursting real estate bubble and subsequent foreclosure crisis.) A quick visit to the real estate section of your local paper, or to an online site like www.realtor.org, will show you typical prices in the location where you're interested in buying.

USA TODAY Snapshots®

Neighborhood street vs. Wall Street
Which do you think is the better investment?

Real estate market 69%

Stock market 24%

Don't know 7%

Source: TIAA-CREF survey of 1,001 investors ages 30 and older who help make household financial decisions. Margin of error: ±3 percentage points.

By Jae Yang and Julie Snider, USA TODAY 2006

You'll also need to budget around 2%–3% of the house's price for closing costs, depending on what state you live in, what kind of mortgage you get, and what you can expect to pay in escrow fees, title fees, real estate agent commissions, and taxes and insurance at closing. So if you can put down $80,000 plus pay $12,000 in closing costs, you're well on your way to buying a $400,000 property. If your cash on hand will likely buy a worthwhile rental in your area, keep reading.

> ⓘ **CAUTION**
> **Looking at a fixer-upper?** In that case, you'll need even more cash on hand. Major home improvements always seem to take more time and money than originally expected, so think twice about this strategy if you're not experienced with home repairs or construction.

How large a loan you'll qualify for

You'll probably be taking out a loan with which to buy your property (unless you're among the approximately 35% of real estate investors who pay all cash). That means you'll need to show a lender that you can afford the monthly payments. One of the tests that lenders use is your credit history and score, or your record of paying debts on time. We're not going to discuss credit scores in detail here—for more information, see the free articles in the Debt Management section of www.nolo.com.

The other test that lenders use is the comparison between your income and your debt load, called your "debt-to-income" ratio. The more debt obligations you already have hanging over you, the less likely the lender is to let you take on more. In fact, the lender may be stricter than when you bought your first home, because lending practices have tightened and mortgages on investment properties are considered riskier.

USA SNAPSHOTS®

Tougher times

Is it more difficult to buy a home now than it was for your parents' generation?

Yes **80%**

20% No

Source Prudential Real Estate Consumer Outlook survey of 2,500 adults

JAE YANG AND PAUL TRAP, USA TODAY

● **USA TODAY** 2014

> ⓘ **CAUTION**
> **Evaluate your monthly expenses even more strictly than your lender does.** What we're discussing here is how much mortgage you'll qualify for. But if you tend to spend everything you earn each month—and perhaps aren't even sure where the money is going—you need to get your first house in order before taking on a second one.

The concept of "debt-to-income ratio" isn't as complicated as it sounds. The lender looks first at your household's gross monthly income (the amount you earn before taxes and other monthly withdrawals, plus income from all other sources, like rents, royalties, alimony, or investments). Then it makes sure that your combined minimum debt payments on the property—going toward your PITI (principal, interest, taxes, and insurance), plus any community association fees, credit card payments, car debt, student loans, and more—don't eat up more than a certain percentage of that gross income. See the "Sample Debt-to-Income Ratio Worksheet," below.

How high can your debt-to-income ratio go? Traditionally, lenders said that your PITI payment shouldn't exceed 28% of your gross monthly income (sometimes called the "front-end ratio"), and your overall debt shouldn't exceed 36% (the "back-end ratio"). Although that formula was largely tossed out during the real estate boom of the early 2000s, it's not only back in full force, it's more stringent than ever. As of 2014, federal guidelines say that a home borrower's total debt-to-income ratio for a "qualified mortgage" should not exceed 43%.

With that ratio in hand, the lenders set your maximum monthly mortgage payment. Using the calculators listed below, you can arrive at roughly the same figure—and then decide whether that amount is enough to buy a rental property in your chosen area.

Sample Debt-to-Income Ratio Worksheet		
Gross monthly income:	$4,000	
Gross monthly income x .28	$1,120	= Maximum monthly PITI payment
Gross monthly income x .36	$1,440	= Maximum monthly debt overall

RESOURCE
Ready to run some real numbers? Find online affordability, as well as household budget, calculators at www.nolo.com/legalcalculators, www.hsh.com, and www.interest.com. Make sure any calculator you use factors in the amount of your down payment, income and debts, and estimated taxes and insurance.

Apartment Rents Projected to Rise in 2014

Higher rents are ahead in 2014 for the nation's apartment dwellers, but some cities will see smaller bumps than in recent years, market researchers say.

Rents will increase 3.1% nationally in 2014, about the same as in 2013, apartment market researcher Axiometrics says. Meanwhile, researcher Reis sees rents rising an average of 3.3% in 2014.

Tight supply and rising demand are still the key drivers.

"The construction pipeline really closed during the recession. We're still clawing our way back," says Ryan Severino, Reis chief economist.

Cities that have seen some of the sharpest increases will see rents rise a little more slowly in 2014, says Jay Denton, Axiometrics vice president of research.

Since the end of 2009, rents have soared 43% in San Francisco, including an 8% jump in 2013, Denton's data show.

In 2014, they'll rise 5.1% given still strong demand and limited new supply.

Seattle, which posted a 6.5% increase in 2013, will rise 4.4% in 2014. Austin, which rose 5.2% in 2013, will see an increase of 3.7%

Construction has been uneven across the country. Some major metros that have led the way in new construction are now at risk of having an oversupply of apartments.

Washington, DC "has probably already gone over that cliff," Denton says. Rents there will fall 2.5% in 2014, Axiometrics predicts.

Austin also has seen a lot of construction. "It'll be difficult to raise rents there," Severino says.

Nationwide, almost 230,000 new apartments will be added to the supply, Axiometrics says. That's up from 170,000 in 2013 and only 87,000 the previous year.

Half of all U.S. renters paid more than 30% of their income for rent—a traditional measure of affordability—in 2010, up 12 percentage

Apartment Rents Projected to Rise in 2014 (cont'd)

points from a decade earlier, according to a study from Harvard's Joint Center for Housing Studies.

Apartment rents have risen every year since 2010, market data shows.

Meanwhile, the share of Americans who rent grew from 31% in 2004 to 35% in 2012, the study says, driven in part by the foreclosure crisis.

Trevor Coccimiglio, 24, is looking to rent a room in a shared house in San Francisco for less than $1,200 a month. That's about what his father pays to rent an entire house in suburban Salt Lake City.

"That's just the cost," says Coccimiglio, who has taken a new investment banking job.

He recently looked at a $900-a-month room in a 3-bedroom, 864-square-foot apartment. The parking space costs $75 extra a month.

 USA TODAY "Apartment rents will keep rising next year," by Julie Schmit, USA TODAY, December 15, 2013.

Keep in mind that interest rates are higher on investment properties, so your calculations shouldn't assume that you'll qualify for the rock-bottom rate offered to buyers with stellar credit who are buying primary residences. You won't be offered these rates, because lenders know they're in a riskier position when their borrower is paying two mortgages: If you hit hard financial times, you'll pay the mortgage on your primary residence first.

Some investors with lots of equity in their primary residences get around these higher rates by doing a cash-out refinance (drawing out cash from their main home to pay for a second) or taking out a home equity loan. This strategy is beyond the scope of this book; in general, while you can use it to get a lower interest rate, the lender will subject you to the same financial evaluation discussed above.

Fortunately, lenders will allow you to include your expected income from the rental property in your calculations. This will help you qualify for a bigger loan. However, lenders will probably be conservative in estimating your likely income, for example, by figuring a higher-than-expected vacancy rate.

You'll need to know how much loan you qualify for so you can estimate what kind of property you can buy, how much it will cost you each month, and how much you can expect it to bring in. Later in this chapter, we'll cover whether it's profitable to buy based on these factors.

Buying a Foreclosed Property

Although the flood of home foreclosures has turned to a trickle, many savvy buyers have braved the uncertainties and frustrations associated with such sales to buy homes for use as investments.

Foreclosure properties tend to be in rough shape (there's a reason they're known as "distressed"), and some come with resident tenants and even recalcitrant former owners. You'll need to be prepared for the special challenges that come with obtaining a distressed property that you intend to rent out. But first, here's a brief description of how to find and secure a distressed property.

The main advantage to buying a foreclosure is price—you're likely to get a good bargain, whether you buy from the owner (preforeclosure), at a foreclosure sale, or directly from the bank (known as "real estate owned," or REO). The main disadvantages to buying foreclosure properties are:

More people buy foreclosure properties as investments or second homes than as homes in which they'll live!

In 2010, according to the National Association of Realtors, foreclosures accounted for 12% of investment sales and 10% of vacation-home sales, but a mere 2% of primary home sales.

- **Going without the usual buyer protections.** As we'll explain further, below, at most stages in the foreclosure process you'll forgo at least some of the normal protections available in a typical transaction. For example, you may not get to see the property before you buy, have to accept it "as is," and have to go without title insurance.

- **Waiting to make sure the owner's rights are protected.** All states have laws to make sure banks can't rip properties out from under late-paying owners on a moment's notice. For buyers, that means deadlines, delays, court rules, and uncertainty—particularly in the many states that allow the former owner to "redeem" or buy back the property within a certain period of time after it was sold in foreclosure (usually from ten days to one year). Of course, if the owners redeem the property, you'll get your money refunded. But as attorney Fred Steingold notes: "Do you really want to be held in limbo, unsure of whether you'll ever be able to occupy the house?"

RESOURCE
To find out your state's redemption period and get other summaries of your state's law regarding foreclosures, see www.nolo.com (choose Foreclosure and then Foreclosure Laws).

- **Competition from experienced real estate investors.** If there are good deals to be had, you can bet real estate investors will be lined up in front of you, with cash at the ready.
- **Risks of undisclosed repair needs, tax liens, or other issues with the property.** Remember, these homeowners were probably financially stressed for a while. They may have held back on maintenance, gotten behind on their taxes, or used the house as collateral for other debts.

Still interested in pursuing foreclosed properties? Find an agent who specializes in them—most don't handle them at all, while some go so far as to arrange bus tours of local foreclosures. A good source is www. reonetwork.com. If you still have a regular real estate agent, explain to both agents what you're doing, so that you can agree on each agent's limited role. You'd also be wise to hire a real estate attorney to help navigate this somewhat touchy area.

Buying a house in preforeclosure

When a house is in preforeclosure, this means that the homeowner has fallen behind in payments and the lender has filed a notice of default or started a lawsuit to officially begin the foreclosure process. The foreclosure sale has not yet taken place; this is simply an early stage of the foreclosure process. During the preforeclosure period, the homeowner typically has a certain amount of time in which to either catch up on past-due mortgage payments plus fees, sell the home to pay off the loan, or work out an alternative to foreclosure, like a mortgage modification, short sale, or deed in lieu of foreclosure.

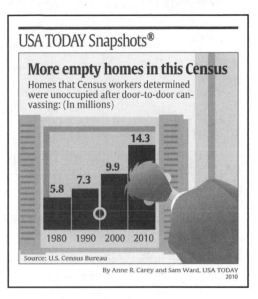

Preforeclosure listings are publicly available even if the homeowner hasn't listed the property for sale. Online services like foreclosures.com or realtytrac.com compile this information from public records, and members pay a modest monthly fee ($30–$50) to get the information. Some aggressive home buyers or investors use this information to find homes in preforeclosure and then approach the defaulting homeowners to make an offer. Of course, investors prefer properties that are worth more than the homeowners owe, because they'll be able to offer less than market value while still helping the homeowners get out from under the mortgage. (If the seller owes more than the property is worth and can't make up the difference or negotiate an agreement with the lender, the only alternative short of foreclosure is a short sale, in which the bank agrees to the sale of the home for less than what the owner owes on the loan.)

If you find a homeowner ready to sell, you can negotiate just as you would any other transaction (although with a short sale you'll also be negotiating with the bank). However, you could be very pressed for time. Depending on the state you're in, the homeowner could have as little as a few weeks between the time the notice of default is filed and the foreclosure sale date (meaning you'll have to close the deal by then), or the lender will put the house up for auction.

Buying a house at public sale or auction

If the seller doesn't pay what's owed or work out some other agreement with the lender and the lender forecloses, the property will be sold at a public sale or auction. This doesn't always offer the bargains you might expect, for several reasons.

First of all, the lender will probably make the first bid on the house, likely for the amount owed on the mortgage. Unless the amount owed is low in relation to the home's value (rarely the case), you won't want to bid any higher. And if the price is right and you want to bid, you'll be competing with savvy real estate investors who know what they're do-ing. Even if you're the highest bidder, you have another giant hurdle to overcome: You'll be expected to have cash in hand, without relying on a traditional loan or financing.

Add to this the fact that you'll know very little about the house itself. You may never have even seen the place on the inside, and you'll have to take it "as is," without the benefit of an inspection. It isn't uncommon for disgruntled homeowners to trash their former homes or to strip them of all valuable assets when foreclosure happens (light fixtures, appliances, even copper wires). Or if the house has been sitting vacant for a long time, thieves may have done the same thing. Even worse, you may have to go without title insurance, leaving you open to the risk of an unpaid lien or a later claim to title.

Unlike a preforeclosure, when you buy a foreclosure, you aren't work-ing directly with the homeowner anymore. But that doesn't mean the homeowner isn't involved. If a stubborn homeowner hasn't moved out, you will likely have to proceed with an eviction action or exchange "cash for keys"—that is, give the former owner some money to vacate the place to avoid the hassle and expense of the eviction.

Buying a bank-owned house

If no one else buys the property at the foreclosure sale, the bank will then own it and likely try to sell it, usually by listing it with a local real estate agent. You may come across these deals if you browse MLS listings. At this point, the bank may be willing to sell the house for less than the seller owed, because it isn't in the business of owning property and needs to get as much of its cash out of the place as possible. Still, lenders want to get as close to market value as possible, and that may mean it's not such a great deal for you.

USA TODAY Snapshots®

Mortgage shopping
How many loan quotes did you get when shopping for your current mortgage?

More than one
61%

Only one
39%

Source: LendingTree survey of 2,113 adults 18 and older. Weighted to represent actual population

By Jae Yang and Veronica Salazar, USA TODAY 2011

Even if the price is a little lower than you'd find on a house that isn't bank owned, a bank-owned property comes with additional complications. By the time the bank gets to selling it, it may have been vacant for months, which means it probably won't be in the best shape. Banks usually do little more than pick up debris and do a basic cleanup. You may find that the lower price is balanced by the hard work you'll have to put in to make the house liveable.

Also, banks usually sell properties "as is." At this stage, you'll at least have the benefit of an inspection contingency. That means that while you can't expect the bank to do anything about needed repairs, you'll at least be able to have the property professionally inspected and back out of the deal if you don't like what you see.

If you find a good deal on a bank-owned home, chances are you're not the only one. It isn't unheard of for well-priced bank-owned properties to garner as many as ten to 20 offers. (Your real estate agent should be able to find out this type of detail on properties you're interested in, with a little legwork.) To make your offer stand out, you may have to pay more than other bidders. You'll definitely want to be preapproved for a loan, and it could help if your preapproval letter comes from the selling lender—they'll trust their own assessment of your finances better than anyone else's.

> **RESOURCE**
> **For information on foreclosures, see the following sites:**
> - www.propertyshark.com (you'll need to register for some information)
> - www.realtytrac.com (includes state-by-state statistics)
> - www.homesales.gov (includes listings of houses foreclosed upon by the federal Department of Housing and Urban Development after owners failed to pay their FHA loans)
> - www.foreclosure.com, and
> - www.foreclosures.com (note the "s" after "foreclosure").

Consider the neighborhood

As important as the condition of the house is the condition of the neighborhood. In general, a rental in an area dotted with foreclosures is likely to command less rent when foreclosed properties remain unsold and, more importantly, unoccupied. These forlorn properties are likely to be unmaintained and are targets for vandalism and even squatters. Few tenants will want to join the ranks in such a neighborhood, and those that do may expect the rent to reflect these negative attributes. When making a bid on such a property, factor in the realistic rent the house can command.

A neighborhood of foreclosed homes bodes ill even if the homes have been purchased and are in relatively good shape. Not all of these homes are going to be occupied by the owners—many will be rented out, just as yours will be. That makes for a concentration of rentals—in short, a glut on the market, which will drive rents down. The same property in a different part of town might fetch a higher rent simply because it's up against less competition.

A foreclosed property in good condition located in a neighborhood with few other foreclosures will most likely fetch higher rent. Of course, such a property may command a higher selling price as well.

Investigate the home's maintenance history

Turn your attention to the house itself and its history. If you are buying at preforeclosure, the current owners should (depending on the laws in your state) give you a filled-out disclosure form and answer any questions you might have. (And of course, before closing the deal, you'll want to have the house inspected.) There's a good chance that you're dealing with a home that has already been a rental.

If you don't have access to the prior owner, ask the neighbors about the house's maintenance history. Did the owners take pride in their home and leave it in good shape? Or was the home occupied by malicious tenants who were unsupervised by an owner already demoralized by the property's imminent loss? Or was the home occupied by resident owners who spitefully trashed the home before moving out?

No matter whom you talk to, be prepared for disappointing news. As neighbors, brokers, banks, and eventual new owners of distressed properties have learned all too well, the prospect of losing one's property —whether owned or rented—spurs some to acts of vengeful destruction. Refurbishing these properties will involve considerable expense.

Even if the property was a rental that escaped the wrath of its last occupants, think about the extent of wear and tear it has undergone. Often, rental properties suffer more deterioration than owner-occupied homes. Take this into consideration when setting your purchase bid.

Dealing with former owners

Occasionally, you'll find former owners still in residence right through the foreclosure proceedings—and beyond. Some of these folks simply have nowhere to go, and figure that they'll stay on as long as possible. The sight of a new owner may be the last straw that will trigger their departure, but maybe not.

If you inherit former owners, you'll need to evict them. (Do not resort to self-help measures, which can turn nasty.) But you may not be able to evict using the same methods as you would to evict ordinary tenants. (Under normal circumstances, tenant evictions are very quick compared to other types of civil cases; many states provide simple fill-in-the-blank forms, making it possible to handle the matter on your own.) Instead, evicting a former owner may involve a more complex lawsuit, for which you will probably need a lawyer.

Dealing with current tenants

It's possible that the house you're considering will come with resident tenants who were renting from the prior owners. Until recently, most tenants lost their leases when a rental property was foreclosed on, which gave the new owners the option to keep the tenants (under a new lease) or evict them. But that changed on May 20, 2009, when President Obama signed the "Helping Families Save Their Homes Act." This legislation specifies that all leases will survive a foreclosure, except when new owners intend to personally occupy the premises (in that case, the current tenant's lease may be terminated with 90 days' notice). Month-to-month tenants may be terminated with 90 days' notice (which is longer or as long as any notice period required by the states).

According to this law, if you are buying a home that you intend to use as a rental, if it was foreclosed on after May 19, 2009, and it comes with a lease-holding tenant, you must honor the lease. You can terminate month-to-month tenants with 90 days' notice, but keep in mind that if the home is subject to local rent control requiring landlords to have a "just cause," or good reason, to terminate a tenant (or is in New Jersey or Washington, DC, which impose statewide "just cause" eviction protection), you cannot give the tenant a notice to vacate the property. You'll be stuck with these tenants for as long as you use the property for rental purposes, or until you fit within one of the rent control ordinance's allowable reasons for termination.

Evaluating resident tenants

If you're inheriting month-to-month tenants in a non-rent-controlled city, should you allow them to stay? Evaluate these tenants as you would any others. If they've been paying rent on time (which, admittedly, might be hard to find out unless you can talk to the prior owner), and have been taking reasonable care of the property, you might decide to keep them and negotiate your own new rental agreement or lease (after giving the tenants 90 days' notice).

But if you sense trouble, particularly if the property comes with tenants who have lots of time left on a lease, think twice about purchasing this property. You don't want to be saddled with tenants whom you'd never have rented to in the first place. If you go ahead and purchase the property, while counting on evicting the residents, understand that if these tenants refuse to leave, you'll need to begin an expensive and drawn-out eviction. This is hardly the way to begin your new rental business.

What Will Your Monthly Profit Be?

Earning steady profits from the rent stream off your investment property should be at the top of your goals list. So don't just guesstimate or hope for the best. Do the research and run through the analysis below to determine whether you'll make money each month.

Calculate rental income

Wouldn't it be nice if you could just add up your expenses for the property, tack on a little extra for profit, and call the result your monthly rental amount? Unfortunately, it doesn't work that way (except by coincidence). The local rental market largely sets the prices, based on how many properties are available and what amount tenants are willing and able to pay. That's why many landlords must settle for rental amounts that don't actually cover their costs, hoping that long-term appreciation in property value will make their investment worthwhile.

As a first-time landlord, your safest bet is to rent out your property only if the rent you can charge will cover your expenses (unless you have no other realistic choice). To figure out whether that's feasible, look at local ads for comparable properties of the same size and condition, in the same neighborhood and school district. Or check www.rentometer.com, which provides median rent amounts by area.

If the house is already being rented, the existing landlord will of course tell you what the monthly rent has been—and will continue to be, if the tenant has a lease that lasts beyond the property transfer. (You can't raise the rent until you renew the lease.) But if the tenant will be leaving, your outside research will come in handy, because the landlord may have kept the rent below market rates, perhaps in order to keep a good tenant. And even a tenant who wants to stay may have only a month-to-month rental agreement, which you are free to either terminate or renegotiate (unless your state or local laws add restrictions).

USA TODAY Snapshots®

Hours a day Americans in debt worry about money

1–3 hours **63%**
4 hours or more **22%**
0 hours **15%**

Average hours: **3.3**

Source: FreeScore.com survey
By Anne R. Carey and Paul Trap, USA TODAY 2011

For more on rentability, see "What gives a property 'tenant appeal'?" above. And see Chapter 3 for ideas on how to spiff up your house for added appeal. When setting your rental policies (which we'll detail in Chapters 3 and 5), consider whether you might be willing to, say, allow pets or charge a lower security deposit in trade for a higher rent. Depending on who your likely tenants are, a furnished property might also allow you to raise the rent—for example, if you'll be renting out a downtown condo to busy young professionals. This will be particularly handy if you inherited a fully furnished property.

Also visit other rentals (say, during open houses) to see how yours stacks up. There's no need to be undercover about it—identify yourself as a new landlord researching the market, and you may find a fellow landlord who's eager to share tips and stories.

After figuring out a likely market rent, your next task is to check into the local vacancy rate, usually expressed as a percentage. A real estate or property management company should be able to tell you how many rental houses like yours are sitting empty. You can also get a sense of likely demand for your house by considering factors such as whether your area is growing economically (so that new employees need housing), whether there's a steady stream of likely renters (such as students), and whether home prices are out of reach for the average local resident, who will turn to renting instead. Nationwide, a rental vacancy rate of up to 10% of the year is not uncommon, according to U.S. Census Bureau figures. Of course, this is just a ballpark, and you can lower this rate by using some of the methods in this book to find and keep long-term tenants.

TIP
Consider setting your rent slightly below market rates. In the experience of Gordon, a landlord with a single-family property in San Jose, California, "It's important to not charge as much as you can get away with. If you charge top dollar, you're more likely to have a tenant not take care of it. But if you give them a fair rent and they feel you're treating them fairly, they'll return the favor by taking care of the place."

Putting it all together, you should be able to come up with a monthly and annual dollar figure that your rental is likely to command—the monthly rent figure times twelve, minus expected vacancies. Assume that your vacancy rate will be the same as the average where you live, even if you expect to have a long-term renter.

Subtract expenses

If you're already a homeowner—most people are before becoming landlords—you know that keeping up a home isn't cheap. Your regular annual expenses will include the mortgage (both principal and interest, assuming it hasn't already been paid off), homeowners' insurance, property and other taxes, and property management services if you decide to use them. You'll also face less predictable expenses, such as maintenance and improvements, accounting fees now that you're in business, and more.

When Will You Be Able to Raise the Rent?

After you're in full swing as landlord, keep an eye on changes in your local rental rates, by watching the ads and talking to local real estate management experts. If rents go up, then you may be able to renegotiate a raise at the next lease renewal, or, if you have a month-to-month rental agreement, within the next month or two (depending on your state's requirements for giving the tenant advance notice). Local rent control laws, if any, will also affect when and by how much you can raise the rent.

The next question is whether you'll want to raise your rent. Dennis (the long-time landlord mentioned earlier) says, "I usually don't raise the rent on anyone in the property. I raise it when I rent to someone new. Maybe I can save 50 bucks a month by raising the rent, but I can save thousands by not having it vacant. I have one set of tenants whose rent I haven't raised in 12 years. They're the nicest, neatest people. They put in their own blinds; they garden and mow."

Now's the time to draw up a budget, estimating what it will cost to keep your property. The worksheet below will help with this task. We've broken it down so that you enter monthly figures—of course, you'll need to fiddle with some of the numbers, for example dividing your annual property tax payment by 12.

CAUTION

Double the amount you think you'll spend on maintenance. If you base your likely maintenance figures on what you usually spend on your own home, you'll probably come out low. Tenants tend to be harder on houses than owners and blind to minor maintenance issues until they become major. And habitability laws will require you to make some repairs that you might otherwise have delayed.

If the property is already being rented, the departing owner is a valuable source of financial information. Ask for:

- a copy of the lease or rental agreement
- details on security deposits (location, amount, and whether the old owner will be returning them to tenants, in which case you'll need to recollect them)
- service contracts (such as for gardening—these can be canceled, but you might not want to if the seller is getting a good bargain)
- utility bills and maintenance and repair records for at least the last year (preferably longer), and
- all other paperwork relevant to the property.

And if the current tenant plans to stay, figure out which expenses you can cut out of your budget accordingly. Advertising and screening are the obvious ones, but you may be able to reduce the number of repairs and improvements you otherwise would have done before a new tenant moved in.

> **TIP**
> **If you want existing tenants to stay, encourage them.** During a transfer, tenants may worry that the new landlord will be difficult to work with and will raise the rent or change other lease or rental agreement terms as soon as legally possible. Some will start looking for a new place, just in case. As soon as you can, meet with the tenants to explain your policies and establish some personal rapport.

Our expense worksheet also includes some categories that you may not be able to estimate yet, such as gifts (for example, flowers to your tax accountant for dealing with your shoebox of receipts). Leave these blank if you can't imagine paying them—but use them as a reminder of possible unexpected expenses.

Monthly Property Expense Estimate	
Expense Description	**Amount**
Advertising and tenant screening	$
Local transportation	$
Out-of-city travel, meals, lodging	$
Cleaning and maintenance	$
Homeowners' insurance (if not included in mortgage payment)	$
Legal and other professional fees (accountant, property manager)	$
Mortgage payment (principal and interest, plus property taxes and insurance, if included)	$
Other loan payments	$
Repairs	$
Appliances and furnishings (irregular but major expenses, such as a refrigerator)	$
Supplies (for office and rental property)	$
Income tax	$
Property tax (if not included in mortgage payment)	$
Utilities and phone (if not covered by tenant)	$
Gifts and entertainment	$
Licenses	$
Homeowners' association dues (in condos and some developments)	$
Landlords' association dues, if you choose to join one	$
Educational publications, subscriptions, and memberships	$
Tools and equipment	$
Construction and improvements	$
Other, miscellaneous expenses	$
Total estimated expenses	$

> **CAUTION**
>
> **Costs can mount if you're unable to make regular visits to the property.** Amy explains, "My property tax bill recently went up significantly, and I decided it wasn't worth the time and expense to fly from California to Texas to appeal it. But if more surprise costs like this come along, I'll probably have to either raise the rent or sell."

Estimate short-term profits

Continuing with the simple calculations, let's say you can afford to buy—or you already own—a house that's suitable for renting. Now you need to estimate whether the rent will cover your costs. Do that by filling in the chart below.

	Estimated Monthly House Profit or Loss	
A	Expected rental income (based on "Calculate rental income," above)	$
B	Estimated costs (based on "Monthly Property Expense Estimate" worksheet, above)	$
C	Profit or loss (A minus B, or expected income minus estimated costs)	$

This chart will tell you whether you stand to make money on such a property in the short term. If the income comes out ahead of the costs, great. But remember that if you're buying, you'll probably have put in a large down payment, and may eventually want to sell the place. That's why it's worth figuring out the ultimate return on your investment, which we'll discuss next.

If the property's expected income isn't enough to cover its costs and more, we recommend walking away (if you can—see our discussion for people trying to avoid foreclosure, below). Sure, the place might make a good long-term investment if and when property values rise, but that's a different ball game—we're assuming you picked up this book because you wanted to earn regular money as a landlord, not aim for one-time profits.

CAUTION

This calculation doesn't include tax benefits. These benefits—depreciation and other tax deductions—can reduce your tax liability by thousands of dollars. If your calculations look borderline, skip ahead to Chapter 6, where you'll learn more about what these tax benefits are and how they help you increase your profits.

Another thing worth considering is the value of your own time. We can't calculate that for you, but we will discuss some of the tasks that go into being a landlord in this book.

Added financial concerns when trying to avoid foreclosure

It may be that you aren't trying to make a profit, but are just trying to avoid losing a home that has become unaffordable—perhaps one you don't think you can sell for what you owe on it. In that case, you might avoid foreclosure by renting the place to someone else. Most likely, you'll rent another place of your own until the situation changes.

In that case, you should continue your calculations as follows:

A	Profit or loss from rental (from above)	$
B	Cost of renting another house for yourself	$
C	A minus B = Total cash you'll need to spend on housing (after paying other bills)	$

EXAMPLE: Samuel's monthly mortgage is $1,000, but after paying his other bills, he has only $800 left with which to make the payment. He discovers that he can rent out his house for $1,200. That amount covers the mortgage and other house-related expenses ($200 per month) so that he breaks even, neither profiting nor losing money on the rental itself. If he can find a smaller place to rent for $800 a month, he may be able to pay the bills and keep his house.

> **CAUTION**
> **You may need to inform your tenants about defaults or imminent foreclosures.** Several states, including Oregon, Nevada, and Minnesota, require a landlord to inform tenants, before signing a lease, if the property is subject to a notice of default or pending foreclosure. Other states are sure to join the trend.

Added financial concerns when buying for a college student

Buying a house for a college-bound child has become an increasingly popular option, with dorm costs often prohibitively high. The average annual room and board for public, four-year, in-state schools rose to $9,498 in 2013–2014 (up 3.6% over the previous school year), while private school room and board averaged $10,823 (up 3.5%). (Source: the College Board.) But before you assume buying a place for your college kid will be cheaper, make sure you'll truly come out ahead.

Step One is to find out what the actual room and board at your child's college will likely be. Then research both the rental and the real estate market in the

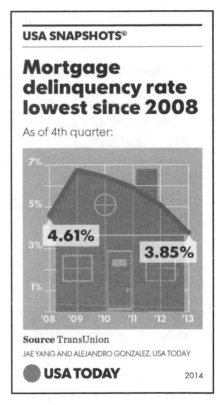

USA SNAPSHOTS©

Mortgage delinquency rate lowest since 2008

As of 4th quarter:

4.61%

3.85%

'08 '09 '10 '11 '12 '13

Source TransUnion

JAE YANG AND ALEJANDRO GONZALEZ, USA TODAY

● **USA TODAY**   2014

area. If you're lucky, your child will be attending school in an area where average rentals are high enough to offset average mortgages and other costs (the reverse may be true, although the demand for housing in college towns has a tendency to drive up rents). By renting out some rooms to other students, you may come out ahead even before your child graduates.

Of course, citywide averages may not be enough. You'll need to look at property values right around the college, which will naturally be affected by student demand for housing. With a couple of sample home prospects in mind, run the profit-or-loss calculation described under "Estimate short-term profits," above, then compare it to how much you'd be spending on room and board. If it comes out about the same, then you should buy the property only if you like the idea of a long-term investment, or think it will bring in a high return when you sell (as discussed next).

What Will Your Long-Term Gain Be?

Whether you're an accidental landlord or are actively looking to buy a house to rent out, your research so far will help you analyze your house's worth as a long-term investment—taking into account up-front costs, ongoing costs versus income, property appreciation, and profits from the sale. Now you can:

- estimate the house's likely appreciation, or increase in value over time, and
- calculate the likely return on your investment (ROI), or the expected value of your investment in your property.

Appreciation: Will your rental property rise in value?

We've already discussed the general tendency for homes to rise in value over time. But to get a true picture of your home's prospects, you'll need to look at local home prices. Ask your real estate agent to calculate the change in median prices for the past ten or more years, or call or visit the town clerk or assessor. The more local your research, the better—one neighborhood's house values may rise or remain steady while another one's drop.

If the price trend looks to be heading upward, you're probably on safe ground buying. If it's heading downward, you'll have to make a tougher decision—will you be getting a bargain just before prices tick upward again, or will you be entering a depressed housing market in which you'll have little choice but to hang onto the property for years trying to make the most of your rental income? Talk to your real estate agent and read the local media before making your decision.

Also remember that slow real estate markets sometimes increase demand for rental units, because people are skittish about buying, or have left a house due to foreclosure. And if you can charge enough rent to offset the monthly costs from the beginning, it's a solid investment by any measure.

To figure out the actual amount by which your house

Parental home buyers are a campus trend! Many real estate agents see significant numbers of parents investing in homes for their children to live in while going to college. The top college towns in which to invest, according to a 2012 Realtor. com analysis of rental rates versus average monthly mortgage amounts, include Boston, MA; Princeton, NJ; Chicago, IL; Washington, DC; Houston, TX; Philadelphia, PA; Atlanta, GA; Pittsburgh, PA; Providence, RI; and Los Angeles, CA.

is likely to go up in value year by year, take the appreciation rate that you researched above and use it to create an analysis like the one in the chart below. (It looks complicated at first, but is actually quite obvious when you follow it line by line.) The example shows the projected appreciation of a $400,000 house over a five-year period in an area with 5% appreciation.

Sample Projected Appreciation on $400,000 House									
Year	Current house value		Local appreciation rate		Appre-ciation amount		Current house value		Appreciated house value
1	$400,000	x	5% (or 0.05)	=	$20,000	+	$400,000	=	$420,000
2	$420,000	x	5% (or 0.05)	=	$21,000	+	$420,000	=	$441,000
3	$441,000	x	5% (or 0.05)	=	$22,050	+	$441,000	=	$463,050
4	$463,050	x	5% (or 0.05)	=	$23,153	+	$463,050	=	$486,203
5	$486,202	x	5% (or 0.05)	=	$24,310	+	$486,203	=	$510,513

Return on investment: How much will you get back?

Let's look years down the road, to estimate whether your total investment in the property will be worth it after paying all the associated expenses. The term to describe this is "return on investment," or ROI. It's usually expressed as a percentage. You can calculate ROI on other investments as well (such as stocks and bonds), and see how they're all doing relative to one another.

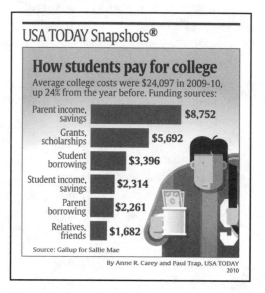

USA TODAY Snapshots®

How students pay for college

Average college costs were $24,097 in 2009-10, up 24% from the year before. Funding sources:

Parent income, savings — $8,752
Grants, scholarships — $5,692
Student borrowing — $3,396
Student income, savings — $2,314
Parent borrowing — $2,261
Relatives, friends — $1,682

Source: Gallup for Sallie Mae

By Anne R. Carey and Paul Trap, USA TODAY 2010

The basic idea is to take your estimated annual profits (including rents plus home appreciation—which are only paper profits until you sell, but that's okay), and divide it by your total investment in the property (down payment, annual costs, total mortgage principal paid that year, and anything you spent for major home improvements). That means filling in the following calculation (simplified to leave out tax deductions and depreciation):

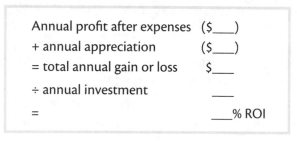

Annual profit after expenses   ($___)
+ annual appreciation   ($___)
= total annual gain or loss $___

÷ annual investment   ___

=   ___% ROI

EXAMPLE: Kira bought a house for $400,000 (putting $80,000 down), and began renting it out immediately. In her first year, she earned $2,000 in income (after expenses including mortgage interest, plus maintenance, utilities, and the rest), plus another $5,000 in home appreciation (paper profits until she sells). Dividing that by her investment amount (her $80,000 down payment plus $5,000 in mortgage principal payments over the year), her ROI would be approximately .082, or 8%.

So, what does the ROI percentage mean? It means that, continuing with our example, if Kira sold her home after the first year, she'd have earned an 8% return on her initial investment. She's probably doing pretty well compared to the returns on her stocks and other investments. Of course, we're using artificial numbers, and your returns may be far less.

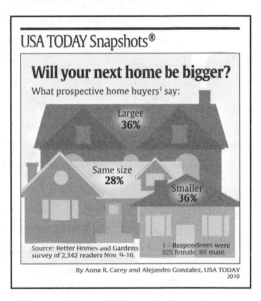

USA TODAY Snapshots®

Will your next home be bigger?

What prospective home buyers[1] say:

Larger **36%**

Same size **28%**

Smaller **36%**

Source: Better Homes and Gardens survey of 2,342 readers Nov. 9-16.

1 – Respondents were 92% female, 8% male.

By Anne R. Carey and Alejandro Gonzalez, USA TODAY 2010

At this point, we suggest you do the ROI calculation using projected numbers, for the first year as well as later years that you plan to own the property. If it's positive, that's another green light—but again, don't be too swayed by the prospect of home appreciation if your actual profits are negative. An ROI that's lower than you could get with other investments after several years may be a sign to look elsewhere.

Return to the ROI calculation once you have actual numbers, to see how reality compares with your projections. It might actually be a source of comfort if you're not earning a profit on your rents but home prices are appreciating. You may still come out ahead.

It's Tough to Buy a House in an Area With Rapid Appreciation

If your hope is to rent a house for a while and then sell it, you're going to want to look at areas where home prices are trending upward—but not too quickly if you hope to get a foot in the door, as explained by USA TODAY's Julie Schmit:

"The housing recovery hit high gear in 2013 with bigger than expected price gains and solid home sales. This year isn't likely to be as exciting. Rising mortgage interest rates will price out some potential buyers. Instead of double-digit price gains, look for single-digit ones, economists say, while existing home sales remain at last year's level."

Sound boring? "You want boring in the housing market," says Svenja Gudell, Zillow director of economic research.

Look for fewer bidding wars and a less frantic market, says Glenn Kelman, CEO of brokerage Redfin. Its data show bidding wars recently falling to one of two offers handled by Redfin agents, down from three of four at the peak in March.

Slowing price gains wouldn't be a bad thing, says John Burns, CEO of John Burns Real Estate Consulting.

Rapid appreciation encourages flipping—when homes are bought and resold in short intervals for fast profits—and pushes home prices into unaffordable territory as wage gains lag. If prices keep rising as fast as they have been, "It will create a bubble," Burns says.

Zillow's panel of 106 economists and real estate experts predicts home values will end this year [2013] up 6.7%. Appreciation will slow to 4.4% next year [2014], the panel says.

Kelman even expects prices to flatten or decline in some markets this fall as inventories increase. "It isn't just going to be up, up and up," he says.

 Excerpted from, "Housing market gets more buyer friendly," by Julie Schmit, August 18, 2013; and "What's ahead for 2014 housing market," by Julie Schmit, January 1, 2014.

Setting Your Goals

It's decision time: Having explored some of the basics of owning rental property, you must decide whether it's truly right for you. To help you in this process, answer the following questions:

- **How committed are you to holding onto the property?** If you're hoping for, say, a year's trial run, it's safest if you already own the property. Buying a property that you might not keep for at least three to five years is a recipe for loss (especially because of the transaction costs: 5%–6% for the real estate agent's fees alone when you sell).

> **Who's buying investment homes?**
>
> The typical investment-home buyer in 2012 was 45 years old, earned $85,700 per year, and chose a property that was relatively close to his or her own home—a median distance of 21 miles away.

- **What are your short-term financial goals?** After running the calculations above, decide what amount of property income will make it worth your while to pursue this project. Balance this against your long-term goals, below.

- **What are your long-term financial goals?** At some point, you may want—or need—to sell the house. What amount of profits are you expecting or hoping to make? If your sales profits aren't likely to be high, then it's even more important that you're satisfied with the anticipated monthly rental income.

- **How much time are you willing to put into this project?** If being a landlord will take precious hours you can't spare, then it may not be worth making a priority right now.

Take a careful inventory of your objectives as a landlord and property owner, both in the short term and the long term. Discuss them with your family, especially if you expect them to help maintain the property, deal with your absences, or travel with you for that purpose. Then keep track of where you are vis-à-vis those goals from year to year. We'll help you track your profits and expenses, in Chapter 6. ●

So Happy Together: Landlording With Family or Friends

After evaluating all the pros and cons of being a landlord, you may feel like it's too much for any one person to handle. Good news! You don't have to do it alone. Today, many people share the responsibilities and benefits of co-ownership with family members, friends, or professional associates.

In this chapter, we'll talk about investing together and divvying up the responsibilities of being a landlord, including:

- the pros and cons of co-owning rental property
- how to decide whether co-landlording is right for you
- ways to take title together, and
- what to cover in a co-ownership agreement.

Whether you're undertaking these responsibilities with your spouse, your sister, a long-time professional associate, or a distant cousin with whom you've inherited a property, this information will help you decide how to manage the property and finances.

We use the term "co-owner" throughout this chapter, assuming that most people will be sharing landlording responsibilities with only one other person. But in some situations—for example, if you and three other siblings inherit your parents' house and decide to rent it out—you might have multiple co-owners. For practical, financial, legal, and emotional reasons, it's crucial that you have a carefully thought-out written agreement that specifies everyone's responsibilities, as well as how you'll divide expenses and profit and make key decisions. You may find that outside professional help—a lawyer, mediator, financial adviser, or even a family therapist, if needed—will help craft a plan that works for everyone.

The Pros and Cons of Co-Owning Rental Property

Sharing the experience of being a landlord with someone else is like any situation with multiple cooks in the kitchen—some things are easier to do with the help of another person, and some things just seem to get more complicated. Here are some of the advantages you can expect:

- **Fewer responsibilities.** As we'll discuss in the next section, you and your co-owner may choose to divvy up landlording responsibilities according to your skills. Working on projects you're good at should mean that you can accomplish them efficiently and quickly. You may be able to avoid—or at least share—some of the tasks you don't like, if your co-owner is willing to do them.

- **Lower expenses.** You and your co-owner can share expenses, most likely in proportion to your ownership interest. For example, if you own 50%, you would pay only 50% of the replacement cost if the water heater broke.

- **Greater buying power.** You may be able to increase your buying power by co-owning with someone else. For example, by pooling resources you might purchase a more expensive and lucrative property, such as a multiunit building instead of a single-family house.

USA SNAPSHOTS©

Would you recommend working with a significant other?

Yes **57%**

No **43%**

Source Manta survey of 1,147 small-business owners
JAE YANG AND ALEJANDRO GONZALEZ, USA TODAY

● **USA TODAY**   2013

- **Lower risk of vacancy.** If a tenant doesn't pay the rent or the unit sits vacant for a month or two, the loss won't fall entirely on you— you'll share it with your co-owner.

But before you start scouting around for a co-owner, consider these drawbacks:

- **Lower income.** As nice as it may be to share the responsibilities of landlording, you also have to share the proceeds. If you each own

50% and split profits that way, you'll get half as much as you would otherwise. You'll also make less when you sell.

- **Less independence.** When you're the only landlord, you can decide who moves in, how much rent they pay, who will do repairs, and more. You'll probably lose some of this autonomy, and you and your co-owner may even disagree about some issues.

- **Less stability.** When you own with someone else, you must rely on that other person to do a designated share of the work—and pay a share of the bills. If your co-owner doesn't pay the appropriate share of the mortgage, for example, you may have to pay the whole thing or risk being foreclosed on.

- **Difficulty selling.** Depending how you and your co-owner take title (discussed further below), you may each be free to sell your interest in the property at any time. But because there isn't a huge market in partial ownership shares, it may be difficult to sell only your share.

Having a Compatible Co-Owner

Whether sharing the risks and responsibilities of landlording is right for you depends on more than the objective pros and cons. The biggest predictor of success is your ability to actually work with a co-owner to accomplish your goals. You'll want to co-own with someone who sees things the same way you do.

Of course, your choice may have already been made for you, for example if you and your sister have jointly inherited a house, or you and your spouse are moving out of the house you already own but plan to rent. But in other situations, you may actively decide to buy together and co-own with someone else, perhaps even someone you don't know very well.

What to look for in a co-owner

If you're thinking about looking for a co-owner—or just want to know what to expect if you're planning to work with your spouse—carefully consider the following factors:

- **Finances.** You and your co-owner should be willing to share the minute details of your finances with each other, including the amount of money you have coming in and where it's currently being spent. You'll probably each want to know as much as you can about the past, current, and anticipated debts, income, and expenses of your co-owner.

USA TODAY Snapshots®

Spouses and secret spending

Percentage of spouses who:

Make secret purchases **80%**

Have credit cards their spouse doesn't know about **19%**

Source: CESI Debt Solutions survey of 200 married men and women

By Jae Yang and Alejandro Gonzalez, USA TODAY 2010

- **Location.** It will be much easier to share the experience of landlording if you're both near the property in question. If you're both far away, you may want to discuss hiring a property manager, covered in Chapter 10.

- **Goals.** It's best if you and any co-owner have the same goals in mind. Do you want to buy a house your college kids can share, then sell it when they're done with school? What if your son decides to stick around a few extra years? Or are you hoping to buy out the co-owner's share in a few years, so you can retire in the place? You'll need to make sure you are on the same page about both short- and long-term goals.

- **Personality.** You'll want to choose a co-owner who you're sure you can get along with professionally. That may mean that you don't discuss the possibility with your best friend, who's a great pal but absentminded and has trouble balancing a checkbook.

Finding a co-owner

To find a co-owner, start by making your intentions known. If you have a particular co-owner in mind, you can approach that person with your proposition. It may be a vague idea about an eventual purchase or a specific plan to buy a property you've already identified. The more detail you provide, the more likely you are to look like—and find—a serious investor. If you don't have anyone in particular in mind, you can discuss your ideas more generally with people you know, getting the word out that you're looking.

If you're willing to work with someone you don't know, ask local real estate professionals and attorneys whether they know others interested in similar investments. Buying with someone you don't know is beyond the scope of this book, but suffice it to say that all the factors above— finances, location, goals, and personality—become even more important when the person isn't someone you're already acquainted with.

Sharing duties with your co-owner

Early on, you and your co-owner should talk about the various duties that co-owning a rental property will require, and who will do them. You may decide on a formal arrangement where each of you takes on certain tasks, perhaps using the "Landlording Duties" list, in Chapter 1. Or you may decide to be more flexible ("If you can handle maintenance problems on the weekdays, I'll take them on the weekends"). And married couples can take flexibility to the extreme, like Sarah, a San Francisco landlord, who explains, "I'll generally say to my husband something like, "The doorbell's not working, do you wanna call Tom or shall I?" In any case, it's a good idea to discuss the different possibilities so you can decide how to proceed before you make a purchase together.

Once you've decided who will do what, each of you should stick to your responsibilities and give each other the freedom to handle the assigned tasks as desired (unless it's going to have major negative effects, such as decreasing the property value or subjecting the tenant to uninhabitable conditions). For example, while Amy attended school in Berkeley, California, her partner Phil remained in Texas for awhile, and agreed to help manage her rental property in Austin. However, Amy explains, "After a hailstorm, Phil said he'd take care of communicating with the insurance company and the roof repairperson. But I got so anxious, I kept stepping in, which only caused confusion. Finally Phil had to remind me of our agreement."

There may also be some tasks you handle together. Gordon and Connie, for example, who co-own a house in San Jose, California, always make a point of interviewing potential tenants together. They find they each recognize different flaws and strengths in the applicants. Gordon, a lawyer, pays more attention to whether the applicants appear willing to abide by contractual obligations and can afford the rent. Connie tends to focus on whether people will pay on time, regardless of whether they can afford it, and whether they'll care for the property as if it were their own. Working together, they're able to select better tenants than if they worked singly, and they are less apt to lay blame if one of the tenants doesn't work out.

How to Take Title

When you own property with another person, you'll need to decide how you take title—that is, how you own the property together. This isn't a decision to procrastinate or flip a coin over, because it needs to be stated on your deed. Unless you're married, you have two main options for taking title in your own names: as tenants in common or as joint tenants. A third alternative is to form a business entity, such as an LLC, which will take title to the property in its name.

> **CAUTION**
> **How you hold title affects your rights to use, rent, and sell the property.** The information provided here will give you some basic information about your choices, but it's a good idea to talk to your attorney or tax adviser about your own situation before deciding which form of ownership is right for you.

Tenants in common

A tenancy in common (TIC) is probably the most popular way for unrelated co-owners to take title. As a tenant in common, you and your co-owner can own unequal shares of the property—for example, you could own 40% and your co-owner 60%. (You can also have more than one co-owner, with each of you owning different shares.) This is a big advantage if you have different amounts of cash to invest or are looking for different levels of return.

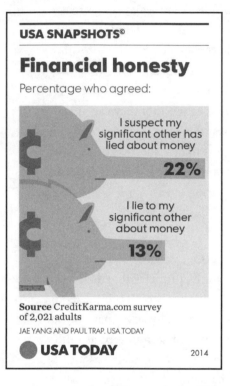

USA SNAPSHOTS®

Financial honesty

Percentage who agreed:

I suspect my significant other has lied about money

22%

I lie to my significant other about money

13%

Source CreditKarma.com survey of 2,021 adults

JAE YANG AND PAUL TRAP, USA TODAY

● **USA TODAY**   2014

Owning a share doesn't mean you own a particular slice of the pie, however. Your portion is called an "undivided interest," which means all co-owners have the right to use and enjoy the entire property. Let's say, for example, that you and your friend decide to split your ownership 60/40, and you'd like to apply your 40% share toward ownership of the smaller downstairs part of the house, while your co-owner owns the more spacious upstairs. That's not going to work in terms of legal ownership rights. If you ever want to separate your ownership share and your co-owner disagrees, you'll have to request that a court "partition" the property—that is, legally split it into separate parcels, owned individually. Because physically dividing property isn't feasible in most cases, the usual result is that the property is sold and the proceeds split. It's a lengthy and expensive process, which you're better off avoiding.

Another potential problem with owning as tenants in common is that either you or your co-owner can transfer your interest at any time. That means that your friend might suddenly decide to sell that 60% interest in the property—and can legally do so without your consent, to any interested buyer.

And then there's the matter of what happens if one of you dies. In a tenancy in common, a deceased person's share passes under the terms of that person's will or, if there isn't one, the inheritance laws of the state. You could find yourself sharing with a new co-owner (your current co-owner's long-lost daughter in Indonesia, for example).

Perhaps even more troublesome, co-ownership gives owners the right to "encumber" the property, which means take out loans against it. If your co-owner takes out a large equity loan against the property and doesn't pay it back, he or she can put your ownership at risk. You could get stuck making payments to stay out of foreclosure, even if your co-owner has taken the cash and skipped town.

Fortunately, you can draft an agreement to deal with some of these possibilities before they ever happen, which we'll discuss later in this chapter.

Joint tenants with right of survivorship

Another way to take title is as joint tenants with right of survivorship (JTWROS). Like tenants in common, joint tenants own an undivided interest in the entire property, and can't, for instance, draw a line down the middle. However, unlike tenants in common, joint tenants in most states must own equal shares—that is, if there are two of you, you each own 50%.

The other main difference between joint tenants and tenants in common is that if a joint tenant dies, the property immediately passes to the other tenant, even if the person's will says otherwise. That means you should own property this way only if you want your co-owner to own the entire property if you die. This is a common way for married couples, domestic partners, and those in committed relationships to take title. It's probably not the best option if you're buying with an unrelated investor.

Other options for married couples

In addition to the ownership methods described above, married couples have a few more options when it comes to taking title. In several states (Alaska, Arizona, California, Idaho, Louisiana, Nevada, New Mexico, Texas, Washington, and Wisconsin), married couples (and in some states, registered domestic partners) can own community property. Couples who own property this way each own half the property, which they can pass to whomever they please through their wills. While living, they can't sell or give away their share unless the other spouse consents.

A few states (Alaska, Arizona, California, Nevada, and Wisconsin) offer the additional advantage of community property with the right of survivorship. Property held this way doesn't have to pass through probate when one spouse dies, but instead goes straight to the other spouse (or, if the state allows, the registered domestic partner).

Finally, about half the states allow married couples (and sometimes, those in registered domestic partnerships or other "official" relationships) to take title as tenants by the entirety. In this case, you and your spouse or partner each own the entire property and can sell it only with the other's consent. In most states, if one of you is in debt, creditors can't come against that person's share of the property. Like joint tenancy, if one spouse dies, the other gets the property without probate hassles.

Holding property as a business entity

One final option for co-owners is to form a separate business entity and take title in its name. All co-owners would, in turn, own shares or a membership interest in the business.

Probably the most popular choice for people interested in forming a business entity is the limited liability company, or LLC. An LLC combines some of the best features of corporations and partnerships, offering these advantages:

- **Limited liability.** The LLC protects your personal assets (your house, car, and such) from business debts. That means a creditor claiming to be owed money by the business (the rental property) won't be able to come after you personally. Similarly, if a tenant is injured on the property, the tenant will be able to recover only from the LLC, not from you.

- **Tax benefits.** LLCs benefit from what's called "pass-through" tax status. That means the business's tax liabilities are paid directly by the members. The entity itself does not separately pay taxes.

Making It Work Over the Long Haul

Managing a property with a co-owner takes a lot more than just similar goals and objectives and a good solid contract. It takes patience, understanding, and a longstanding relationship that is nurtured over time. For example, Sergio Raddavero and his co-owner have owned a single-family home in Burlingame, California, for 20 years. They have an oral agreement that has never been put on paper. Sergio says the secret to their success is that "we understand each other and complement each other."

"He does more on the handyman side. I do more on the management side," says Sergio. "I'm better at managing the rentals, and I organize the finances. Every month, I print out a financial statement and send it to him. Keeping your partner informed and in the loop makes him feel comfortable and secure." The fact that they have had positive cash flow for most of those 20 years has also made it easier. They repaint the house every six years, put on a new roof every ten years or so, and remodeled the kitchen once—always using a reserve account set aside for such repairs, and never having to dip into their own pockets.

The point is, while we highly recommend having a written co-ownership agreement, sometimes the mutual understanding and respect you have for each other is enough to create a good property management relationship. Regardless, being aware of your expectations before crafting an agreement, and having a clear understanding of each other's strengths and weaknesses, are keys to making the rental property business a success.

- **Less formality than other business entities.** Relatively speaking, LLCs have to comply with fewer paperwork and meeting formalities than other business entities, such as regular "C" corporations.
- **No right of partition.** A property held in an LLC cannot be partitioned—the LLC owns it fully. You can decide in your operating agreement how any individual's membership interest can be sold, but you are protected from a partition action.

However, LLCs also have disadvantages, such as:

- **Complex tax rules.** If you form an LLC with another person, you will be treated as a partnership for tax purposes. Tax rules governing partnerships are significantly more complicated than rules for individuals. You will need to hire a tax professional to help you deal with these complexities.
- **Cost.** Forming an LLC will take extra cash. You'll have to follow the process outlined in your state, and spend as much as several hundred dollars for filing fees alone. Costs will be even greater if you get the help or advice of a professional.
- **Formalities.** Although the formalities associated with forming and running an LLC are fewer than with a corporation, they're still more than with a simple co-ownership agreement between two people. For example, you must file some paperwork to form the LLC (usually called the articles of organization), and then will want to prepare an operating agreement (covering a lot of the same topics a co-ownership agreement normally would).
- **Difficulty obtaining financing.** You may find it difficult—and more expensive—to find a lender willing to loan money to your LLC. Even if you find a willing lender, you'll probably have to provide a personal guarantee (undercutting the limited liability that made an LLC attractive in the first place). Some people get around this by taking title in their own names, then transferring title to the LLC. But most mortgages have a "due on sale" clause, making the mortgage fully payable when the property is sold. You risk the mortgagor "calling" your loan as a result of the transfer, forcing you to repay it in full or refinance the property.

For more information on various types of business entities, including state-by-state rules on forming an LLC or a corporation, see the Business Formation section of Nolo.com.

> ⚠ **CAUTION**
> **If you operate as a business entity, you may not be able to do a 1031 exchange.** A 1031 exchange, discussed further in Chapter 11, is a tax strategy that allows you to defer capital gains taxes when you sell investment property and purchase other investment property with the proceeds. If you think you may want to do a 1031 exchange in the future, discuss the possibility with your tax adviser.

Because limited liability is one of the primary benefits of forming an LLC, you should consider forming one if you are particularly concerned about protecting your assets. Another way to protect yourself is to purchase an umbrella insurance policy. Unless you own several rental properties, adequate insurance will probably be the more cost-effective way to deal with the risk of being sued. For more information on obtaining insurance, see Chapter 8.

If you've inherited property with family members and keeping the property in the family is a primary goal, you might also consider an LLC. In that case, an LLC can protect the property, because your co-owners won't be able to sell or encumber it. If interested, talk to your attorney about how to best convert ownership into an LLC.

> 📖 **RESOURCE**
> **Need to form an LLC?** To form an LLC online right now, use Nolo's Online LLC formation service. You complete a comprehensive interview online, and Nolo will create a customized LLC operating agreement and file your articles of organization with the state filing office. Your LLC will come into existence the day the articles are filed. See www.nolo.com/llc.cfm.

Creating a Co-Ownership Agreement

As we've already explained, there are many logistics involved in working with another person to co-own and manage rental property. Many of these details can be worked out—and potential problems can be avoided—if you and your co-owner start out with an agreement that specifies what each of you will be responsible for.

If you form an LLC, much of this will probably be covered in your organization's operating agreement. And if you're taking title in a form available only to married couples, you and your spouse may not face the same legal risks of other forms of shared ownership. Here, we're assuming you're taking title as tenants in common or joint tenants with a co-owner you aren't married to. A good co-ownership agreement should address:

- **How you'll choose tenants.** As co-owners, each of you has a right to use the property. Technically, each of you could rent it out to whoever you'd like. But to avoid stepping on each other's toes, create a system for choosing tenants. You may set certain (non-discriminatory) criteria (such as income, job stability, or lease length minimums), or provide a system for reviewing applications (for example, each person gets the right to veto one applicant who otherwise meets all minimum stated requirements).

- **Whether each of you will have the right to use the property personally.** Ownership as a tenant in common or joint tenant also entitles you to use of the property in question—if one of you occupies the place, the law won't assume that your possession is "adverse" to the rights of the other owner (in other words, your occupancy will be assumed legal). But neither of you wants your co-owner, or your co-owner's best friend, moving in rent free. Make sure the agreement specifies what happens if one of you wants to use the property personally.

- **The responsibilities each of you will handle.** As discussed above, you and your co-owner will want to lay out the exact duties each of you will be responsible for. The more detail you provide, the less there will be to disagree about later.

- **How you'll divide expenses and profits.** Make sure the agreement specifies that you'll split expenses and profits in relation to your ownership shares. (If you want another arrangement, discuss it with a tax adviser first—it could mean you're functioning as a partnership for tax purposes.)

- **Improvements.** Unlike regular maintenance expenses, you may not be legally entitled to reimbursement from your co-owner if you make any improvements to the property. Address how you will decide to make improvements and how you will pay for them.

- **Responsibility for the mortgage.** Usually but not always, co-owners purchase with a single mortgage. You

USA TODAY Snapshots®

All in the family
Do you plan to bring your children into the family business?

Father & Son PIZZERIA

No **43%**

Undecided **31%**

Yes **26%**

Source: SunTrust Bank Private Wealth Management survey of 201 business owners of companies with revenue of $10 million or more.

By Jae Yang and and Bob Laird, USA TODAY
2007

must decide what to do if one of you does not pay the promised share. For example, you may agree that the nonpaying party must make up payments with interest and is not allowed to participate in decisions about managing the property until current.

> **TIP**
>
> **Look for an assumable loan.** If you have a joint loan and anticipate that one of you might sell before the loan is paid off, consider getting an assumable loan. This will allow a subsequent purchaser to take the seller's place with the loan, meaning you won't have to refinance when that happens.

- **Making sure the property is adequately insured.** Agree that you will always maintain adequate insurance so that you're not relying on each other's resources in the event of damage or a loss (discussed in Chapter 8).

- **The lease or rental agreement.** Your lease or rental agreement will contain many terms you choose—for example, whether you will allow pets, the amount of the security deposit, and how long a lease term the tenant must agree to (see Chapter 5). You may wish to discuss these terms with your co-owner first, then agree how you'll handle any changes.

- **What to do if one of you wants to sell.** To avoid getting stuck in business with a complete stranger (because either of the original owners may have the right to sell your interest to whomever they please), spell out what you will do if one of you wants to sell. For example, you might determine that each of you has the "right of first refusal"—that is, the right to purchase the other's share before it's offered to anyone else. You'll have to determine how to value the property if you go this route—to keep things simple, you might agree to pay to have the property appraised, and for the purchasing party to pay the fair market value as determined by the appraiser.

- **What to do if one of you dies.** If you own property as joint tenants and one of you dies, the other will own the property. But if you are tenants in common, ownership will pass according to the terms of the deceased person's will or trust (or state inheritance laws, if there is no will or trust). In your agreement, you can specify that if either of you dies, the other has the right to purchase the deceased owner's share from the estate, and that each of you will add this to your will or trust documents.

- **How you will resolve disputes.** Even if it's hard to anticipate now, it's possible that you and your co-owner won't always agree. If that happens, you may want to try to resolve problems without going to court, for example using mediation. You can set up the requirements for this in your agreement.

As you can see, the issues you will need to cover in a co-ownership agreement are many. Because these agreements can get complicated, we suggest you hire an attorney to help you draft one or review one you've drafted. Better to spend a little up front if it helps save money and hassle in the long term.

Inherited a House? Watch Out for Flying Apples

How wrenching is it to let go of the family homestead? Anne Hyde Hyland, the youngest of five siblings, is finding out. The home in question is a rambling seaside house near Bath, Maine, used as a summertime gathering place for four generations. It is rife with memories and in grave need of repair.

When the family matriarch died last summer, the house was left to the eldest sister, who plans to rent it out this summer for the first time to pay for a new furnace and roof.

"My kids don't get it," says Hyland, who, as the only sibling living nearby, is being hit the hardest. "They say, 'What do you mean we can't come to our house anymore?'"

As the generation that produced the baby boomers dies or downsizes, people are increasingly likely to inherit a home.

The Hydes' mother had hoped to prevent disputes among her children, reasoning that leaving the home to one child, who could share it with the others, was more harmonious than splitting it five ways. Unfortunately, "our mother was thinking about it in a fairy-tale sense," says Hyland. One brother feels disenfranchised. Another objects to renovating the antiquated kitchen. Hyland was alarmed to find her sister had locked away a ship painting that hung above the fireplace, fearing it might be stolen. The siblings are "struggling" to schedule use of the house around the renters, and to negotiate a family rate, says Hyland.

Elizabeth Arnold, a lawyer in San Francisco who specializes in estate planning, tells of one family with a vacation home in the Pocono Mountains that squabbled after one in-law painted the bare two-by-fours on the walls. Later, at a family meeting, "two wives started voicing all their frustrations," and one pelted the other with apples from the fruit bowl.

It was the wake-up call they needed.

Inherited a House? Watch Out for Flying Apples (cont'd)

Arnold helped resolve disputes about the broken burner on the stove (fixed), the buck's head on the wall (removed), the newly painted two-by-fours (covered with paneling) and the lime-green shag carpeting (replaced by hardwood floors).

The family also started a new tradition: gathering one night each summer "to share memories and talk about what the place meant to them," says Arnold.

"This stuff is completely avoidable if the families get together and talk about it," she says.

 "Inheriting a house, but not the squabbles," by Joyce Cohen, April 11, 2003.

Preparing and Marketing Your Rental Property

Before you open the doors to prospective renters, you'll need to make sure the rental home is ready for showing. Particularly in competitive markets, your place should look as good as it can, to attract the best tenants at the best price. As John, who's been a landlord since 1975 explains, "It took me many years to discover that there's competition among landlords for the good tenants. The good tenants take away all your problems—they aren't breaking things and making up stories—and they let you stay ahead of the game."

This chapter explains the prep work involved, from scrubbing the toilet to painting the living room to making sure the house is fully up to code. Particularly if you're renting out a house that you or your parents have lived in for many years, you may have a lot of work to do.

This chapter also covers your choices for advertising and marketing your rental house and how to deal with renting out property that's still occupied. We'll also discuss why it's important to make a number of key decisions—such as how much rent you'll charge or whether you allow pets—before you run your first ad or talk with potential tenants.

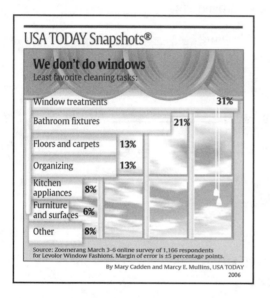

USA TODAY Snapshots®

We don't do windows
Least favorite cleaning tasks:

Window treatments	31%
Bathroom fixtures	21%
Floors and carpets	13%
Organizing	13%
Kitchen appliances	8%
Furniture and surfaces	6%
Other	8%

Source: Zoomerang March 3-6 online survey of 1,166 respondents for Levolor Window Fashions. Margin of error is ±5 percentage points.

By Mary Cadden and Marcy E. Mullins, USA TODAY 2006

Make Sure Everything Is Up to Code

Your first order of business is to make sure your house complies with all local and state housing codes. Chapter 7 discusses your legal duty to rent out habitable housing and your repair and maintenance obligations, and explains how to find out the extent of your responsibilities.

If you recently bought the property, you doubtless obtained an inspection report, which hopefully chronicled the structure's condition and repair needs. But if you're about to rent out a home that hasn't been inspected recently, you may not be sure what kind of shape it's in or what repairs it could use. It's worth hiring a professional inspector—just like you'd do when buying a house—to check the place out and identify potential problems, such as a leaky roof or faulty electrical circuits.

Look for an inspector who will give you a written, narrative report that helps you understand which issues need immediate attention and which you'll need to follow up on in the future. Common and significant code compliance issues include insufficient smoke detectors and the absence of ground-fault circuit interruption (GFCI) outlets.

RESOURCE
More information on home inspections. The Real Estate section of Nolo.com includes many useful articles on home inspections. Also check out the website of the American Society of Home Inspectors (ASHI) at www. ashi.com.

Should You Make Major Repairs or Improvements?

If your property is in really bad shape (perhaps you've inherited your parents' 75-year-old house), it might be easier to sell it than to turn it into a rental. At the very least, preparation for renting means making sure that the house is safe and habitable. And, particularly in competitive markets, you may need to spend some big bucks on optional upgrades (such as on modernizing the kitchen or bathroom) before finding a renter. Unless you have the cash to pay for such upgrades, you may end up having to add repayments on a home equity loan to your monthly expenses—making it even less likely that the rent will cover the costs.

Start by talking to contractors and getting cost estimates. Then look again at the calculations in Chapter 1, to see how your short-term profits and long-term investment prospects will shake out. If you'll be going deep into debt with no hope of profiting until years later when you sell, putting the place up for sale now might make as much sense. (See Chapter 11 for tips on selling your house.)

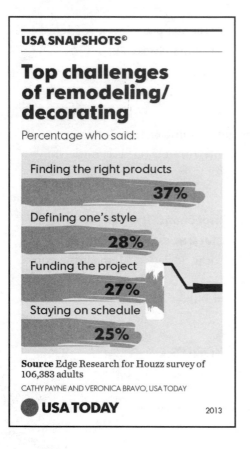

USA SNAPSHOTS©

Top challenges of remodeling/decorating

Percentage who said:

Finding the right products
37%

Defining one's style
28%

Funding the project
27%

Staying on schedule
25%

Source Edge Research for Houzz survey of 106,383 adults

CATHY PAYNE AND VERONICA BRAVO, USA TODAY

USA TODAY   2013

But what if you can't or don't want to sell right now, or think the property won't sell without some improvements anyway? That might change the analysis. After all, a renter might be willing to pay more once the place is improved. And in competitive markets, you may have little choice: If competing rentals (particularly in a planned unit development where units look alike) offer more amenities such as built-in dishwashers, you might need to install one, too.

Do your homework, however, before deciding which improvements to make. Major home improvements almost never return 100% of their value. Remodeling a kitchen or adding a deck tends to do the most to boost a sales price, but you're still unlikely to recoup the entire amount spent. For a breakdown by project, see the National Association of Realtors® annual "Cost vs. Value" report (go to www.realtor.org and search for "cost vs. value").

Prepare the Rental for an Attractive Showing

First impressions count, and when interested renters first lay eyes on your rental house, you want their reactions to be positive. No amount of, "I'm going to take care of that … and that … and that … in the next few weeks" will dispel the negative impression left by dirty windows, peeling paint, or an unkempt front yard. Basic cleanup doesn't cost much, but it can make all the difference to prospective tenants.

If you're too busy to do the work yourself, hiring a handyperson or cleaning service may well pay for itself by cutting down the amount of time your place is vacant and attracting good tenants.

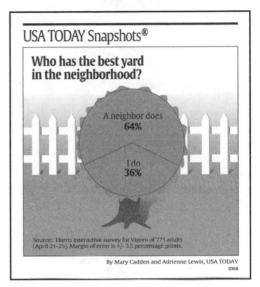

USA TODAY Snapshots®

Who has the best yard in the neighborhood?

A neighbor does **64%**

I do **36%**

Source: Harris Interactive survey for Vigoro of 773 adults (April 21-25). Margin of error is +/- 3.5 percentage points.

By Mary Cadden and Adrienne Lewis, USA TODAY
2008

> **TIP**
>
> **Keep your receipts.** Much of your prep work will be tax deductible, as discussed in Chapter 6.

Clean up the outside

The true first impression is made while your prospective tenants are getting out of their car or walking up to your property. If it looks run down or bedraggled, some people may just turn around and leave. Make sure your property looks welcoming and demonstrates your attention to maintenance. Here are the basics:

- Sweep the sidewalk and clear paper and debris from the yard, porch, driveway, and entryways.

- Mow the lawn, prune the shrubs, and pull up weeds.
- Wash all the windows.
- Check that the doorbell works.
- Make sure the property is well lit, and the address is visible from the street. Replace the porch light bulbs, and consider adding lights with sensor detectors that go on automatically when someone approaches the house.
- Add greenery, such as flowering potted plants that you can place strategically.
- Put out a nice welcome mat or add other decorative touches such as a bench on the porch or a birdhouse in the tree.
- Paint the exterior of the house if it's looking bad.

Spruce up the inside

No matter how good the outside looks, tenants will ultimately focus on picturing their daily life inside your property. Here's how to create a clean, tidy, and attractive interior:

- Make sure all rooms (especially the bathroom and kitchen) are spotless (including all appliances, cabinets, and fixtures).
- Clear all hallways and counters.
- Sweep or vacuum the floors or carpets. Replace any flooring that's torn, badly stained, or mildewed. Remove slippery throw rugs.
- Make sure everything works—from the shower to the ceiling fan to the front door lock.
- Replace the window coverings if they're in bad shape. And leave curtains open when prospective tenants visit, to let in lots of light.
- Repaint all rooms, especially if it's been a year or two since the last paint job. As *USA TODAY*'s Noelle Knox found, "Dark walls make the house look smaller. Walls should be off-white, or have earthy tones if the room has lots of light."
- Get rid of ants and any pests that may be roaming the rental.

- Cover electrical outlets, especially if families with small children will be visiting the place. Coil long electrical or phone cords to get them out of the way. Block off or child proof any dangerous areas for kids, such as pools and stairways.

- Check that smoke detectors and fire extinguishers are in place (and in working order).

- Bring in a few nice pieces of furniture, including a chair or two that will give people a chance to sit down and imagine what it might be like to live there. A coffee table with flowers and a few magazines or books will make the living room appealing.

- Put a new shower curtain in the bathroom.

- Put a pot of spiced apple cider on the stove, a tried-and-true trick to make the house smell good.

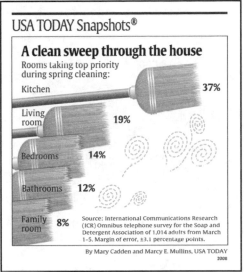

USA TODAY Snapshots®

A clean sweep through the house
Rooms taking top priority during spring cleaning:

Kitchen — 37%
Living room — 19%
Bedrooms — 14%
Bathrooms — 12%
Family room — 8%

Source: International Communications Research (ICR) Omnibus telephone survey for the Soap and Detergent Association of 1,014 adults from March 1–5. Margin of error, ±3.1 percentage points.

By Mary Cadden and Marcy E. Mullins, USA TODAY 2008

"The rental property should be absolutely spotless," says Sharon, who owns a rental property in Chico, California, and also manages two other properties in Sonoma County. "There should be no litter, no trash that needs to be emptied, no dust, no mildew, no paint that doesn't look fresh, and no lawn that needs mowing. In short, it should look like the kind of place you would live in!"

> **TIP**
> **Do the work now.** No matter how anxious you are to get new tenants moved in, take the time to repair and refurbish first. By waiting to deal with things like a ratty carpet or a bad paint job, you'll just end up paying bigger bucks later, when the job has gotten bigger. Plus, you'll irritate or inconvenience your tenants.

Set the Rent and Other Important Terms

Before you place your first ad, talk with prospective tenants, or prepare your lease or rental documents, you'll need to make a number of key decisions, including:

- the amount of rent you're going to charge (see Chapter 1)
- your requirements for tenants' minimum income and credit

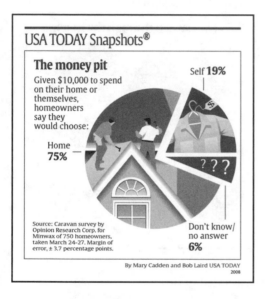

USA TODAY Snapshots®

The money pit

Given $10,000 to spend on their home or themselves, homeowners say they would choose:

Home **75%**

Self **19%**

Don't know/ no answer **6%**

Source: Caravan survey by Opinion Research Corp. for Minwax of 750 homeowners, taken March 24-27. Margin of error, ± 3.7 percentage points.

By Mary Cadden and Bob Laird USA TODAY 2008

- how much security deposit you're going to collect
- number of occupants
- whether pets are allowed (and, if so, what kind and any size limits)
- whether to offer a fixed-term lease or a month-to-month tenancy
- when the rental will be available
- what utilities (if any) you'll pay for, and

- any other important issues, such as whether you'll allow a home business, a cosigner on the lease, or smoking in the rental property.

Good rental policies are a combination of the practical ("What will work for this property?") and the legal ("May I legally require or forbid this?"). Showing your rental property (or even having an initial phone conversation) without a firm idea of how you'll handle the above issues is a real mistake and will waste everyone's time. Plus, you may get into legal trouble, such as a fair housing complaint, if you provide certain terms for some tenants, but not others.

Setting your rental priorities dovetails with writing your lease (a topic we'll cover in Chapter 5).

Balance Tilts From Owning to Renting

Since the real estate bubble burst, the American dream of home-ownership has fizzled. A growing number of Americans, called a new class of renters, can afford to buy a home but are renting by choice, says Tara-Nicholle Nelson, consumer educator at Trulia.com.

In August of 2010, 72% of people said they feel that homeownership is part of their American dream, down from 77% in January, according to a survey by Trulia.com. One out of four renters said they never plan to own a home.

In the past, renters tended to be college students and young married couples who were saving money for a home down payment. Now many older families who have been homeowners for years are returning to the rental market.

It's a confusing time in the market. On one hand, mortgage rates are at record lows, and in many cities, home prices have plummeted. But on the other hand, home foreclosures continue to rise, and the economy remains weak.

No wonder some people are sitting on the fence, trying to decide if it's better to buy or rent.

Oscar Martinez, who is married and has three children, has been a renter since he sold his home in Tempe, Arizona, about two years ago and used the money to expand his business.

"We wonder if my business is now stable enough to buy a home," says Martinez. "But instead of putting money into a down payment, I may keep investing in the business—for at least another year."

In the past, apartments and condos were the primary rental options. But now single-family homes are more available.

Many homeowners who can't sell their homes have become landlords. And some investors have purchased foreclosed homes and turned them into rental property, says Jim Gaines, economist at the Real Estate Center at Texas A&M.

Balance Tilts From Owning to Renting (cont'd)

If the rental vacancy rates are high, renters may be able to negotiate better deals. Some landlords have been willing to offer incentives, including flat-screen TVs, tickets to sporting events, free parking or a lower deposit, says Peggy Abkemeier, president of Rent.com.

Pros and cons of different cities

In some cities, it is much cheaper to rent than buy. But in another city in the same state, it could be less expensive to buy than it is to rent.

Trulia.com provides a quarterly Rent vs. Buy Index that is based on the 50 largest cities. For example, two cities in Texas are in the top lists: While Arlington is the best city in which to buy a home, Fort Worth is one of the best cities for renting. The ratio is determined by multiplying rent times 12 months and dividing that figure into the average list price. A low ratio indicates that it's less expensive to own than to rent.

 "Balance tilts from owning to renting," by Christine Dugas, October 8, 2010.

Get to Know the Neighbors

While you're puttering around the property, take the time to introduce yourself to neighbors in the surrounding houses. Some of them may be concerned about the house becoming a rental, given the widespread reputation that renters have for taking worse care of a property than homeowners do.

Reassure them that you're doing your best to find excellent tenants and plan to maintain regular oversight of the property. Sometimes just knowing that the landlord is a real person goes a long way toward making neighbors feel comfortable.

> ⚠ CAUTION
> **Let neighbors know how to reach you with complaints about your tenants.** Laura, a Bellevue, Washington, landlord, for example, says: "I like to meet the neighbors, give them my phone number, and say, 'If you have a problem, give me a call.' That happened with a Bellevue property—in fact, I wish they'd called me sooner. The tenants were leaving garbage on the back deck, and the neighbors had to look at dirty diapers and stuff. I went and talked to the tenants: Problem solved." (If a tenant later does cause trouble, our advice in Chapter 9 will explain how to act swiftly.)

Come on Down! Advertising Your House for Rent

A little word-of-mouth among your friends or colleagues, and posting on Facebook and other social media, may be all you need to find the perfect tenant, particularly if the market is tight and you have a competitively priced rental. For example, Laura describes how she found one of her best tenants: "The existing tenant (who needed to get out of the lease early), placed an ad in her mom's club's newsletter. I've also heard of landlords offering tenants money if they bring in a good replacement tenant."

For wider choice, however, you'll need to advertise publicly. Possible ways to do that include:

- if you live in one of the many areas served by Craigslist (www.craigslist.org), using that free online service (or other local online services you may find)
- putting a "House for Rent" sign in front of the property or in one of the windows
- posting flyers on neighborhood bulletin boards
- hiring a property management company (discussed in Chapter 10) that will advertise your rental as part of the management fee

- posting a notice with a university, alumni, or corporate housing office
- advertising in a local newspaper, and/or
- working with a local real estate broker who handles rentals.

The method of advertising that will work best depends on your particular rental house (its rent, size, amenities, and location), your budget, the saturation of the market, the type of renter who will likely be your tenant (such as students versus families), and whether you're under time pressure to rent your place out. If, for example, your rental is near a popular park or shopping area, a For Rent sign in the window is a must. In many markets, Craigslist is the only way to go. Longtime landlord Dennis has found that, "What does work is Craigslist. I don't use the newspapers anymore. You don't get many calls from the paper."

TIP

A picture really is worth a thousand words. One of the great advantages of online advertising services is that you can post digital photos of your rental, inside and out.

Your ads should contain a clear (and accurate) description of the property, including basic details, such as:

- rent
- size—particularly number of bedrooms and baths
- location—either the general neighborhood or street address, including proximity to public transportation and shopping areas and the school district
- whether you're offering a fixed-term lease or a month-to-month rental agreement
- the date the rental house is available
- special features—such as fenced-in yard, view, washer/dryer, fireplace, remodeled kitchen, furnishings, garage, parking, hardwood floors, wall-to-wall carpeting, or security system
- any important rules, such as no pets, and

- your phone number and/or email for more information, or the date and time of any open house.

> **CAUTION**
> **Avoid discrimination complaints—or a lawsuit.** Be sure your ad never mentions sex, race, religion, national origin, disability, or age (unless your property meets the legal requirements of senior citizens housing). See Chapter 4 for a discussion of antidiscrimination laws.

How to Show Your Property

Prospective tenants may start phoning as soon as you've advertised your vacancy. Be ready to tell them how they can come for a visit. You have three basic choices:

- individual appointments, in which you meet at the property and conduct personal tours
- private open houses attended by multiple prospects who have been invited by you, or
- public open houses, where anyone who has seen your ad or sign or knows of the vacancy can show up.

During that first phone call, provide complete details on the property and your policies. Sure, some prospective tenants will say "No thanks" on the spot, but that's fine. You'll avoid wasting your time showing your rental to someone who wouldn't have been interested in it anyway (or won't meet your requirements). Also, as John, an experienced California landlord, reminds us, "Give prospective tenants clear, simple driving directions, so they're not feeling frustrated by the time they arrive—if they find their way there at all."

Your decision whether to show your rental by appointment or by open house depends on market factors and your own time and preferences. For example, in a soft market, where good tenants are hard to find, you'll need to schedule appointments at the prospective tenant's convenience. In a hot market, with lots of interested applicants, one or two open houses may do the job. If you hold an open house, be sure it's at a convenient time, such as during two or three hours on a Saturday afternoon.

> **TIP**
> **Prepare the rental unit for a secure showing.** If you'll be allowing strangers into a rental house that no one is currently living in, consider bringing at least one other person with you. If you'll be holding an open house and expect a mob scene, sign up more than one person, ideally people who can answer questions and promote your rental to its best advantage. If someone is still living on the property, ask that they hide all valuables and prescriptions.

As you show your rental to prospective tenants, be polite and informative to everyone, even those whom you're pretty sure are not in the running. For example, after hearing someone's laundry list of needed cosmetic upgrades, you could fairly cross that applicant off your list. Still, while it's fine to tell the person that you won't be making those upgrades anytime soon, beware of doing so in a way that might cause offense. For one thing, you need to preserve (or begin creating) your reputation as a businesslike landlord. Perhaps more importantly, you never want to give a disappointed prospect an opening to accuse you of a fair housing violation, as may happen if the demanding prospect concludes that your tone and demeanor had more to do with race, religion, sex, or another protected characteristic than it did with your unwillingness to go along with the demands.

USA TODAY Snapshots®

Stirring things up
What Americans do in the kitchen aside from cooking:

Pay bills	48%
Do work/homework	44%
Do a hobby or craft	38%
Socialize & entertain guests	37%
Read	34%

Source: Electrolux Home Products survey of 1,024 adults. Margin of error is ±3.1 percentage points.

By Cindy Clark and Suzy Parker, USA TODAY 2006

Pardon Those People: Renting Property That's Still Occupied

Many first-time landlords buy or inherit property with tenants in place. Hopefully, yours will be a good tenant who wants to keep renting. But what if the tenant plans to leave, or you decide not to renew the lease or rental agreement for a tenant who is less than ideal? If possible, wait until the current tenant moves out to show a rental unit to prospective tenants. (This is especially a good idea if your elderly parents are the current residents and they're leaving their long-time home for a nursing home or assisted living.)

Waiting until the place is vacant gives you the chance to spruce it up. It also avoids problems such as promising the house to a new tenant, only to have the existing tenant not move out on time or leave the place a mess.

Nevertheless, to comply with a lease that's still valid for many weeks or months, or to eliminate any gap in rent, you may need to show your property while its current tenants are still there. Follow these suggestions to minimize the disruptions to current tenants and maximize your chances of having a successful showing:

- **Communicate.** Before advertising, discuss your plans with outgoing tenants so you can be as accommodating as possible.
- **Warn tenants about showings.** Give current tenants as much notice as possible before entering and showing a rental house to prospective new tenants. In all states, you have a right to show the still-occupied property to prospective tenants, but your current tenants are still entitled to a reasonable level of privacy and appropriate notice (typically 24 hours—for details, see the discussion of the notice-of-entry clause in leases and rental agreements in Chapter 5).
- **Don't overdo showings.** Try to limit the number of times you show the house in a given week, and make sure your current tenants agree to any evening and weekend visits.

- **Offer something in return.** Consider offering a restaurant gift certificate or another perk. As a last resort, for situations where showing the rental will be a major imposition or the tenants refuse to cooperate, you might reduce the rent slightly.

- **Avoid putting a sign on the rental property itself.** This almost guarantees that your existing tenants will be bothered by strangers. Or, if a sign seems like an important advertising method, make sure it clearly warns against disturbing the occupant and includes a telephone number for information: for example, "For Rent: Shown by Appointment Only. Call 555-1700. Do Not Disturb Occupants." If you're using a real estate agent to help with the renting and showing, do not allow the use of a "lockbox," which results in unannounced (and often illegal) property showings.

> **TIP**
>
> **You don't want a tenant who violates the "Do not disturb" sign.** Catherine, a Berkeley landlord who rents a cottage behind her own house, looked out her window one day to see a woman wandering through her back yard. Catherine says, "It turns out she was a prospective tenant who just chose to ignore the sign. I figured this didn't bode well for her ability to follow my rental agreement terms, so of course I didn't rent the place to her."

If, despite your best efforts, the current tenants are uncooperative or hostile, avoid hassles and wait until they leave before showing the rental. Also, if the current tenant is a complete slob or has damaged the place, you're better off applying paint and elbow grease before trying to rent it again. Never advertise or rent a unit in which the current tenant is ignoring a termination notice or, worse, fighting an eviction. Better to clear the decks before embarking on your search for a new tenant. ●

Screening and Choosing Good Tenants

After all your work preparing, showing, and marketing your new property, the day will come when a prospective tenant looks around and says, "It's great, I'd like to rent it." Is that your cue to set a move-in date and watch the rent checks start to roll in? Not so fast.

Choosing tenants is the most important decision you'll make. A bad choice can result in damage and lost rent. And tenant turnover is invariably expensive: By the time you factor in lost rental income (depending on how long the property sits vacant), advertising and screening costs, and the value of your time to plan and run the whole tenant selection show, one change of tenants can easily cost two to three times the monthly rent. And nothing can destroy a profitable year more quickly than an eviction lawsuit, even one that you ultimately win.

Every landlord we talked to in preparing this book was eager to tell us horror stories about tenants who didn't work out—and how he or she learned to find the best tenants (and avoid legal hassles) through a fair and thorough screening process. This chapter shows how your common sense and business moxie, coupled with a clear understanding of the law, will keep your rental income steady and safe. It will help you meet the all-important goal of finding (and keeping) good tenants who pay their rent on time, take good care of your property, and are considerate neighbors.

Hate to Choose? A Property Manager Could Handle This

Many landlords decide to contract with a property management company, which will take care of advertising your property and screening tenants, as well as collecting rent, handling tenant complaints, arranging repairs and maintenance, and evicting troublesome tenants (usually for an additional fee). But not all management companies will deliver on their promises—like prospects, they too have to be researched and screened. See Chapter 10 for details.

> **TIP**
> **Lesson learned the hard way: Nice guys aren't always what they seem.** As Darla in Seattle found, "When I tried to rent my house out, I had plenty of people interested. One guy seemed really nice, and looked good on the application he filled out. So I didn't bother to do a financial background check. Bad move—he was a total loser, with a lousy credit record and past evictions. I wound up with a big utility bill after I evicted him for nonpayment of rent."

Creating a Rental Application

If you were to ask a group of landlords whether their "gut reactions" to prospective tenants have always panned out, chances are you'd find some whose instincts have never failed them. Alas, you'd also find a fair share of rueful stories, chronicling the disappointments or even disasters that resulted from trusting skin-deep impressions. To avoid being misled, ask each prospective tenant to fill out a rental application that includes:

- the applicant's employment, income, credit, and rental housing history
- up-to-date references from landlords and employers
- identifying information, such as the applicant's Social Security number (SSN), driver's license number, passport, or Individual Taxpayer Identification Number (ITIN) which is issued by the

USA SNAPSHOTS®

Value of minimum wage

The federal minimum wage hit its inflation-adjusted high point in 1968 (2013 dollars):

$10.74
$9.49
$7.89
$7.89
$7.25

1960   1968   1978   2009   2014

Source Business Insider analysis of Labor Department data

ANNE R. CAREY AND PAUL TRAP, USA TODAY

USA TODAY   2014

IRS to persons who are required to file income taxes but who can't obtain a Social Security number, and

- details on past bankruptcies, evictions, or criminal convictions (you'll also get much of this information from a credit report, as discussed below).

You can either hand over the blank rental application in person when showing your rental or email a copy to interested applicants. If more than one person plans to live in your property, each one over the age of 18 needs to fill out his or her own, separate application. This is true whether you're renting to a married couple or unrelated roommates, complete strangers or the cousins of your current tenant.

> **CAUTION**
>
> **Don't pick and choose who gets a rental application.** After explaining the basic terms of the tenancy (such as the length of the rental, the rent, deposit, maximum number of occupants, and pet rules), give a rental application to anyone who appears to be qualified and interested—even if you think they can't afford your place. Be sure applicants understand that they must fully complete the application in order to be considered.

Your prospect's signature at the bottom of the rental application is crucial. It authorizes you to verify the information and references and to run a credit report. (Some employers and banks require written authorization before talking to you about a person.)

> **TIP**
>
> **Information on the rental application will also help you track down a tenant who later skips out.** This doesn't happen often, but it happened to Thai, a first-time landlord. He explains, "Eight months into a one-year lease, the tenant just picked up and left. She changed her phone number and didn't respond to my emails. Now I'm much more careful to get references, and ideally a family member's address, which can work like a 'permanent address.'"

Renting to Section 8 Tenants

"Section 8" is a federally run and financed housing assistance program of the federal department of Housing and Urban Development (HUD). ("Section 8" refers to Section 8 of the U.S. Housing Act of 1937, 42 U.S. Code § 1437f.) One-third of a tenant's income is paid to the landlord; the local housing authority makes up the balance of the rent. In most states, you aren't obligated to accept a Section 8 tenant, but can choose whether to participate in the program. Your local public housing agency can provide details. If you have property in a low-income neighborhood, you may find that most of your applications are from Section 8 renters, and you may need to accept them in order to stay in business.

There are pluses and minuses to participating in Section 8. Although many landlords are leery of accepting tenants whose ability to pay the rent is already marginal, Phil, a first-time landlord who shares his Berkeley triplex with two Section 8 tenants, says, "It's worked out fabulously. The fact that they're getting a rental subsidy helps them pay on time. Plus, it's a good deal for them and they want to keep it that way, so if anything, they're more responsible than regular tenants might be."

RESOURCE

More information on rental applications. The Rental Applications and Tenant Screening area of the Landlords section of Nolo.com includes several articles on how to screen and select tenants based on a rental application and credit report (discussed below). A sample rental application published by Nolo is shown below. (Source: *Every Landlord's Legal Guide*, by Marcia Stewart, Ralph Warner and Janet Portman (Nolo).) This book is available in both hard copy and electronic form at www.nolo.com. An online rental application form is also available on the Nolo site.

Rental Application

Separate application required from each applicant age 18 or older.

Date and time received by landlord _____

Credit check fee ___$38_____ Received _____

THIS SECTION TO BE COMPLETED BY LANDLORD

Address of Property to Be Rented: _____178 West 81st St., Apt. 4F_____

Rental Term: ☐ month-to-month ☑ lease from __3/1/20xx__ to __2/28/20xx__

Amounts Due Prior to Occupancy

First month's rent.. $_____3,000_____

Security deposit .... $_____3,000_____

Other (specify):__Broker's fee_____ $_____3,000_____

TOTAL.................. $_____9,000_____

Applicant

Full Name—include all names you use(d): __Hannah Silver_____

Home Phone: _609-555-3789___ Work Phone: _609-555-4567__ Cell _609-555-6543_

Email: __hannah@coldmail.com_____ Fax*: _____

Social Security Number: _123-00-4567__ Driver's License Number/State: _D123456/NJ___

Other Identifying Information: _____

Vehicle Make: ____Toyota____ Model: __Corolla___ Color: __White_____ Year: __2008___

License Plate Number/State: _____NJ1234567/New Jersey_____

Additional Occupants

List everyone, including minor children, who will live with you:

Full Name	Relationship to Applicant
Dennis Olson	Husband

Rental History

FIRST-TIME RENTERS: Attach a description of your housing situation for the past five years.

Current Address: _39 Maple St., Princeton, NJ 08540_____

Dates Lived at Address: _May 2008–date__ Rent $ _2,000_ Security Deposit $ _4,000__

Landlord/Manager: _Jane Tucker__ Landlord/Manager's Phone: _609-555-7523____

Reason for Leaving: __New job in NYC_____

* By providing this fax number I agree to receive facsimile advertisements from the landlord or management company.

Previous Address: 1215 Middlebrook Lane, Princeton, NJ 08540

Dates Lived at Address: 6/2003–5/2008 Rent $ 1,800 Security Deposit $ 1,000

Landlord/Manager: Ed Palermo Landlord/Manager's Phone: 609-555-3711

Reason for Leaving: Better apartment

Previous Address: _____

Dates Lived at Address: _____ Rent $ _____ Security Deposit $ _____

Landlord/Manager: _____ Landlord/Manager's Phone: _____

Reason for Leaving: _____

Employment History

SELF-EMPLOYED APPLICANTS: Attach tax returns for the past two years

Name and Address of Current Employer: Argonworks, 54 Nassau St., Princeton, NJ

_____ Phone: 609-555-2333

Name of Supervisor: Tom Schmidt Supervisor's Phone: 609-555-2333

Dates Employed at This Job: 2000–date Position or Title: Marketing Director

Name and Address of Previous Employer: Princeton Times

13 Junction Rd., Princeton, NJ Phone: 609-555-1111

Name of Supervisor: Dory Krossber Supervisor's Phone: 609-555-2366

Dates Employed at This Job: 5/1996–2/2000 Position or Title: Marketing Associate

ATTACH PAY STUBS FOR THE PAST TWO YEARS, FROM THIS EMPLOYER OR PRIOR EMPLOYERS.

Income

1. Your gross monthly employment income (before deductions): $ 8,000

2. Average monthly amounts of other income (specify sources): $ _____

    Note: This does not include my husband's income. $ _____

    See his application. $ _____

    TOTAL: $ 8,000

Bank/Financial Accounts

	Account Number	Bank/Institution	Branch
Savings Account:	1222345	N.J. Federal	Trenton, NJ
Checking Account:	789101	Princeton S&L	Princeton, NJ
Money Market or Similar Account:	234789	City Bank	Princeton, NJ

Credit Card Accounts

Major Credit Card: ☑ VISA ☐ MC ☐ Discover Card ☐ Am Ex ☐ Other: _____

Issuer: _City Bank_____ Account No. __1234 5555 6666 7777__

Balance $ _1,000_____ Average Monthly Payment: $ _1,000____

Major Credit Card: ☐ VISA ☐ MC ☐ Discover Card ☐ Am Ex ☑ Other: _Dept. Store_

Issuer: _City Bank_____ Account No. _2345 0000 9999 8888__

Balance $ _2,000_____ Average Monthly Payment: $ _500____

Loans

Type of Loan (mortgage, car, student loan, etc.)	Name of Creditor	Account Number	Amount Owed	Monthly Payment

Other Major Obligations

Type	Payee	Amount Owed	Monthly Payment

Miscellaneous

Describe the number and type of pets you want to have in the rental property: _____
_None now, but we might want to get a cat sometime_____

Describe water-filled furniture you want to have in the rental property: _None_____
_____

Do you smoke? ☐ yes ☑ no

Have you ever: Filed for bankruptcy? ☐ yes ☑ no How many times _____

Been sued? ☐ yes ☑ no How many times _____

Sued someone else? ☐ yes ☑ no How many times _____

Been evicted? ☐ yes ☑ no How many times _____

Been convicted of a crime? ☐ yes ☑ no How many times _____

Explain any "yes" listed above: _____
_____

References and Emergency Contact

Personal Reference: ___Joan Stanley___ Relationship: ___Friend, coworker___

Address: _785 Spruce St., Princeton, NJ 08540_

_____ Phone: _609-555-4578_

Personal Reference: ___Marnie Swatt___ Relationship: ___Friend___

Address: _82 East 59th St., #12B, NYC_

_____ Phone: _212-555-8765_

Contact in Emergency: _Connie & Martin Silver_ Relationship: ___Parents___

Address: ___7852 Pierce St., Somerset, NJ 08321_

_____ Phone: _609-555-7878_

Source

Where did you learn of this vacancy? _Ryan Cowell, Broker_

_____

I certify that all the information given above is true and correct and understand that my lease or rental agreement may be terminated if I have made any material false or incomplete statements in this application. I authorize verification of the information provided in this application from my credit sources, credit bureaus, current and previous landlords and employers, and personal references. This permission will survive the expiration of my tenancy.

Hannah Silver _February 15, 20xx_

Applicant Date

Notes (Landlord/Manager): _____

_____

_____

_____

_____

_____

_____

_____

_____

_____

Check References and Run a Credit Report

If you're lucky, you may easily find one or more potential tenants whom you like personally, and whose written applications look good. Should you sign one of them up yet? Sorry, those written applications can lie

USA TODAY Snapshots®

The lies have it

Overall, 42% of high school students think a person has to lie or cheat sometimes to succeed. By gender:

Male
50%

Female
33%

Source: Josephson Institute's 2006 Report Card on the Ethics of American Youth, a questionnaire survey of 36,000 high school students ages 14-19 from 114 schools, January-June; margin of error is ±1 percentage point.

By Tracey Wong Briggs and Alejandro Gonzalez, USA TODAY 2006

or cover up a rental or financial history that would make the applicant a poor risk. Even after 20 years as a landlord, Dennis says, "It's hard to judge people just by meeting them—are they going to pay bills, are they going to take care of property, are they going to be a nuisance to the neighborhood?" So your next step is to choose your top two or three applicants and confirm the representations on the application.

> **TIP**
>
> **Best thing I ever did: Weed out tenants by charging first and last months' rent.** Kyung bought a three-family house in New Haven, Connecticut, and lived in one of the units (the two rents paid the entire mortgage). "But," she explains, "because we had a small child, and were going to be sharing the driveway and laundry area, we needed tenants we could trust. We not only interviewed people carefully, but we asked them to sign a one-year lease, plus put down first and last months' rent. That ruled out a lot of people who didn't have money or were bad risks. We decided we'd rather go months with no one living there than regret saying yes to someone. It worked out great; we found good, long-term tenants."

Collect Holding Deposits Carefully

Eager applicants will often ask you to accept a holding deposit pending your review of their rental application. (A holding deposit is supposed to guarantee that the applicant will get the rental if his or her credit and references check out.) These tenants want you to know that their money is where their mouths are—if their rental, employment, and credit histories meet your satisfaction, they'll move in.

Holding deposits should be accepted warily and handled with care. Some states impose disclosure requirements on landlords who collect them, by requiring you to explain the circumstances in which you'll keep or return the deposits (or credit the deposit to the first month's rent). Beyond these technicalities, however, consider the added bookkeeping. Are you prepared to keep track of these deposits? It's generally a bad idea to require holding deposits—many tenants who are otherwise perfectly good candidates will not have cash available to sideline into a holding deposit.

Check with previous landlords

Who better to tell you about a tenant than the person's past landlords? In particular, a former landlord has no reason to paint a deceptively rosy picture of a problem tenant in order to unload that person onto you. When you call, ask targeted questions such as:

- Did this person pay the rent on time (and, if not, what were the circumstances)?
- Did the person ask for repairs when appropriate (but not every time there was a minor problem)?
- How easy was it to communicate with this person?
- Was he or she considerate of neighbors (no loud parties)?
- Did the person take good care of the property?
- Would you rent to this person again?

Assuming you're dealing with a candid, businesslike landlord, you want to hear positive answers to your questions. But what if you sense that you're talking to an unreasonable landlord, whom even you wouldn't want to rent from? If so, or if your prospect has alerted you to this possibility, consider the landlord's statements, but be sure to contact other, past landlords to get a more complete picture.

TIP

Check out pets, too. If the prospect has a dog, cat, or other pet, ask landlord references whether the pet caused any damage or problems for other tenants or neighbors. It's also good to meet the pet, so you can make sure that it's well groomed and well behaved. That will avoid situations like the one Gordon, with property in San Jose, California, faced: "One tenant told us they had a small dog, and they didn't, they had a big one. And the dog basically killed all the grass in the back yard and destroyed the landscaping." You must, however, accommodate an applicant with a legally recognized disability whose pet serves as a support animal—no matter what your pet policies otherwise might be.

Verify income and employment

You no doubt want a tenant who will pay the rent each month. That's why you need to find out whether, in raw numerical terms, the tenant has the income with which to do so. Call the prospective tenant's employer to verify income and length of employment. (The employer might require written authorization from the employee, which you'll have on the rental application or on a separate, stand-alone consent form—fax or email either one to the employer.) You may also ask the prospective tenant to document other sources of income, such as Social Security, disability payments, workers' compensation, welfare, child support, or alimony. Ask self-employed applicants to provide copies of recent tax returns.

How much income is enough? Think twice before renting to tenants where the rent will take more than one-third of their income, especially if they have a lot of debts or financial obligations, if their job is seasonal, or they have a history of bouncing from job to job.

> CAUTION
>
> **Boring tenants can be better than ones you'd want to hang out with.** As Sarah, a San Francisco landlord, explains, "We've rented to people we wanted to give a break to—we identified with them, because they were young and having trouble finding a place. Of course, being young, their plans changed, and they moved on quickly, and broke the lease. If we could do it all over again, we'd choose the boring tenants with the more stable financial situation."

Check credit reports

A handy way to check prospective tenants' financial circumstances (in particular, their debt load) and on-time payment record is to get each person's credit report from at least one credit reporting agency (CRA). John, who's been a landlord since 1975, puts it another way: "If you don't run credit checks, you're crazy."

USA TODAY Snapshots®

Most think dogs count as company

People who say that someone at home with their dog is not alone, even if no other people are there:

Non-owners
Alone 29%
Not alone 63%
8%
Don't know

Dog owners
Alone 18%
Not alone 79%
Don't know 3%

Source: Kelton Research for the American Kennel Club

By April Umminger and Frank Pompa, USA TODAY 2005

A good credit report contains a gold mine of information, such as the person's history of paying rent or bills late, past bankruptcies, some criminal convictions, and sometimes past evictions. (Your legal right to get information on evictions, however, may vary from state to state.) Credit reports may also give you a FICO score, which is a number between 300 and 850 that purports to reflect the chances that the consumer will fulfill his or her future financial obligations. A low number indicates a poor risk; most landlords will reject applicants with scores under 550 or 600.

Credit reports usually cover the past seven to ten years. To obtain one, you'll need a prospective tenant's name, address, and Social Security number or ITIN (Individual Taxpayer Identification Number). Technically, as long as you're requesting the report for a valid business reason, which includes evaluating the credit risk of a prospective tenant, you don't need the prospect's consent. But, because many people believe that you need their okay, it's simpler to ask for it (for convenience's sake, get it in writing).

Three CRAs have cornered the market on credit reports:

- Equifax, www.equifax.com

- Experian, www.experian.com, and

- TransUnion, www.transunion.com.

However, you can't order a credit report for someone else directly from one of these big three. Instead, you'll need to work through a credit reporting or tenant screening service (type "tenant screening" or "credit report" into your browser's search box). Look for a company that operates in your area, has been in business for a while, and provides you with a sample report that's clear and informative.

USA TODAY Snapshots®

Many Americans unprepared

How long could you cover household living expenses with your current liquid savings?

17% — Less than one week

14% — One week to less than one month

24% — One month to less than three months

10% — Three months to less than six months

19% — Six months or more

17% — Declined to answer

Note: Total doesn't add up to 100 due to rounding

Source: LexisNexis Martindale-Hubbell's Lawyers.com survey of 2,318 adults 18 and older. Margin of error ±3 percentage points.

By Jae Yang and Marcy E. Mullins, USA TODAY 2006

It's legal in most states to charge prospective tenants a fee for the cost of the credit report and your time and trouble. Any credit check fee should be reasonably related to the cost of the credit check itself—$20 to $30 is common. (And you must really run the credit check—you can't just pocket the fee.) Check your state law for any limits and rules as to what you must do when accepting credit check and application-screening fees.

Check Database of Sex Offenders

Not surprisingly, most landlords don't want tenants with criminal records, particularly of violent crimes or crimes against children.

Checking a prospective tenant's credit report is one way to attempt to find out about a person's criminal history, but not all convictions will show up on a credit report. Self-reporting is another: Rental applications typically ask whether the prospective tenant has ever been convicted of a crime.

"Megan's Law" databases may also be a useful source of information. Named after a young girl killed by a convicted child molester who lived in her neighborhood, this federal disclosure law charges the FBI with keeping a nationwide database of persons convicted of sexual offenses against minors and violent sexual offenses against anyone. (42 U.S.C. §§ 14071 and following.)

Every state has its own version of Megan's Law, requiring certain convicted sexual offenders to register with local law enforcement officials, who keep a database on their whereabouts. For information on accessing this database, and restrictions on your use of information derived from it, contact your local law enforcement agency or check www.parentsformeganslaw.org.

TIP

Keep good records. Take notes of all your conversations with applicants and references and keep them on file, along with applicants' credit reports. (See our advice on record keeping, in Chapter 5.) You'll need these records in order to survive a fair housing challenge if a disappointed applicant files a discrimination complaint. Take special care to store credit reports in a safe place, such as a locked filing cabinet, where only you and those who "need to know" can access them. Under the "Disposal Rule" of the Fair and Accurate Credit Transactions Act of 2003, you must destroy the report when you no longer need it.

Check college transcripts

If you'll be renting to college students, the credit reports may not show much—they may be just signing up for their first credit cards! But you can ask to see a copy of a recent school transcript. (If they're freshmen, a high school transcript will do.)

A transcript can reveal a lot. If it shows no "incompletes," a full load, and good grades, you're probably looking at a person who can follow through with a commitment. Even so, you may want to consider requiring a cosigner (as discussed in Chapter 5) if the student depends on parents for substantial support.

Avoiding Illegal Discrimination

Although you can exercise personal choice in deciding who lives in your rental house, there are limits on the reasons for which you can exclude someone. Federal, state, and local laws specify illegal reasons to refuse to rent to a tenant, and limit what you can say and do in the tenant selection process. The federal Fair Housing Act and Fair Housing Amendments Act (42 U.S.C. §§ 3601-3619, 3631) prohibit discrimination on the basis of race or color, religion, national origin, gender, age, familial status (pregnancy or children), and physical or mental disability (including recovering alcoholics and people with a past drug addiction). These are called protected classes. Many states

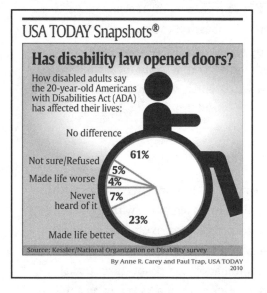

USA TODAY Snapshots®

Has disability law opened doors?

How disabled adults say the 20-year-old Americans with Disabilities Act (ADA) has affected their lives:

No difference 61%
Not sure/Refused 5%
Made life worse 4%
Never heard of it 7%
Made life better 23%

Source: Kessler/National Organization on Disability survey

By Anne R. Carey and Paul Trap, USA TODAY 2010

and cities also prohibit discrimination based on marital status, military status, sexual orientation, gender identity, and/or source of income.

Renting to Undocumented Immigrants

It's not against the law to rent to someone who is in the United States illegally. Then again, it's not against the law to refuse to rent to someone who is here illegally. Some landlords recognize that many undocumented immigrants have been here for years, hold stable jobs, and are unlikely to become the target of hit-or-miss immigration raids. Others assume, whether rightly or not, that people who are here without proper documentation, and subject to deportation, are more likely to skip out on a rental than others.

If you decide to rent to legal residents only, you'll need to advise all applicants that they must supply proof of legal residence. Asking only those who appear to be "foreign" will open you up to a charge of discrimination based on national origin, race, or color.

Next, you'll have to review and understand the documents that applicants give you. You'll quickly discover that the various visas, work permits, receipt notices, and other documents issued by United States Citizenship and Immigration Services (USCIS; www.uscis.gov) are indecipherable, to say the least. And that's before you deal with the possibility of fake documents. Short of being shown a U.S. passport, many landlords throw up their hands.

In recent years, several localities around the United States have passed ordinances making it illegal to rent to people who aren't legal residents. Every such ordinance has either been withdrawn or struck down by a court. Landlords in California and New York City must heed their state and local rules forbidding landlords from demanding proof of legal residence, but if the landlord learns of an applicant's illegal status through any other means, the landlord may decline to rent on that basis.

The federal antidiscrimination laws mentioned above don't apply to owner-occupied rental housing of four units or less, but they do apply to single-family home rentals, unless you go without advertising or the services of a real estate broker. Don't fasten onto this exception without considering the practicalities involved: Rarely will you be able to rent the home without some sort of advertising or help from a broker. And even if you end up continuously renting via word of mouth, your state or local antidiscrimination laws may cover this loophole in the federal rules. It's far more efficient to comply with fair housing laws from the get-go and not open yourself up to a charge of discrimination which, even if you prevail, will cost you plenty in time, money, and a sullied reputation.

To minimize the chances that you'll need to answer to a fair housing charge, treat all applicants more or less equally. For example, don't set tougher standards (such as a higher income level or a credit score) for renting to a member of an ethnic minority or a single parent. Base your decisions on where you advertise, what you say, and how you screen and choose tenants on sound business reasons, devoid of stereotypes or your personal feelings.

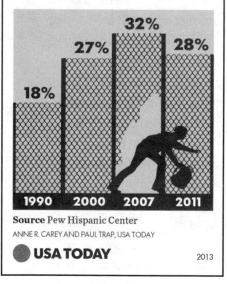

USA SNAPSHOTS©

Living in the U.S. illegally

Undocumented immigrants as a percentage of the foreign-born in the U.S.:

18% — 1990
27% — 2000
32% — 2007
28% — 2011

Source Pew Hispanic Center
ANNE R. CAREY AND PAUL TRAP, USA TODAY

● **USA TODAY**   2013

For further protection, keep a paper trail (such as copies of all credit reports and references from previous landlords) for all applicants. Be organized about filing the applications and other materials and notes on prospective tenants, and keep these for at least three years after you rent a particular unit.

Can You Reject a Prospective Tenant Based on Information From a Google Search?

Many landlords, following the lead of countless employers, do a Google search on rental applicants as part of the screening process. Depending on how active the person is online, you may find a wide variety of personal information; particularly on someone who posts regularly in social media such as Facebook, Twitter, Pinterest, or a personal blog. You may even discover things that you couldn't legally have asked a prospective tenant—such as the person's sexual orientation, race, ethnicity, or religion.

If, however, you use information found online to reject someone who is in a legally protected class and is otherwise a qualified tenant, you may face a discrimination lawsuit. (See "Avoiding Illegal Discrimination," above.)

On the other hand, if you learn that your applicant lied on the rental application (for example, by answering "No" to a question about previous evictions, but posting a request for apartment leads because her former landlord evicted her), you can factor that information into your decision. The reason is that material misrepresentations on an application are sound business reasons to reject an applicant. To protect yourself, be sure your rejection is based on a legitimate business reason, such as in the example above, and document it (print out the Web page and attach it to your applicant's file).

That said, it remains risky to reject an applicant even for legitimate business reasons, when that applicant is a member of a protected class; for example, has a mental disability. Say you learn about the disability on the person's Facebook page, but reject him because of less-than-stellar landlord references. If challenged by the rejected applicant, you'll be on the defensive, trying to convince a fair housing judge that you ignored the legally irrelevant information (the applicant's mental disability) and focused solely on the proper information (negative references).

Can You Reject a Prospective Tenant Based on Information From a Google Search? (cont'd)

For this reason, many landlord attorneys, taking a cue from their employer-side attorney counterparts, counsel landlords not to do a Google search, period. An "old-fashioned" screening process will uncover most of the information you'll need, and you'll have unassailable sources, such as a poor credit history, to back up your reasons for rejecting. See "Whom to Reject," below.

CAUTION

You can't use your property's inaccessibility as an excuse not to rent to a tenant with a disability. The Fair Housing Amendments Act requires all landlords to accommodate the reasonable needs of tenants with disabilities, in many cases at the landlord's expense. (42 U.S.C. § 3604(f)(3)(B).) You're expected to adjust your rules, procedures, or services in order to give a person with a disability an equal opportunity to use and enjoy the house, dwelling unit, or a common space (such as a walkway or yard area). Accommodations include such things as providing a close-in, spacious parking space for a wheelchair-bound tenant (if you provide parking). You aren't, however, required to make accommodations that would pose an unreasonable expense for you. For more on the rights of a tenant with disabilities to make alterations, see Chapter 5.

RESOURCE

More information from HUD and state agencies. For information on the rules and regulations of the Fair Housing Act, contact HUD's Housing Discrimination Hotline at 800-669-9777 or check the HUD website, at www.hud.gov. For information on state and local housing discrimination laws, contact your state fair housing agency. You'll find a list on the HUD website (click the tab "State Info"), as well as on www.nationalfairhousing. org, a website maintained by the National Fair Housing Alliance.

Is This the One?
Characteristics of the Perfect Tenant

Armed with the information you've collected, it's time to see how your top pick or picks match up against the "Checklist of Ideal Tenant Qualities," below.

Of course, intangibles will also come into play. If you communicate well with one prospective tenant and not with another, it makes sense to choose the one whose phone calls you won't soon come to dread. That's doubly true if you're sharing the same property, for example in duplex units.

If you're lucky, you'll find someone who meets all of these criteria and will likely be a good, long-term tenant. Or maybe none of your prospects will seem acceptable—all might have either a troubling rental history, insufficient income, or some other quality (such as immediate and unreasonable requests for upgrades) that would lead most any landlord to reject them. We advise against just swallowing your misgivings and picking the least objectionable.

Checklist of Ideal Tenant Qualities

Any tenant you accept should meet all or most of these criteria:

- ☐ ability to meet your basic rental terms, such as number of people living in your space or length of the rental term
- ☐ sufficient income to pay the rent (the industry standard is a monthly gross income that's triple the monthly rent)
- ☐ satisfactory credit report (debt level and bill-paying history)
- ☐ solid to high credit score
- ☐ positive references from other landlords
- ☐ positive references from current employer
- ☐ no recent terminations or evictions
- ☐ clean criminal record, and
- ☐ complete and accurate rental application.

No matter how urgently you want the rent stream to resume, remember that a bad pick can cost you dearly. Go back to the well, and perhaps advertise in different media, drop the rent, spiff up the rental to make it more attractive, or do something else to enlarge the pool of promising applicants.

But once you've identified a good applicant, your next step is to convey the good news to the lucky person and set a date to sign the lease or rental agreement (discussed in the next chapter).

TIP
Best thing I ever did: Choose a known tenant, despite possible overcrowding. Don, who lives in Philadelphia, says, "When I upgraded to a three-bedroom condo, I decided to rent out my original two-bedroom unit, which included a small den. A hard-working janitor I knew was having trouble finding a place he could afford for his family of five. I let them rent my condo, despite the cramped quarters (they converted the den to a nursery). They were so thrilled, they've taken better care of the place than anyone else would have."

When None of Your Prospects Look Financially Solid

Depending on your rental and the market, the pickings may be slim. If you've held off long enough and simply can't find a financially stable tenant, consider requiring a creditworthy cosigner on the lease. (This approach is often used by landlords renting to college students.) If you're renting to someone with bad credit, be extra sure that their references check out. And consider charging a good-sized deposit—as much as you can collect under state law and the market will bear. For more information on security deposit agreements and cosigners, see Chapter 5.

Whom to Reject

You'll probably have people applying for your rental whom you simply don't want to rent to, even if they're the only applicants. You're legally free to reject people for the following reasons (called your "legitimate business interests"):

- poor credit history
- income that you reasonably regard as insufficient to pay the rent
- negative references from previous landlords indicating problems—such as property damage or consistently late rent payments—that make someone a bad risk
- convictions for criminal offenses of any kind (however, you cannot reject someone with a conviction for drug use; you can, however, reject a person who was convicted of manufacturing or selling drugs, or who currently uses illegal drugs)
- inability to meet the legal terms of a lease or rental agreement, such as someone who can't come up with the security deposit or who wants to keep a pet and your policy is no pets, or
- more people than you want to live in the unit—assuming that your limit on the number of tenants is clearly tied to health and safety or legitimate business needs. (See the discussion of occupancy limits, in Chapter 5.)

These are the candidates whom you may safely and legally reject. If you have a bunch of equally qualified applicants and need to pick one, it's safest to choose the person who applied first. You can also apply tie-breaking criteria that are less hard-and-fast. You might, for example, pick the one you feel you'll communicate best with, or who appears to have the skills necessary to take care of your house and garden. But be sure to examine your motives to make sure your preference for one applicant over another isn't based on discriminatory assumptions about people who are in a protected class.

If your reasons for refusing to rent to someone are, in fact, based on information in a credit report or tenant-screening report, you can't just say "Sorry, I found a more qualified tenant." In that case, you must give the applicant the name and address of the agency that reported the negative information or furnished the report. You must tell the applicant that he or she has a right to a copy of the file from the agency, by requesting it within the next 60 days, or by asking within one year of having asked for their last free report.

You must also tell the rejected applicant that the credit reporting agency didn't make the decision to reject the person and can't explain the reason for your rejection. Finally, you must tell such applicants that they can dispute the accuracy of their credit reports and add their own consumer statement to their reports. These notices are known as "adverse action reports" and are a requirement of the federal Fair Credit Reporting Act (FCRA). (15 U.S.C. §§ 1681 and following.)

USA SNAPSHOTS®

A clutter-free existence?

How long it would take to get rid of your household clutter:

30-59 minutes
19%

29 minutes or less
41%

60 minutes or more
40%

Source Snapware survey of 1,000 U.S. adults

ANNE R. CAREY AND PAUL TRAP, USA TODAY

● USA TODAY   2014

RESOURCE

More information on rejecting tenants. For details on when and how to prepare an adverse action report, see the article, *Using Consumer Reports: What Landlords Need to Know*, on the Federal Trade Commission's website Business Center at business.ftc.gov. (Under "Privacy & Security," click "Credit Reporting," then scroll down.)

Tenant Screening Checklist

Did you:

☐ Deal with current tenants fairly and respectfully?

☐ Know and comply with fair housing laws, and act consistently?

☐ Give every applicant over age 18 a rental application to fill out?

☐ Thoroughly check out the information on the applications of your top most-likely tenants (check references, get credit reports, and so forth)?

☐ Keep good records documenting your decision to choose (or reject) a particular tenant?

Preparing a Lease and Getting the Tenant Moved In

Many landlords believe that if they've checked a tenant's credit and references, any additional paperwork isn't all that important. So they spend a few bucks to buy a one-size-fits-all lease from an office supply store and feel they're covered. Or worse, they simply shake hands with a cheerful, "See you on the first!"

Their casual approach couldn't be riskier. "Getting it in writing" may seem formal and unfriendly, but it's the only way to really run a profitable business and avoid problems on both sides. Many of the disputes that landlords face with tenants—over rent, deposits, repairs, roommates, pets, or rights to entry—have little to do with whether the tenant is a decent person and everything to do with whether the basic rules of the tenancy were covered in a lease or rental agreement.

"If the lease spells out what can and can't happen, most people are responsible," says Dennis, a longtime landlord from Petaluma, California. And because state law (and in a few instances, federal and local law) dictates many aspects of the landlord-tenant relationship, it's crucial that your rental document include them, so that both you and the tenant understand the rules of the game.

USA TODAY Snapshots®

Areas in the home most in need of organization

Office	24%
Bedroom	19%
Garage	19%
Closet	13%
Kitchen	10%

Source: Avery Dennison, survey of 2,182 adults by Greenfield Online.

By Michelle Healy and Karl Gelles, USA TODAY
2010

This chapter will get you started by explaining the key provisions to include in your lease or rental agreement, including the state laws that come into play, and other aspects of preparing this crucial document. And we'll guide you through handling other paperwork and records, such as a move-in checklist inventorying the condition of the rental house, and payment and repair records (to form a paper trail should disputes surface later).

Is the Property Already Rented?

If you've recently bought or inherited rental property, you may also inherit tenants who have existing rental agreements or leases. If they have a lease, you'll need to wait until it expires before changing any of its terms, such as the rent. If they have a rental agreement, you can make changes (such as increasing the rent) with appropriate notice (typically 30 days), following your state rules and any rent control restrictions.

Purchasers. If you're a purchaser, be sure the last owner gives you copies of the lease or rental agreement, plus details on deposits (more on this below), house rules, maintenance and repair records, and all other relevant paperwork.

Inheritors. If you've inherited the property, work with the former owner's executor or trustee (the person in charge of winding up the owner's affairs) to see if the information and documents can be found.

Take special care that the security deposit is accounted for. In some states, landlords must segregate the funds, provide tenants information as to their location, and periodically pay interest. Some states require sellers to either refund the deposit, letting the new owners collect them anew, or transfer the deposits to the new owners, with notice to the tenants.

Even if your state doesn't specifically set forth the procedure for handling deposits, it makes sense to do one of the two things described above, even in an inheritance situation. If the deposit isn't properly transferred or returned when you take over, and the tenant later looks to you, the current owner, for its return, you'll probably be stuck returning it, even if you never got it in the first place.

> CAUTION
> **Watch out for mass-produced, preprinted leases and rental documents.** Many ignore state-by-state differences, use illegal or unenforceable clauses, or are poorly written and full of hard-to-understand legal language. For a solid lease or rental agreement that's valid in your state and easy to create, check out "Helpful Nolo Resources for Landlords," further described in the introduction to this book.

Which Is Better, a Lease or a Rental Agreement?

Here's a key question to ask when making your first decisions about renting out your property: For what length of time will you and your tenants be mutually committed to your rental arrangement? Do you want to lock both of you in for a year (or more), or do you want to give both sides the ability to call it quits after giving approximately a month's notice?

Leases and rental agreements have a lot in common: Both cover basic issues, such as the amount of rent, security deposits, and who can live in the rental unit. The primary difference between them is the length of the tenancy—leases typically last for a year, while rental agreements normally go month to month. Often, but by no means always, your choice will depend on how long you want a tenant to stay. But, because other factors can also come into play, carefully read what follows before deciding.

How a rental agreement works

A written rental agreement commits you and your tenant to a short rental period, typically a month. It automatically renews each month, unless you give the tenant the proper amount of written notice. State laws usually require 30 days to increase the rent or change another term or to terminate a rental agreement (subject to notice requirements and any restrictions imposed by local rent control ordinances and anti-retaliation and discrimination laws). The tenant can also terminate the agreement on short notice (typically 30 days, although this varies).

TIP
Use a written agreement, even if you're friends. When Amy first moved to California and began renting out her Austin, Texas, home, she thought she had the perfect tenant: the roommate she'd been living with all along, plus a friend of his. She says, "We agreed orally that the two would pay a certain rent each month and give 30 days' notice before moving. So I was pretty surprised when I got an email saying he'd be moving in ten days, and then discovered they expected me to go without half the rent until the other tenant's girlfriend moved in two months later. I eventually got most of the rent covered, but the friendship hasn't fared so well."

How a lease works

A lease obligates both you and the tenant for a set rental period—usually a year, but sometimes longer. With a fixed-term lease, you can't raise the rent or change other terms of the tenancy until the lease runs out. The only exception is when the lease itself allows specific future changes (such as, "The monthly rent will increase by $100 on October 1, 20xx"), or if the tenant agrees in writing to the changes.

Although a lease offers the security of a long-term tenancy, it can be frustrating to landlords who discover they'd be happier if the tenant departed early. Under ordinary circumstances, landlords can't ask a tenant to move out or convince a court to order an eviction before the lease term expires. There are exceptions here too, however, such as when the tenant fails to pay the rent or violates another significant term of the lease, or breaks the law, such as by repeatedly making too much noise, damaging the rental unit, or selling drugs on your property. (We'll explain how to deal with such situations, in Chapter 9.)

Which is better for you?

If you're balancing landlording with a full-time job, you're probably best off looking for high-quality, long-term renters who will sign a lease for a year or more. While leases restrict your flexibility, they offer big pluses.

For one, tenants are likely to think hard and make a serious personal commitment before entering into a long-term lease, in part because they think they'll be liable for several months' rent if they leave early. (They're not entirely correct in that fear, but we'll get to that later.) And people who plan to live in the property for a long time have an incentive to treat it well.

Many landlords also prefer long-term leases in order to avoid the hassles and expenses of regular turnover, such as cleaning, advertising, showing the unit, checking out applicants, and possibly spending months with no rental income. As Sergio, with rental property in Burlingame, California, puts it, "We look for long-term strong tenants who will pay the rent on time and take care of the place. We're not aggressive at raising rents at the end of the year's lease term."

If your area has a high vacancy rate or local landlords have trouble finding tenants for during certain seasons of the year, a lease can be especially good protection. For example, if you're renting near a college that's in session for only nine months a year, or in a vacation area that empties out during summer or winter months, you're far better off with a year's lease. This is especially true if you have the market clout to charge a large deposit, so that a tenant who wants to leave early has an incentive to find someone to take over the tenancy.

Other landlords prefer month-to-month rental agreements, precisely because they offer flexibility, allowing the landlord to increase the rent or end the tenancy on relatively short notice and without giving a specific reason. Kathy, with property in Florida, says, "We don't use a lease, since tenants often need to break it anyway." And Catherine, a Berkeley landlord, explains her preference, "I'm using a month-to-month rental agreement because I used a tenant-matching service and wasn't sure they'd found me someone I'd like to keep over the long term. I've been burned before, by tenants whose life circumstances took a turn for the disastrous."

Also, you may prefer to rent month to month if you're hoping to sell the property within the coming months. Prospective buyers may be put off by the presence of long-term tenants, especially if they hadn't been planning on renting out the property, or if the tenants are paying less than market rental rates. (The new owner takes on the obligations of the previous owner, including leases.) You may also prefer a rental agreement if your house is in a tight rental market where new tenants are easily found and rents are trending upward.

Why a Verbal Agreement Isn't Really Enough

Legally speaking, oral leases or rental agreements are perfectly valid for both month-to-month tenancies and for leases of a year or less in most states. You and your tenant could, in theory, sit down over coffee and say, "A one-year lease at $1,000 a month, okay?" "Okay." And if you got into a legal spat about the rent, a judge could rule for one of you based on oral evidence alone.

But while oral agreements are easy and informal, using one is never wise. As time passes, people's memories (even yours) have a funny habit of becoming unreliable. You can almost count on tenants claiming that you made, but didn't keep, certain oral promises—for example, to repaint their kitchen or to not increase the rent. Tenants may also forget their own key agreements, such as no subletting. And you probably won't even think to cover certain other issues, such as how deposits may be used. Oral leases are especially dangerous, because they require both of you to accurately remember one important term—the length of the lease—for a considerable length of time.

If something goes wrong with an oral rental agreement or lease, you and your tenants are all too likely to end up in court, arguing over who said what to whom, when, and in what context. This doesn't mean your written agreement needs to be multiple pages long, especially if you know and trust your tenant. But at least get the basic terms written down, including the rent, the length (or term) of the rental, when and where rent is due, and other important matters you've agreed on, such as whether pets will be allowed.

CAUTION

A lease guarantees less income security than you'd think. As experienced landlords know, it's usually not hard for a determined tenant to break a lease and avoid paying the remaining rent. A few states allow this without penalty in specific circumstances, such moving to a health care facility. And nationwide, tenants who enter military service are entitled to break a lease. Most states also require landlords to "mitigate" (minimize) their losses—meaning that if a tenant moves out early, you must use reasonable efforts to find another suitable tenant at the same or a greater rent. If you rent the place immediately (or if a judge believes you could have done so with a reasonable effort), the lease-breaking tenant is off the hook—except, perhaps, for having to pay for the few days or weeks the unit was vacant plus your costs of renting it again.

For your state's law, see the "State-by-State Rules on Tenants' Rights to Break a Rental Lease" chart, under State Landlord-Tenant Laws in the Landlords section of Nolo.com.

State Laws to Know When Preparing a Lease or Rental Agreement

As described below, conscientious landlords spell out details in their leases or rental agreements regarding matters governed by state law, such as:

- late rent fees
- bounced check charges
- security deposit limits and uses, deadlines and procedures for returning deposits, interest requirements, and other rules (including types of properties that are exempt from state law)
- a tenant's rights, such as to withhold rent if you fail to make necessary repairs
- a landlord's notice requirements to enter rental property
- notice by tenant required to end a tenancy, and
- required landlord disclosures, such as for mold, recent flooding, or details on where the security deposit is being held.

You can find these and other key state laws relevant to preparing a lease or rental agreement, getting a tenant moved in (and out), and running a rental business under State Landlord-Tenant Laws in the Landlords section of Nolo.com.

Typical Provisions in Leases and Rental Agreements

Most leases and rental agreements contain a standard set of rental provisions or clauses, often set out as numbered paragraphs. This section explains common terms you should include in your lease or rental agreement, and notes where state laws come into play. Except for the term of the tenancy, leases and rental agreements will usually include the same basic clauses.

Names and addresses of landlord and tenants

Every lease or rental agreement should identify the tenant and the landlord or property owner—called the "parties" to the "agreement." (Agreement is a synonym for contract and may refer to either a lease or a rental agreement.) The tenant is usually called the "lessee" and the landlord is the "lessor." If a property manager or company is authorized to receive notices and legal papers for you, your lease or rental agreement should also include its name and address.

All adults who will live in the rental house, including both members of a couple, should sign the lease or rental agreement. This underscores your expectation that each tenant is legally responsible for the rent (the whole rent, even if roommates have left), for the use or misuse of the property, and all terms of the agreement (a concept known as "joint and several liability").

> **TIP**
> **Gathering signatures is extra important when renting to unrelated roommates.** As Laura, who owns properties in three states, explains: "It can be a hassle when people want to switch roommates— inevitably, one of them takes a job somewhere else, while the other wants

to stay. I make sure the lease says I need to preapprove the new person. I also make clear that the remaining tenants need to keep paying the entire rent, and that I'm not going to refund the security deposit if one roommate leaves early. If you're renting to college students, be ready for a lot of this."

If you're signing the lease together with your spouse or other co-owners, you may want to put both names on the lease, particularly if both of you plan to actively participate in managing the property.

Number of occupants

Most leases and rental agreements will specify that the rental property will be the residence of only the tenants and their minor children and let the tenants know that they may not move anyone else in as a permanent resident without your consent. Rental documents usually set a limit to the number of people who can live in the rental property.

However, you are not free to set unreasonably low figures (for example, permitting no more than three people for a three-bedroom house) in order to maintain a "quiet atmosphere" or to reduce wear and tear. Federal law requires landlords to allow two persons per bedroom unless you can point to legitimate business reasons justifying a lower number. (Some states are more generous: California, for example, allows two per bedroom plus one more, and Texas and Oklahoma make special allowances for small children. New York City has a unique "roommate law" that allows current tenants to add roommates.)

Also check your state and local health and safety codes, which probably set a maximum number of tenants based on the size of the property and the number of bedrooms and bathrooms.

> **CAUTION**
> **You can't discriminate against families with children.** Legally establishing reasonable space-to-people ratios is okay, but you can't use overcrowding as an excuse for refusing to rent to tenants with children, especially if you'd rent to the same number of adults. Discrimination against families with children is illegal, except in housing reserved for senior citizens only.

Rental home address and furnishings

The property address is often called "the premises," and this section of the lease should include details on any furnishings, parking space, storage areas, or other extras that come with the property.

If a particular part of the rental property that a tenant might reasonably assume to be included is not, such as a garage you wish to use yourself, be sure you explicitly exclude it from your description of the premises.

Term of the tenancy

The term is the length of the rental. Your agreement should include the beginning date (when the tenant has the right to move in) and whether it's a month-to-month tenancy or a lease. If it's a lease, the ending date should also be specified.

Rent

Your lease or rental agreement should provide specific details on the rent, including:

- **Amount due each month.** Unless you're in a rent-controlled area, you can legally charge as much rent as you want (or, more practically speaking, as much as the market will support). Chapter 1 includes a discussion of how to set rent.

> **TIP**
> **Raising the rent.** If you sign a lease, you won't be able to raise the rent until it expires. You'll have more flexibility with a month-to-month rental agreement.

- **When and where rent is due.** This is your choice, but traditionally rent is due by the first of the month and is mailed to you. If the first falls on a weekend or legal holiday, then rent is usually due the first weekday after that.
- **Acceptable forms of payment.** Specify personal or cashier's check, or other form of payment, such as money order. Accepting cash is a bad idea, because it's risky to regularly handle large amounts of cash.

- **Late fees when rent isn't paid on time.** Late fees can motivate your tenant to make on-time payments. The amount must closely approximate the actual losses you suffer when your tenant pays late, not act as a penalty for late rent. These losses can include the value of your time (or your employee's time) in dealing with the late rent, such as preparing and delivering the notice, plus the interest you're losing because the rent isn't in your bank account (probably minimal). But they can't include indirect consequences, such as late fees on your car payment because you couldn't pay it without receiving the rent check. Also check into (and follow) your state's laws, which might place a legal maximum on the amount of the late fee, and dictate when you can impose it. If your state hasn't set rules, you'll be on solid ground if you: (1) don't apply the late fee until at least three to five days after the due date; (2) charge no more than 4%–5% of the rent; and (3) keep the increases moderate if you want the late fee to increase each day the rent is late (cap them with an upper limit). An acceptable late charge on rent of $1,000 per month would be $10 for the first day rent is late, plus $5 for each additional day, up to a maximum of 5% of the rental amount.

> ! **CAUTION**
> **Don't try to disguise excessive late charges by giving a "discount" for early payment.** When the "discount" is substantial, it's simply a roundabout way of charging an excessive late fee, which will make it illegal if challenged.

- **Grace period (if any) before you charge a late fee.** Many landlords don't charge a late fee until two or three days after rent is due, but in most states, you can legally impose the late fee on the due date (that is, you don't need to give a grace period).
- **Bounced check charges.** If your state's law doesn't say how much you can charge, plan on charging what your bank charges you, probably $15–$35 per returned check, plus a few dollars for your trouble.

See Chapter 9 for advice on dealing with tenants who pay rent late or violate another lease term such as moving in extra roommates.

Rent Control

Laws in communities in only five states—California, the District of Columbia, Maryland, New Jersey, and New York—limit the amount of rent landlords may charge and how and when rent may be increased. Typically, only a few cities or counties in each of these states have enacted local rent control ordinances (also called rent stabilization, rent regulation, or a similar term), but often these are some of the state's largest cities—for example, San Francisco, Los Angeles, New York City, and Newark. For details on rent control in your state, see the "State-by-State Basic Rent Rules" chart on the Paying Rent page of the Landlords section of Nolo.com.

Rent control laws commonly regulate much more than rent. For example, owners of rent-controlled properties must often follow specific "just cause" eviction procedures. And local rent control ordinances may require that your lease or rental agreement include certain information—for example, the address of the local rent control board. In some rent control cities, properties with rents over a specified amount are not subject to rent control (known as "luxury decontrol"), nor are single-family homes.

If you own rental property in a city that has rent control, get your hands on a current copy of the ordinance and any regulations interpreting it. You can count on tenants knowing the rules, and you'll be at a severe disadvantage if you're not up to speed. Check with your local rent control board or city manager's or mayor's office for information.

TIP

And now, for an atypical lease clause: Rent-to-own provisions. In a rare but increasing number of cases, a landlord may agree to grant the tenant an option to buy the property, sometimes at a preset price, at some point during the rental period. See Chapter 12 for details.

Security deposit

All states allow you to collect a security deposit when a tenant moves in, and hold it until the tenant leaves. The general purpose is to assure that the tenant pays rent on time and keeps the rental unit in good condition. Rent that you collect in advance for the first month is not considered part of the security deposit.

It's easy to get into legal trouble over deposits, because they're strictly regulated by state law, and sometimes also by city ordinance. In some states, single-family rentals are exempt from certain aspects of the security deposit rule, such as a requirement to pay interest on the deposit, or to hold it in an account separate from the landlord's personal funds. To avoid disputes, your lease or rental agreement should include details on deposits, including:

- **Dollar amount.** Many states limit the amount you can collect as a deposit to a maximum of one or two months' rent, with the limit sometimes higher for a furnished rental.

- **Restrictions on tenant use of deposit for last month's rent.** Some statutes forbid the tenant from using the deposit as last month's rent. This way, a tenant won't leave you with insufficient funds to cover necessary cleaning and repairs at the end of the tenancy.

- **Where you must keep the deposit and whether you must pay interest.** Several states and cities (particularly those with rent control) require you to put deposits in a separate account and pay the tenant any interest on them. Some states require you to put deposits in a separate "trust" account, rather than mix the funds with your personal or business accounts. Even if you aren't required to keep separate accounts, it's a good idea, as we discuss in Chapter 6.

- **When you must return the deposit.** When a tenant moves out, you'll usually have a set amount of time (in most states, 14 to 30 days) to either return the tenant's entire deposit or provide an itemized statement of deductions and refund any deposit balance.

- **The deductions you may impose.** You can generally withhold all or part of the deposit to cover unpaid rent, damage to the rental property and cleaning costs (outside of "ordinary wear and tear"), or other tenant financial obligations (such as payment of utilities).

> **CAUTION**
> **Be careful about charging nonrefundable fees.** While some states allow landlords to collect a fee that's not refundable (such as for pets or cleaning), most state laws are muddled on the subject. And a few states, such as California, specifically prohibit landlords from charging any nonrefundable fee or deposit. To avoid the legal uncertainties, just factor in the expenses you're worried about when setting the rent, or charge a higher security deposit.

- **How deposit deductions must be itemized when the tenant moves out.** Some states set specific rules and procedures for move-out inspections and preparing itemized statements of security deposit deductions for the tenant.

> **CAUTION**
> **Watch out for liquidated damages clauses.** This item (often found in fixed-term leases) means that a tenant who moves out before the lease expires is supposed to pay the landlord a predetermined amount of money (perhaps the whole security deposit) to replace whatever amount of rent will go unpaid. In some states, liquidated damages clauses are unenforceable—which doesn't mean that the tenant can take off scot-free, just that he or she will be liable only for the landlord's actual damages, which the landlord must prove in court.

How High a Deposit Should You Charge?

Normally, the best advice is to charge as much as the market will bear, within any legal limits (many states limit the deposit to two to three times the monthly rent). The more the tenant has at stake, the better the chance your property will be respected—a particular concern in high-risk situations, like when a tenant has shaky credit or comes with a large pet. And, the larger the deposit, the more financial protection you'll have if a tenant leaves owing you rent. When renting a single-family home, where damage can be more expensive to remedy than similar damage in an apartment, it makes sense to set the deposit as high as you can.

But a high deposit means that prospects need to come up with a large amount of cash that's tied up throughout the tenancy, which may be unattractive to otherwise qualified renters. Here are some alternatives to a high deposit:

- **Higher rent.** Many acceptable, solvent tenants have a hard time coming up with several months' rent, especially if they're still awaiting the return of a previous security deposit from their last rental. These tenants might rather pay a slightly higher rent than an enormous deposit.
- **Installment payments.** You might gain a marketing advantage by allowing a deposit to be paid in installments, rather than as one lump sum.
- **Renters' insurance.** As a term of the lease, in most states you can require the tenant to buy renters' insurance to cover certain damage by the tenant or guests, as well as injury to other people.

Utilities

Your agreement should state who pays for what utilities. Normally, landlords pay for garbage and sometimes for water, particularly if there's a yard. Tenants usually pay for other services, such as gas, electricity, cable TV, and Internet. In single-family rentals, tenants may pay for everything.

Tenant's repair and maintenance rights and responsibilities

A carefully written lease or rental agreement will include a statement that makes tenants responsible for:

- keeping the rental premises clean and in good condition (but not for major maintenance, which should remain part of your responsibility as a landlord)
- reporting defective or dangerous conditions to you, and
- reimbursing you for the cost of repairing damage caused by their abuse or neglect.

Many leases and rental agreements also tell tenants what they can't do in the way of repairs or alterations—such as painting walls, rekeying locks, or adding built-in bookshelves without your permission. Chapter 7 covers landlords' and tenants' rights and responsibilities regarding repairs and maintenance.

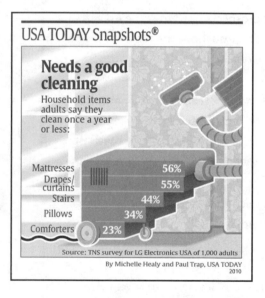

USA TODAY Snapshots®

Needs a good cleaning

Household items adults say they clean once a year or less:

Mattresses	56%
Drapes/curtains	55%
Stairs	44%
Pillows	34%
Comforters	23%

Source: TNS survey for LG Electronics USA of 1,000 adults
By Michelle Healy and Paul Trap, USA TODAY 2010

When and how landlords may enter rental property

Nearly every state clearly recognizes the right of a landlord to enter the premises while a tenant is living there, under certain broad circumstances, for example, such as to deal with an emergency (flooding) or when the tenant gives permission. Your agreement should set forth and explain this right.

Many states have access laws specifying other circumstances under which landlords may legally enter rented premises, such as to make repairs (for example, fix a broken oven), inspect the property, and show the property to prospective tenants and purchasers. State access laws typically specify the amount of notice required for such entry—usually

Step Aside: Tenants May Be Allowed to Make These Repairs or Alterations

In certain narrow situations, tenants can alter or repair the premises regardless of what your lease or rental agreement says. Examples include:

- **Alterations by a person with a disability.** Under the federal Fair Housing Act, a disabled person may, with your prior approval, modify living space if needed to make it safe and comfortable. For example, the tenant might need to have the countertops lowered to wheelchair height. Landlords with certain federally financed properties, and those in Massachusetts, must shoulder the modification expense. However, if the modifications will make the unit unacceptable to the next tenant, the disabled tenant must agree to undo them before leaving. Ask for a reasonable description of the proposed modifications, proof that they'll be done in a skillful and efficient manner, and evidence that the tenant is obtaining any necessary building permits. If you'll need to undo the modifications when the tenant leaves, you can insist that the tenant place enough money to cover the estimated restoration costs in an interest-bearing escrow account (the interest belongs to the tenant).

- **Use of the "repair and deduct" procedure when landlords fail to act.** As explained in Chapter 7, tenants in many states may repair defects or damage that make the premises uninhabitable or substantially interferes with its safe use or enjoyment, and subtract the cost from next month's rent.

- **Installation of satellite dishes and antennas.** Federal law gives tenants limited rights to install wireless antennas and small satellite dishes.

- **Specific alterations allowed by state statutes.** Some states allow tenants to install energy conservation measures (like removable interior storm windows) or burglary prevention devices without the landlord's prior consent.

24 hours (unless impractical—for example, in an emergency). A few states simply require the landlord to provide "reasonable" notice, often presumed to be 24 hours.

Extended absences by tenant

Some leases and rental agreements require tenants to notify the landlord in advance if they'll be away for a certain number of consecutive days (often seven or more). Such clauses may give you the right to enter the property while the tenants are gone for needed maintenance and to inspect for damage. This type of clause is usually most appropriate for rentals in cold-weather places where landlords want to drain the pipes to guard against bursting.

You Can't Ask Tenants to Sign Away Their Rights

Most states have passed tenant-friendly laws covering subjects such as landlords' access to rental property, the amount and use of security deposits, and tenant rights to a livable home. Tenants also have important legal rights under federal law (particularly in the area of discrimination).

You can't get around these rights by asking tenants to waive them—for example, by including a lease clause saying that the premises are acceptable "as is," or not warranted as fit, safe, secure, or in good repair. Most states will not uphold a clause that diminishes tenant rights to habitable property. (Texas is a notable exception; and in Maine, landlords of single-family homes may shift the duty to maintain a fit home to the tenant.)

Limits on tenant behavior and illegal activity

A good lease or rental agreement will contain a clause forbidding tenants from using the rental property or adjacent areas, such as the sidewalk in front of the house, in a way that violates any law or ordinance, including laws prohibiting the use, possession, or sale of illegal drugs. These clauses also prohibit tenants from intentionally damaging the property (called "committing waste," such as by punching holes in the wall), or creating a "nuisance" by annoying or disturbing other tenants or nearby residents—for example, by continuously making loud noise or allowing garbage to pile up.

Basically, you can set any kind of restriction you want—as long as it's not discriminatory, retaliatory, or otherwise violates your state law. For example, you may prohibit smoking in the rental property as well as on the deck, patio, or front porch.

We'll discuss some common restrictions involving pets, home businesses, sublets, and guests in the following sections.

Pets

You have the right to prohibit all pets, or to restrict the types allowed—for example, forbidding dogs or cats, but allowing birds. However, you must allow "service" or "comfort" animals used by people with physical or mental disabilities (protected by the fair housing laws).

USA SNAPSHOTS®

Vive la 'Frenchie'!

Breeds with the largest percentage increase in registrations, 2003-13:

Breed	Increase
French bulldog	+323%
Black and tan coonhound	+155%
Anatolian shepherd dog	+149%
German pinscher	+143%
Wirehaired pointing griffon	+126%

Source American Kennel Club analysis of registration numbers

ANNE R. CAREY AND PAUL TRAP, USA TODAY

USA TODAY   2014

Not every landlord wants to prohibit pets. Allowing them can attract a wider range of tenants. And it offers benefits if you're sharing the property, as Catherine in Berkeley explains: "I had one great renter who had a dog—we took care of each other's dog when we traveled, shared poop patrol, and more."

No matter what you decide, spell out your pet rules—for example, the type and number of pets allowed (such as one cat or one dog under 20 pounds). Also state that the tenants will keep the yard free of all animal waste and keep the dogs on leash and under control (no excessive barking that bothers the neighbors).

See Chapter 8 for a discussion of landlord liability for dog bites and other animal attacks.

> **TIP**
> **You may want to waive your no pets policy.** That's what Sarah, a San Francisco landlord of a single-family home, has done in many instances. She explains, "We've said 'No Pets,' but if we find a good tenant, we'll meet the pet and take it case by case. Dog owners in particular seem to be very responsible, maybe because they already have to walk their animals every day. One dog we let move in chewed some stuff up, but the owner was completely willing to pay for it without question." But be careful about waiving your rules when you own a multifamily property. The last thing you want is for a tenant to observe that you're waiving the rules only for some people and claim that you're refusing to waive the rules for him or her not because the dog appears to be out of control, but because of race, nationality, or another protected characteristic.

Renting to Pet Owners

The San Francisco Society for the Prevention of Cruelty to Animals (SPCA) seeks to show landlords how to make renting to pet-owning tenants a satisfying and profitable experience. The SPCA offers landlords tips and a sample pet agreement.

For details, contact the San Francisco SPCA at 415-554-3000 or via www.sfspca.org/programs-services/open-door/guidelines-landlords. For additional information, including a sample pet application form, see the national Humane Society's website at HumaneSociety.org, and search "resources for rental managers." Also see the Dogs in Rental Housing articles in the Landlords section of Nolo.com, for more information on renting to pet owners.

Restrictions on home businesses

Are you at all worried that your tenant might run a business from your rental property—potentially burdening neighbors by increasing local traffic, and exposing you to liability if a customer or business associate gets hurt? If so, you may prohibit this with a clause in your lease or rental agreement specifying that the premises are "for residential purposes only." For more on the subject, see "Home Businesses on Rental Property," below.

Home Businesses on Rental Property

If a tenant wants to run a business from your rental home, be sure to spell out all the details in your lease or rental agreement. First, you'll need to check local zoning laws for restrictions on home-based businesses, including the type of businesses allowed (if any), the amount of car and truck traffic the business can generate, and other rules about outside signs, on-street parking, number of employees, and percentage of floor space devoted to the business. And if your rental is in a planned unit or a condominium development, check the CC&Rs of the homeowners' association.

Also consult your insurance company as to whether you'll need a different policy to cover the potential liability of tenants' employees or guests. In many situations, a home office for occasional use won't be a problem. But if the business will involve people and deliveries coming and going, such as a therapy practice, jewelry importer, or small consulting firm, seriously consider whether to expand or add coverage.

You may also want to insist that the tenant buy certain types of liability insurance, so that you won't wind up paying if someone gets hurt on the rental property—for example, if a customer trips and falls on the front steps.

Finally, be aware that a residence used as a commercial site may need to meet the accessibility requirements of the federal Americans with Disabilities Act (ADA). You can insist that the tenant pay for any modifications. For more information on the ADA, see www.ada.gov.

CAUTION

What if a tenant wants to run a day-care operation in your rental? You may not be able to stop it. Some states give licensed day-care owners the right to conduct business in a rental. However, landlords in California and New York, for example, may limit the number of children. Also, the business must comply with state fire and health regulations regarding minimum facility size and fire exits. If the property won't pass inspection, and making the property compliant (for example, by adding exits or stairways) is not something you're willing to do, the tenant won't be able to get a permit and won't be able to run the facility.

Restrictions on assignments or sublets

Most leases and rental agreements prohibit "assignments," which happen when your tenant moves out permanently and brings in a replacement tenant for the remainder of the lease. Your rule on prohibiting assignments should state that you won't unreasonably refuse to rent to a proposed newcomer. (That simply reflects your obligation, in most states, to use reasonable efforts to find a replacement once the original tenant leaves.) When you think about it, it's actually to your advantage to have a lease-breaking tenant do the work of finding a suitable replacement.

Your agreement should also prohibit tenants from temporarily renting their (and your) space to someone else (called a sublet), without your written consent. This includes letting someone stay in the rental while the tenant is on vacation or renting out a room to other people, perhaps by using a service like Airbnb, without your consent. And even if you allow a tenant to rent out space on Airbnb or a similar service, local laws may restrict these kinds of short-term rentals. See "Legal Restrictions to Renting Your Home on Airbnb or Other Rental Services" and related articles in the Real Estate section of Nolo.com.

Renting Your Home Seasonally

Here's what Kim Komando, who hosts the nation's largest talk radio show about consumer electronics, computers, and the Internet, tells USAT readers about renting your home out on a short-term basis:

Every winter and spring, swarms of tourists show up in Phoenix, my neck of the woods. Many other parts of the country are popular in summer and fall.

Increasingly, savvy travelers—especially families—prefer to stay in furnished homes. They're larger and more comfortable than a hotel. Private homes and condominiums are usually quieter, and they're generally a better value, too.

Could you make money renting your home to tourists? Keep in mind, you don't need to own a cabin in the Rockies or a cottage on the beach to play this game. Your home could fetch $200 per night or more if it is close to a popular national park or a major tourist attraction. Cities such as Denver, Chicago, New York, Orlando and Washington, DC, are magnets for summer travelers.

Is there a big music or food festival that temporarily swells the population of your town each summer? Or perhaps a major golf tournament or NASCAR races at certain times during the year? These can be excellent opportunities to make your home available.

If you plan it right, you could rent out your home and use the money to take a free vacation of your own! These three websites will help you roll out the welcome mat:

- Airbnb is a good place to start. Just set up a free profile page and start connecting with potential renters.
- Home Away is a subscription-based site that may be a good choice if your home is in a prime location. The subscription also includes a professional review. One of their representatives will visit your rental property and offer tips on how to improve your listing.

Renting Your Home Seasonally (cont'd)

- FlipKey especially caters to professional property managers, but the reasonable annual rate makes it attractive for casual users, as well. FlipKey also offers short-term subscriptions. That's perfect if you want to advertise your home for only a few weeks or even a couple months out of the year.

How much should you charge for your home? These sites double as research tools. Check out listings similar to yours and take a look at the rates. Also pay attention to what extras are offered (Breakfast? Bottles of water? Wine at check in?) and any typical limitations (What times should you set for check-in and checkout? Will you allow children? Pets? Smoking?) You'll soon have a pretty good idea of what's reasonable as well as the decisions you need to make.

Keep taxes and insurance in mind if you decide to become a part-time innkeeper. Your state and city governments may require you to collect sales and tourism taxes. Check with your local government agencies for more information.

The rent you collect is, of course, income—so keep that in mind as you decide what to charge. If you rent your primary home for fewer than 15 days during the year, however, you need not report that as income to the IRS.

Make sure your insurance covers your house as a rental. Though most rental sites will reimburse you for damages or theft, it's just smart to have the added security written into your policy.

USA TODAY "Use the Web to rent your home seasonally," by Kim Komando, Special for USA TODAY, Updated 5/17/2012.

Limits on guest stays

It's common for leases to limit overnight guests. For example, you might allow a guest for no more than ten days in any six-month period, with written approval required for longer stays. The idea is to keep long-term guests from gaining the status of full-fledged tenants, who haven't been screened or approved or signed the lease or rental agreement.

Attorney fees and court costs in a lawsuit

In case of a dispute over the meaning or implementation of a part of your rental agreement or lease, the agreement should specify who will pay the costs of a lawsuit. For example, disputes about rent or security deposits are common. This clause can act as a nice deterrent—even with several properties, Laura says, "I have something in the lease saying the prevailing party will have their legal costs covered, and I've never had a tenant threaten to sue." Attorney fee clauses don't, however, apply to disputes that don't stem from the lease or rental agreement—for example, lawsuits over alleged discrimination.

Grounds for termination of tenancy

This important clause states that any violation of the lease or rental agreement by the tenant, or by his or her guests, is grounds for

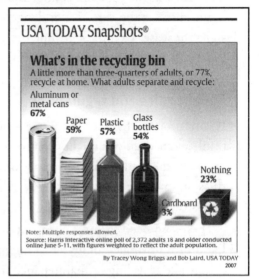

USA TODAY Snapshots®

What's in the recycling bin
A little more than three-quarters of adults, or 77%, recycle at home. What adults separate and recycle:

Aluminum or metal cans **67%**

Paper **59%**

Plastic **57%**

Glass bottles **54%**

Nothing **23%**

Cardboard **3%**

Note: Multiple responses allowed.
Source: Harris Interactive online poll of 2,372 adults 18 and older conducted online June 5-11, with figures weighted to reflect the adult population.

By Tracey Wong Briggs and Bob Laird, USA TODAY
2007

terminating the tenancy according to the procedures established by state or local laws. Chapter 9 provides an overview of how tenancies can be ended.

Lead-based paint and other disclosures

Federal, state, or local laws may require you to disclose certain things about the property before a new tenant signs a lease or rental agreement or moves in, including the presence of lead-based paint (a federal law requirement discussed in Chapter 8). State laws may require other disclosures, too, such as the presence of mold, shared utility arrangements, or recent flooding. And local rent control ordinances often require disclosures, such as the name and address of the government agency or elected board that administers the ordinance.

Some states require landlords to inform tenants of the name and address of the bank where their security deposit is being held, and the name and contact information of the person authorized by the owner to receive legal papers. Check your state and local laws for details on these and other disclosure requirements.

If your property contains a hidden (not obvious) problem that could cause injury or substantially interfere with your tenant's safe enjoyment and use, and the problem is impossible to fix, you're better off legally if you disclose the defective or dangerous condition before the tenant signs the lease. Examples include naturally occurring dangers, such as loose soil, and human-made dangers, such as steep stairs.

Tenant rules and regulations

If your property has more than one unit—even if it's a duplex you share— think about what you might want to require of tenants concerning shared areas like the yard, garage, driveway, or even a pool. Be clear about your rules on smoking, parking, and pets. Also give details on what's considered excessive noise.

There's no need to cover every detail of daily living, however. Landlords of single-family rental houses often find it easier to discuss things like recycling or maintenance tips in a move-in letter, discussed below. To make sure you have some clout, include a clause in the lease or rental agreement giving you the right to terminate the rental arrangement if the tenant repeatedly and seriously violates house rules.

CAUTION

Watch out for conflicts with community association rules. If you're renting out a condo or another property governed by a community association, check to make sure that none of the terms of your lease contradict the CC&Rs or association rules. If, for example, your lease says pets are allowed but the CC&Rs say they're not, your tenant will not be allowed to keep a pet.

Signing a Lease or Rental Agreement

Once your lease or rental agreement is completely drafted, make an appointment with your new tenant(s) to review and sign this important document. Bring two copies to your meeting (one for you and one for the tenant(s)). Of course, this assumes that you're not interested in negotiating any of the terms. In a soft market, or when you're dealing with prospects whom you really want and might be willing to bend the terms for, you may want instead to negotiate selected issues before your signing meeting.

Before you even think about signing the lease, start with this very important step: Ask for the money, and to be extra careful, don't accept a personal check. Until you have the tenant's cash, certified check, or money order for the first month's rent and security deposit in hand, signing a rental commitment is a recipe for trouble. Starting with the second rent payment, of course, you may prefer to accept checks (in fact, insisting on cash is inadvisable), and you'll have to trust that your careful tenant-screening process weeded out those tenants who would have given you checks that bounce.

Next, encourage tenants to ask questions about anything that's unclear on your lease or rental agreement. "Make sure you sit down with each tenant before they move in and go over the lease, so you both have a good understanding from the beginning about what you expect from each other," says Dennis from Petaluma.

Should You Ask for or Accept Cosigners?

Some landlords require cosigners on rental agreements and leases, especially when renting to students who depend on parents for much of their income. The cosigner signs the rental agreement or lease or a separate document, agreeing to cover any rent or damage-repair costs the tenant fails to pay.

In practice, a cosigner's promise may have less legal value than you'd think. Suppose your tenant doesn't pay the rent, and the cosigner doesn't step up. Most landlords will simply evict the tenant, because the alternative (suing in small claims court to force the guarantor to honor the promise) is too much trouble (and is practically impossible if the cosigner lives in another state).

Still, a tenant who thinks you can (and will) notify and sue a cosigning relative or friend may be less likely to default on the rent. Similarly, a cosigner asked to pay the tenant's debts may persuade the tenant to pay, or may (as many parents will) come to the tenant's rescue.

Because of the practical difficulties associated with cosigners, many landlords refuse to consider them, which is legal in every situation but one: If a tenant with a disability who has insufficient income (but is otherwise suitable) asks you to accept a cosigner, you must at least investigate the proposed cosigner's suitability. If that person is solvent and stable, federal law requires you to accept the cosigner, in spite of your general policy.

If you decide to accept a cosigner, you may want to have that person fill out a separate rental application and agree to a credit check—after all, a cosigner who has no resources or connection to the tenant will be completely useless. Should the tenant and prospective cosigner object, you may wonder how serious they are about the arrangement. Once you're satisfied that the cosigner can genuinely back up the tenant, add a line at the end of the lease or rental agreement for the dated signature, phone, and address of the cosigner.

> CAUTION
> **Don't sign until all terms are final and mutually understood.**
> All of your expectations should be written into the lease or rental
> agreement before you and the tenant sign. Never sign an incomplete
> document assuming last-minute changes can be made later. If you've
> altered a preprinted form by writing or typing in changes, you and the
> tenant should initial and date each change when you sign the document.

Be sure all adults (18 years of age and older) who will live in the
rental unit, including both members of a couple, sign the lease or rental
agreement. Doing this makes everyone who signs responsible for all
terms, including the full amount of the rent. As Gordon, a landlord in
San Jose, California, says, "If you have to evict your tenants, you can
evict the guy who signed the lease, but the others may not move out.
A smart attorney can get around that, but you can avoid the problem
from the get-go if they all sign the lease."

After everyone signs, give one copy of the signed lease or rental
agreement to the tenant(s) and keep the other one for your files.

Getting the Tenant Moved In

A clearly written and easy-to-understand lease or rental agreement is critical to starting a tenancy. But there's more that can be done to help establish a positive relationship. On or before the tenant's move-in day, set up
a time to go over your house rules and important information about the
rental, walk through the house, and hand over the keys. Bring a welcome
gift, such as a bottle of wine or a gift certificate for a local restaurant. Be
cordial and allow enough time to answer all the tenant's questions.

Give new tenants a move-in letter and house rules

A good move-in letter will provide all kinds of valuable information for
the new tenants, such as:

- your phone numbers (during the day and after hours), email, and
emergency contacts

- how and where to report maintenance and repair problems
- location of garbage cans, trash pickup days, and available recycling programs
- maintenance dos and don'ts, such as how to avoid overloading circuits and use the garbage disposal properly
- where to find appliance manuals, water shut-off valves, smoke detectors, and other important information
- homeowners' association rules (if any), and
- any other useful information about the property and neighborhood.

Many landlords highlight important lease terms in their move-in letter, such as their policy regarding late fees and adding a roommate or pets.

TIP
Renting out a condo or house in a common-interest development (CID)? Remember to give the tenant a copy of the community association rules (often called CC&Rs), and emphasize that failing to comply with them may give you no choice but to evict.

Inspect and photograph the rental property

To ward off future arguments, it's absolutely essential that you and your tenant (ideally, together) check the place over for damage and obvious wear and tear before the move-in (but after your own prepping of the property, discussed in Chapter 3). You and the tenant should document what you find with an inventory describing the general condition of each room (and any furnishings), backed up with photos or video, and signed by both (or all) of you.

Write down, in as much detail as is practical, both serious problems, such as a broken heater, and minor flaws, such as a stained kitchen counter, dirty drapes, or chipped paint. Ideally, you'll have fixed all major problems before the tenant moves in, but if not, now's the time to do so (especially any habitability or security problems).

This inventory will protect both you and your tenant when the tenant moves out and questions why you withheld all or part of a security deposit. Coupled with a system to keep track of the rental property's condition (as discussed in Chapter 7), your inventory will also be extremely useful if a tenant withholds rent, breaks the lease and moves out, or sues you outright, claiming the unit needs substantial repairs.

USA TODAY Snapshots®

Understanding energy bills

How well do you understand the different sections of your energy/utility bills?

Completely	22%
Mostly	49%
Just the overall costs	22%
Just pay it	8%

Note: Total exceeds 100% due to rounding.

Source: MXenergy survey of 1,739 homeowners conducted by Impulse Research. Margin of error ±3 percentage points.

By Jae Yang and Alejandro Gonzalez, USA TODAY 2007

Besides just being useful, an inventory is sometimes mandatory. Many states require landlords to give new tenants a written statement on the condition of the rental premises at move-in, including a comprehensive list of existing damages, and give tenants the right to inspect the premises to verify the accuracy of the list and note any problems.

RESOURCE

Where to find a room-by-room inventory and relevant state laws. Nolo's book, *Every Landlord's Legal Guide,* includes detailed forms for inspecting and inventorying the rental property at move-in and move-out and making security deposit deductions, and state laws in these areas. Nolo also publishes an online Landlord-Tenant Checklist for documenting the condition of the rental (and any furnishings) at the beginning and end of the tenancy. See Nolo.com.

Organizing Your Rental Records

Making written notes of key events in a tenant's rental history, and organizing your rental documents, will come in very handy if you and your tenant disagree, perhaps in court, about what happened and when. For example, suppose you terminate the tenancy of a tenant who chronically paid rent late. If that tenant claims that your real reason was illegal (say, discrimination on account of race), your records, including late fee notices, requests for rent, and bank records will help you establish your true motive. You never want to be in a position where the only evidence before a judge is your word against the tenant's.

Start by setting up a file folder for the following documents (it's also a good idea to keep electronic copies where possible):

- tenants' contact information, including phone numbers (home and work, plus emergency contacts), plus vehicle make, model, color, year, and license plate number
- a copy of your tenant's rental application, references, and credit report
- your copy of the signed lease or rental agreement
- deposit information, including the location and interest rate terms of your deposit, and
- inventory and photos or video of the condition of rental unit at move-in time.

After your tenant moves in, add these documents to your file:

- your written requests for entry
- rent increase notices and late fee notices
- records of tenant repair requests and how and when they were handled, and
- any other correspondence with your tenant.

Chapter 6 provides advice on keeping important financial and tax records.

> **CAUTION**
>
> **Don't keep copies of tenant credit reports.** Under the "Disposal Rule" of the Fair and Accurate Credit Transactions Act of 2003, you must destroy a report when you no longer need it. Use a shredder or burn the credit report. ●

Manage Your Rental Income to Maximize Tax Deductions

Do you know how to give an accountant a supersize migraine? Put the rental payments from your tenants right into your family bank account, dip into the same account when you need to buy things for the property, don't bother saving receipts or keeping records, and let your kids use the maintenance and office supplies you originally bought in connection with the rental property.

This will guarantee that, at the end of the year, you and your accountant tear your hair out trying to figure out whether your rental property business made or lost money, which expenses will be tax deductible (important if you did make a profit), and whether you were even active enough as a landlord to claim business owner deductions. In the worst-case scenario, you could end up in an IRS audit, perhaps having to pay back taxes and penalties for disallowed deductions.

But wait, there's a better way: Treat your rental property as a business from the beginning, even if it's only half of your duplex or a spare room in your house. That includes:

- drawing a clear line between your business and personal finances
- taking steps to shield you and your family from personal liability for business debts
- learning what tax deductions you're allowed, how to conduct business so you can claim them, and how to prove you deserve them
- keeping your income and expense records in good order
- making sure you're actually earning a profit, and
- getting professional help when needed.

We'll show you how to do all these things in this chapter. You should read it even if you don't expect to turn a profit—that picture may change, and it's worth developing good habits, and keeping clear records, from the start.

TIP
Good financial management translates into a good credit record. Because you're probably operating as a sole proprietor, your ability to pay business bills on time and repay loans is as important to your credit record as how you handle your personal credit card. A good credit record will make it easier to take out loans—which you may need for property improvements or to weather a rough patch. Conversely, a poor credit record will hurt your ability to not only take out loans at reasonable interest rates but accomplish other life goals, like getting a new job. For more on the hows and whys of keeping up a good credit score, see the Bankruptcy section of Nolo's website (www.nolo.com).

Keeping Your Business Finances Separate

It's not hard to keep your personal finances separate from your rental property finances—but it gets harder the longer you wait to create an appropriate system. Start by setting up a separate bank account, which you'll draw on for business expenses.

Opening and using a separate bank account

One of your first steps in becoming a landlord should be to choose your favorite local or online bank and open a separate checking account. If you incorporate your business activities or form an LLC (as discussed below), open the account in the name of that business. If not, just use your own name. (In theory, you could register a separate business name with your state or county government—often called a "DBA," for "doing business as"—but there's little point, because the laws will probably require you to include your last name in your DBA anyway.)

CAUTION
Shop around for bank rates. Look for a low-cost or even free checking account, and read the fine print regarding extra fees for things like going below the minimum balance or bouncing a check. Avoid using the word "business" when asking about accounts—some banks immediately raise their checking account rates for businesses, no doubt imagining the massive profits you'll bring in.

Because you'll probably have to spend money on your property before it earns a dime, it's good to seed your checking account with some start-up cash ("capital contributions") from your personal account. Once you start earning rental income, deposit it into your business account and pay all expenses out of that account (after charging expenses to your business credit card, if you have one). Repay yourself for those capital contributions by writing a check to your personal account. When writing checks, always use the memo line to write what the money is being spent on.

CAUTION
Landlords in certain states must put tenants' security deposits into a separate bank account. Adding them to a separate, business account won't do it in these states. (However, your property manager, if you hire one, may take care of this for you.) Check your state's security deposit laws, available in the Landlords section at www.nolo.com.

Opening and using a separate credit card account

For convenience, you may want to open a separate credit card account for your business. Credit cards are convenient, may offer benefits like cash back, and avoid keeping all of your money in your checking account, which is relatively easy prey for identity thieves.

> **TIP**
> **Already have more than one personal credit card account?** You could simply pay one down to a zero balance and start using it exclusively for your business.

Be scrupulous by making business purchases on your business credit card only, even if you find the perfect plants on sale and forgot to bring the right card. If you must make an exception, save the receipt and write a memo for your files as soon as you're home, then repay your personal account out of your business account.

Do your best to pay off the entire credit card debt month by month—mounting interest can quickly undercut your profits. Credit card interest rates are typically the highest of any type of loan.

> **TIP**
> **What if you buy something for mixed use?** For example, suppose you pick up a tray of ground cover that you'll use partly for business and partly for your home. One option is to ask the cashier to divide the bill between two credit cards. Another is to pull out both your business and personal checkbooks and use separate checks to pay. If you must use only one credit card, go with your personal one, then make a note for your files and repay the proportional share from the business checking account. (After-the-fact conversions of property from personal to business raises eyebrows at the IRS.)

Sharing property between your home and business

There's no need to rush out and buy two sets of everything—a new lawn mower, power saw, or computer, for example. If you already have or need to buy something at home, you can use it for your business, too. The catch is that, if you want a tax deduction, you'll need to keep track of what percentage of the property's use is dedicated toward your business.

With computers and other "listed property" (described below), that percentage must be greater than 50% for the IRS to recognize the business use. The same is true for property you want to deduct under Section 179 (described below). Telephones are a separate case—the first line into a home is always considered personal, so you can't deduct its cost no matter how much you use it for work (though you can deduct long-distance calls). With other property, however, you can simply take a proportional amount of the applicable tax deduction based on your percentage of business use.

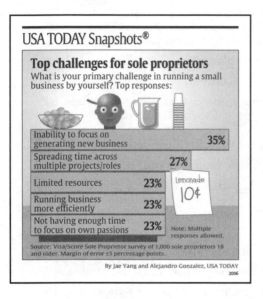

USA TODAY Snapshots®

Top challenges for sole proprietors
What is your primary challenge in running a small business by yourself? Top responses:

Inability to focus on generating new business	35%
Spreading time across multiple projects/roles	27%
Limited resources	23%
Running business more efficiently	23%
Not having enough time to focus on own passions	23%

Note: Multiple responses allowed.

Source: Visa/Score Sole Proprietor survey of 1,000 sole proprietors 18 and older. Margin of error ±3 percentage points.

By Jae Yang and Alejandro Gonzalez, USA TODAY 2006

A related issue is whether you'll actually decide to create a separate office within your home in order to qualify for the home office deduction. We'll discuss that below under "Deducting for use of a home office."

Shielding Yourself From Liability for Business Debts

We're assuming you're currently operating as a sole proprietorship, meaning you haven't done anything special or filed any papers with your state. You create a sole proprietorship simply by going into business by yourself. The same goes for partnerships: Two people going into business together create a partnership. There's no need to register with the state or sign a partnership agreement.

Starting out as a sole proprietorship or partnership is certainly convenient, but there's a catch: As a sole proprietor or partner, you and your business are legally one and the same when it comes to debts and liability. It won't matter how hard you've worked to keep your books and finances separate. If someone claims you owe them money—perhaps a contractor whom you've refused to pay for shoddy work, or your tenant who sues you for medical costs after slipping on the badly lit back porch—your own assets could be on the line.

That's why some businesses that start out as sole proprietorships or partnerships eventually decide to convert to separate legal entities, usually a limited liability company (LLC) or a corporation.

> ⚠ **CAUTION**
> **No business structure can completely shield you from all liability.** Even if you operate as a corporation or LLC, a creditor can go after your personal assets if, for example, you personally guarantee a loan or lease (which many banks require of landlords); your business owes federal or state income, payroll, or other taxes; or you fail to abide by corporate rules (for example, you mix corporate and personal funds and don't keep records of meetings and shareholders).

Pluses and minuses to forming a corporation

Incorporating means that you formally declare that your business is a separate legal entity from you, its owner. Once you incorporate, the corporate entity becomes responsible for your business's debts and liabilities instead of you (with certain limitations).

The process of incorporating can be a bit worky, however. It involves choosing a name, filing articles of incorporation with your state, paying filing and other fees (often hefty), adopting bylaws, appointing a board of directors (most states allow just one director, who can be you), and issuing shares (probably to yourself).

Running a corporation is also more complicated than running a sole proprietorship or partnership. You'll need to comply with federal and state securities laws concerning record keeping, corporate taxation, and more.

The upshot is that forming a corporation may require more time and expense than you want to invest. For many landlords, the personal liability issue can be dealt with in other ways. See "Alternative ways to minimize your risk," below.

Pluses and minuses to forming an LLC

Limited liability companies, or LLCs, are less complex to form and run than corporations. Yet, just like corporations, the owners of an LLC are not personally liable for business debts (with similar exceptions).

To form an LLC, you need to file articles of organization with your state, pay filing and other fees, and draft an internal operating agreement. Although you'll have to pay annual fees, you won't have to deal with many of the other ongoing requirements that corporations face, such as holding regular board meetings and keeping minutes. And your taxes will be much simpler, because you can choose to simply pay them through your individual tax return. Again, however, you may want to look for simpler alternatives.

Alternative ways to minimize your risk

Forming a separate legal entity isn't the only way to deal with unexpected events that require you to dip deeper into your own pockets than you can handle. Another important measure is buying adequate insurance to protect yourself (see our discussion of insurance in Chapter 8).

Also, simply behaving in a responsible manner will help forestall problems before they arise—for example, by signing written agreements with contractors to help head off disputes, following health and safety codes, and making repairs and taking other preventative safety measures on your property before a tenant gets injured (as discussed in Chapter 7). See Chapter 2 for more on the pros and cons of LLCs.

Spent a Lot of Money?
Take More Tax Deductions!

A surprising number of your landlording expenses can be turned into tax deductions. When Lisa first began renting out the Berkeley, California, house she formerly lived in, she says, "I had no idea how much I'd save in taxes—enough that, once I ran the numbers, I went straight to my HR director's office and changed my wage withholding so I could start enjoying the benefits with my very next paycheck. The reason wasn't just the deductions for mortgage interest, property tax payments, and expenses, but the surprisingly large depreciation deduction."

Apart from your day job, you'll hopefully have some new income from the property as well, so you've got every interest in offsetting it with some deductions.

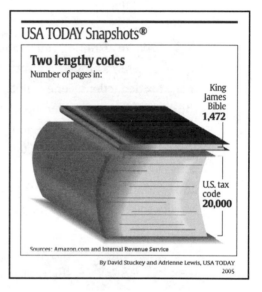

USA TODAY Snapshots®

Two lengthy codes
Number of pages in:

King James Bible **1,472**

U.S. tax code **20,000**

Sources: Amazon.com and Internal Revenue Service

By David Stuckey and Adrienne Lewis, USA TODAY 2005

The basic formula works like this:

- Add up your gross income (mostly rent received over the year).
- Deduct your start-up expenses.
- Deduct your operating expenses (mortgage interest and property tax included).
- Deduct your depreciation and amortization expenses.
- Deduct any Section 179 expenses. (This deduction is much more limited for landlords than other business owners.)
- The result is your taxable income, or the amount the IRS will ask for a bite of (after you report your profits and losses on Schedule E).

Let's take a closer look at the various federal tax deductions available to landlords, and how you can make the most of them. Most states also impose income taxes, which you'll have to research on your own—but state income tax laws tend to mimic the federal system. Our goal here is not to provide every legal detail or prepare you to fill out a tax form, but to raise your awareness of likely tax-reducing strategies—and dead-end tax traps.

TIP

We're assuming you'll really be acting like a business owner. If you're merely a property "investor," you won't have access to as many tax deductions. For example, if you're lax about placing ads, and the property sits vacant for months at a time, the IRS could classify you as an investor (and make you pay penalties and back taxes if you claimed business owner deductions). The key is to earn a profit by actively running a business by working at it regularly, systematically, and continuously. Hiring a property manager to take over much of the activity still counts, for IRS purposes.

Who Gets the Deductions If You Co-Own?

If you share ownership of your property with someone other than your spouse, you can share the tax deductions, as well. For example, if you take title to the property as tenants in common, you'll have to list each of your percentage ownership interests (60%/40%, for example), on your property deed, and the IRS will expect you to share the expenses and tax deductions in equal proportions.

If you've placed ownership of the property into a partnership or an LLC, the deductions will pass through to the partners or members. The deductions can then be allocated among you as you wish, subject to IRS "substantial economic effect" rules (which let the IRS disregard allocations of losses done only to avoid taxes).

This is a complicated area of tax law, so see a tax expert to work out the details.

It's entirely possible—especially if you recently bought the property—that you'll be able to wipe out all your taxable rental income with your expenses, and not have to pay any tax at all on the rental income. Of course, you'll need to keep good records of every penny spent in order to do this. And, unfortunately, one of the most valuable contributions you'll be making to your rental property is your own time—and that's not tax deductible.

If your Schedule E actually shows a tax loss on the property, you may be able to deduct the loss from other income, but this gets more complicated. It's governed by what are called the passive-loss and at-risk rules, which we don't cover in this book.

RESOURCE
For in-depth information on all the topics in this section, see *Every Landlord's Tax Deduction Guide,* by Stephen Fishman (Nolo). It also covers some topics not discussed here, such as the tax implications of employing your children, and how to deduct business losses. For personalized advice, consult an accounting or tax professional—you can deduct that expense, too.

Deducting start-up expenses below $5,000

You can deduct up to $5,000 of your start-up expenses the first year you're in business. Start-up expenses are any expenses you incur before offering your property for rent, so long as they're related to getting your business up and running. Once you're in business (that is, after you've placed an ad or otherwise started offering the property for rent), all your expenses are considered operating expenses, which we'll discuss below.

TIP
You may need a business license. Some cities or localities require that all landlords—or at least those whose properties have more than a minimum number of units—pay an annual license fee and possibly undergo a property inspection. Check with your city for details.

Examples of possible start-up expenses include:

- costs of researching and investigating the rental market
- educational information, including how-to books (like this one), classes, or seminars
- attorney and accounting fees (except legal and other fees paid to complete the purchase of the rental property)
- licenses
- insurance premiums
- meals, food, and lodging if you have to travel overnight to get the property ready to rent
- repairs to get the property ready to rent
- office supplies, such as telephone, paper, and notebooks (but not equipment and other long-term assets)
- printing bank checks
- advertising your property for rent (such as ads and signs), and
- any other operating expenses that you paid before offering the property for rent, such as landscaping and gardening costs, property maintenance, and utilities (excluding utility connection fees).

What's absent from the above list? Some pretty big-ticket items, actually. Not only is the cost of the property itself excluded, but all equipment, furniture, appliances, and other property that's expected to last more than one year. These items are considered long-term assets, and are deductible only in limited amounts per year, via depreciation. Also absent from the list are any expenses directly related to the purchase of the property, such as closing costs, escrow fees, attorney fees, travel expenses related to the purchase, title insurance, and transfer taxes. These costs are added to the property's tax basis and depreciated over time, as described below.

Deducting start-up expenses over $5,000

What if your start-up expenses add up to more than $5,000? You can deduct start-up expenses over $5,000 in equal amounts over the first 15 years you're in business. However, this is a long time to wait to get the full deduction value of your expenditures. One useful strategy is to put the property on the rental market as soon as possible, so that you never run through the $5,000. That automatically triggers the switch into the realm of operating expenses (upon which there's no set limit).

Putting the property on the market doesn't mean you have to do an advertising blitz. Starting with a simple "For Rent" sign on the property will do. Keep proof of your first ad in case of an IRS audit—a date-stamped picture of the "For Rent" sign is all you need.

Another problem with spending more than $5,000 during your start-up period is that if your expenditures end up exceeding $50,000, you won't get to use the full $5,000 start-up deduction. Your allowable deduction is reduced by any amount you spend over $50,000 on start-up expenses. For example, if you spend $54,000 in startup expenses, you'll lose

USA TODAY Snapshots®

A hole in our pockets

Consumers spend an average of $21 per week in cash without being aware of where it goes. That adds up to around $1,092 per year. What consumers could have bought with the money:

About 400 gallons of gasoline

Three months of groceries

791 cups of coffee

Personal physical-training session once a month

Source: Visa

By Jae Yang and Keith Simmons, USA TODAY 2010

$4,000 of your first-year deduction. That means you'll get a $1,000 first-year deduction and you'll have to spread out (amortize) the remaining $53,000 worth of deductions over the next 15 years.

Deducting operating expenses

The operating-expense deduction is sort of a catchall for the many day-to-day costs you'll face as a landlord, for things like upkeep, supplies, taxes, and fees. But it doesn't cover everything you might think of. For one, it excludes long-term capital expenses (such as equipment purchases), which we'll discuss below. For another, it excludes expenses that might be considered excessive or personal. In IRS-speak, you can claim a tax deduction only if an operating expense is ordinary and necessary, current (likely to be used, or used up, within a year), directly related to your rental activity (not for your personal benefit), and reasonable in amount (sorry, no lavish meals, luxury hotel stays, or paying your ten-year-old $100 an hour to sweep the deck).

Here are examples of expenses the IRS recognizes as ordinary and necessary to a rental business:

- **Interest payments on mortgage loans, other loans, and credit cards.** (Discussed below.)

- **Property and other taxes.** (Discussed below.)

- **Professional fees.** For example, attorney, accounting, property management, and rental broker fees.

- **License renewals.** If you must register your rental with a local government, these fees are deductible.

- **Ongoing insurance premiums.** This includes not only homeowners' insurance, but a portion of your car insurance if you regularly use the car for your landlord business.

- **Homeowners' association dues.** If your property is a condo, townhouse, or in a community development, you'll be paying association dues, which cover repairs and maintenance.

- **Local transportation expenses.** For example, you might travel from your home office or other office to make regular property visits, shop for supplies, or transfer garbage to the dump. You can deduct either an IRS amount based on mileage, or actual costs of owning and operating your car. Note that if you don't work from home, trips from your home to your landlord-business office or place of business are considered nondeductible commutes.

> **CAUTION**
> **Got a traffic or parking ticket while on landlord business?**
> Don't try to deduct it. For public policy reasons, taxpayers can never deduct government fines or penalties.

- **Out-of-town travel costs.** You may have to travel overnight and outside your city limits to spend time at the property or attend to related business matters (for example, to attend a real estate seminar or visit an attorney). Transportation, hotel, and related expenses like Internet access, phones, and laundry are fully deductible. Meals and beverages are deductible at 50% of their cost. As an alternative to actual meal expenses, you can deduct a standard daily meal allowance, or "per diem" (which varies depending on your destination). If you plan to mix vacation time into your trip, the value of your deduction may be reduced depending on the percentage of time you spent on rental activities—spending at least four hours a day on rental activities will protect you.

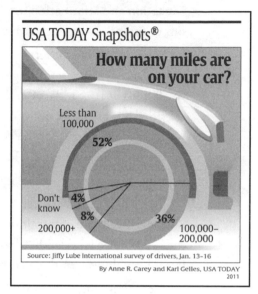

USA TODAY Snapshots®

How many miles are on your car?

Less than 100,000 — **52%**

Don't know — **4%**

200,000+ — **8%**

100,000–200,000 — **36%**

Source: Jiffy Lube International survey of drivers, Jan. 13–16

By Anne R. Carey and Karl Gelles, USA TODAY 2011

- **Keeping up the property.** Upkeep costs include property repairs, maintenance, cleaning, environmental remediation of problems that arose after you bought the property and in the ordinary course of business operations, and gardening. They don't include improvements, or work that makes the property better than it was before —these must be deducted via depreciation, as discussed below.

- **Disability access.** You can deduct the costs of making your property accessible to the elderly or disabled according to the federal Americans with Disabilities Act (ADA) standards (limited to $15,000). This is a special deduction, because such changes would normally be considered "improvements," and subject to depreciation.

- **Office supplies.** You can deduct the cost of supplies you use in your office, including software, paper, postage, and notebooks (but you can't deduct equipment and other long-term assets).

- **Education and information.** Books, magazine or newsletter subscriptions, classes, or seminars are deductible.

- **Advertising and tenant screening.** Unless you rent via word-of-mouth and skip any screening of potential tenants (a risky step), you'll need at least a "For Rent" sign, and will probably pay for classified ads and prospective-tenant credit checks. (Of course, if you charge the tenant for the cost of pulling a report, you cannot also deduct this expenditure.)

- **Utilities.** If you (not your tenant) pay the gas, water, garbage, electric, or other utility bills, you can deduct them.

- **Business meals and entertainment.** For example, you might take the head of the local landlord association to lunch to get some free advice. However, these costs are only 50% deductible.

- **Business gifts.** These are limited to $25 per gift recipient per year (however, if you give a gift to all the employees of a business, such as a holiday fruit basket delivered to your gardening service, you may deduct the entire cost, as long as it's reasonable).

- **Membership fees.** Joining a landlords' association would be considered reasonable. But don't try deducting fees for country, social, or athletic clubs.

- **Home office expenses.** You may deduct these expenses, but it's tricky—see the discussion below before deciding to take the home office deduction.

TIP

Renting a unit that's attached to your home? If, for example, you live in half of a duplex, or have a cottage on your property, you'll need to figure out what portion of the property expenses are personal, and what portion can be called rental operating costs. The easiest way to do this is to calculate the percentage of square footage occupied by the rental unit, then apply that percentage against your overall costs for household operating expenses like insurance, utilities, mortgage interest, landscaping, and repairs and maintenance. Of course, some items can be separately calculated. For example, if you have separate yards with a fence in between and the gardener charges separately for each, or separate utility meters, use these figures.

Deducting mortgage and other loan interest

In most cases, interest you pay on loans taken out to pay expenses on your rental property are tax deductible. By contrast, if you took out a loan using your rental property as security, but spent the money on personal things, the interest wouldn't be deductible.

Unless you've inherited a paid-off property, or converted a house you lived in for many years, the mortgage interest on your rental property may be among your biggest expenses. Your monthly mortgage payment is composed of principal (a direct repayment of what was borrowed) and interest, or the amount you pay the lender for the privilege of using its money. You can't, unfortunately, deduct your principal payments as an operating expense.

However, your interest payments are tax deductible in the year you pay them. This includes any private mortgage insurance (PMI) premiums that your lender requires (which is likely if you made a low down payment, because this insurance protects the lender against your default). The deduction for PMI expired at the end of 2013, but as this book went to press, Congress was expected to extend the deduction at least through 2015. You may not deduct, at least for the current year, the points you paid to get your mortgage (unlike the rules for primary homes); these must ordinarily be spread out over the term of the loan before you can deduct them.

Will you be taking out a loan to improve the property (for example, add a room or remodel)? Your interest payments on this loan are also deductible.

Loans you take out to repair the property, such as a home equity loan, are treated slightly differently. In these cases, you may deduct not only the interest paid, but the principal amount during the years that you repay it.

Finally, interest paid on your business credit card can be deducted (but remember, you should be paying your card off monthly, except in emergencies). You can also deduct interest on a car loan if you use your personal car for business—just figure out what percentage of the time you use the car for business, and then deduct that percentage of the loan interest.

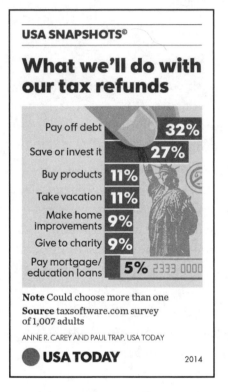

USA SNAPSHOTS©

What we'll do with our tax refunds

Pay off debt	32%
Save or invest it	27%
Buy products	11%
Take vacation	11%
Make home improvements	9%
Give to charity	9%
Pay mortgage/ education loans	5%

Note Could choose more than one
Source taxsoftware.com survey of 1,007 adults

ANNE R. CAREY AND PAUL TRAP, USA TODAY

● **USA TODAY**   2014

Deducting property tax payments

Although the United States has no federal property tax, your state, local, and municipal governments may all be poised to extract property taxes from you. Fortunately, you can deduct these as an operating expense.

How much you'll have to pay in property tax each year usually depends on the value of your house, but thousands of dollars a year is common. The availability of a tax deduction will offset only a fraction of the full cost, so always check whether you're being overcharged. Your state will allow you to appeal the assessment within a certain time period, which is worth following up on if the assessment is demonstrably off base. Unfortunately, you can't count on your assessment going down when house values do.

> **RESOURCE**
> **Interested in your state's assessment rules?** Go to the tax assessor's page on your local government's website (www.netronline.com is a useful portal for individual counties) or view summaries on websites like www.retirementliving.com.

Deducting for use of a home office

If you use part of your own home regularly and exclusively for your rental property business, you may be able to deduct a portion of the related home expenses—such as your mortgage interest, utility bills, cleaning, and home repair costs. And the home office deduction would let you deduct the full amount of any expenses that are solely and directly connected to your home office, such as painting the room and adding a carpet. Office furniture, like a desk or chair you use for your rental business, is deductible whether or not you qualify for a home office deduction.

But there's a major catch to this deduction. Unless you can really set aside space and equipment in your house for exclusive business use, you'll have trouble qualifying for the deduction. It doesn't have to be a whole room. If you can at least set off part of a room for exclusive use, you may yet qualify—but you'll get less of a deduction, due to the small size of the area identified as your home office. And even in a small section of a room, you may need the same desk area and computer to manage your landlord business as to handle personal bills, not to mention surf the Web and send personal emails—so you couldn't meet the exclusive-use test.

If you sell your house, you'll have to pay capital gains tax on the profit earned from the area used as a home office within the last two years. Normally, without your home office, the capital gains tax exclusion of $500,000 for married couples filing joint returns and $250,000 for singles would shield a nice chunk of your profits. But if, for example, you claimed one-fifth of your home as a home office, you'd lose the benefit of that exclusion for one-fifth of your sale profits, which would become fully taxable.

Deducting for depreciation

Depreciation deductions can be complicated—but lucrative enough to be worth spending time learning about. In any case, depreciation is not an optional deduction. Even if you choose to ignore it, the IRS will dock you when you sell the property (in effect, by adding the depreciation you should have claimed to your sales profits, upping your capital gains tax bill).

The basic concept of depreciation is that the cost of certain assets are not everyday operating costs—yet deserve some sort of tax deduction—because the asset will:

- last for over a year
- get worn out or used up over time
- remain in your hands as owner for more than one year, and
- be used in your rental business.

Examples of common depreciable assets for landlords include the rental building and its structural components, personal property bought for the rental property (such as appliances, furniture, and carpets), and personal property bought for use on the rental property, such as tools and equipment.

However, the IRS says that you may currently deduct any item you purchase for your rental activity that costs $200 or less, even if is a long-term asset. For example, you could currently deduct a $50 lamp you buy for your rental activity, even though it is a long-term asset that will last longer than one year.

> CAUTION
> **Receipts aren't always enough.** For certain types of depreciable property, called "listed" property, the IRS will want to see documentation showing that you actually used it for your business, not for your personal life. Listed property includes cars and other vehicles, motorcycles, boats, airplanes, computers, and property used for entertainment, recreation, or amusement, such as cameras and stereos. You'll need to keep a log book showing when and how the property is used. (One exception to the record-keeping requirement is for computers used 100% for business— you don't need to keep records.)

You can either combine the depreciation of your rental property (all buildings, components, and improvements) with the personal property assets inside it (such as appliances), or depreciate them separately. Separating them is harder, but although it won't increase your total deductions, it can give you higher deductions in the early years of ownership.

How long the depreciation period lasts. Instead of deducting your asset costs in the year you pay them (as with a regular deduction), you spread out your deductions over a certain number of years (the "recovery period"). The IRS provides preset recovery periods, based in part on how much time it thinks will pass before the asset wears out or gets used up.

The IRS also offers more than one possible method for divvying up the total depreciation amount for each year. These methods go by names like "straight-line" (the same amount every year) and "accelerated" depreciation. We're not going get into their details here; you can find more information in *Every Landlord's Tax Deduction Guide*, by Stephen Fishman (Nolo), and in IRS Publication 946, *How to Depreciate Property*.

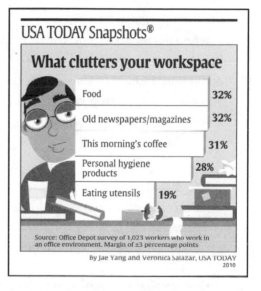

USA TODAY Snapshots®

What clutters your workspace

Food	32%
Old newspapers/magazines	32%
This morning's coffee	31%
Personal hygiene products	28%
Eating utensils	19%

Source: Office Depot survey of 1,023 workers who work in an office environment. Margin of ±3 percentage points

By Jae Yang and Veronica Salazar, USA TODAY 2010

In the case of residential real estate and structural components, the deduction is spread over 27.5 years—by which time the buildings are assumed to have "worn out." Of course, the land itself won't wear out, which is why land can't be depreciated—you have to subtract its value from your purchase price before taking the depreciation deduction. (This is true even for condo owners. Despite the fact that you don't personally have title to any land, you still own an interest in commonly held land, the size of which should be listed on your deed.)

Other assets have a much shorter recovery period, in most cases five or seven years, and only three years for software. The shorter the recovery period, the sooner you get the full value of your deduction. For that reason, you'll probably need to do some research before deciding how to claim your deduction. You'll soon realize there's a history of arguments between taxpayers and the IRS about issues like whether carpeting is personal property (with a five-year recovery period) or a structural component (with a 27.5-year recovery period). (The current view is that carpeting is a structural component if it's glued down, while it's personal property if it's tacked down. But the conclusions aren't that consistent on other property, like tiles.)

When the recovery period ends prematurely. If you sell your property before the recovery period is up, you can't continue to take the deduction. In fact, you must stop taking depreciation for any asset that you either sell, destroy, dispose of, or stop using for your rental business before the recovery period ends.

> **CAUTION**
>
> **Buying art, collectibles, or antique furniture for your rental?** Don't expect to depreciate it. Although such items might eventually wear out, the fact that they're increasing in value in the meantime make them ineligible for depreciation.

How to calculate each depreciable asset's true cost. As mentioned earlier, the cost of buying a house is more than its purchase price. You can add in attorney fees, closing costs, transfer taxes, and the cost of making later improvements to the property. Added together, these are called the property's "basis." The full basis of a piece of property can be depreciated.

What if you inherited the property, and so didn't pay a dime for it? You're still expected to claim depreciation deductions for it. Because you obviously can't use its purchase price as your starting point, your "basis" is instead its fair market value at the time of the previous owner's death. Of course, you still need to subtract the value of the land.

Rather than buying or inheriting property that they decide to rent out, some owners convert a property that they previously lived in to rental use. In this case, your basis for depreciation purposes is either the property's fair market value on the date of the change, or your own adjusted cost basis in the property on that date, whichever is less.

RESOURCE
See IRS Publication 551, *Basis of Assets*, for more detail on calculating cost basis.

How to depreciate additions and improvements. When you add to or improve your rental property, you must separately depreciate the new structures or components. Examples of additions or improvements might include adding a new room, replacing the roof, remodeling, replacing appliances, adding fences or other structures, or installing new plumbing or wiring. The recovery period for these is 27.5 years. A simple repair (which returns the property to the condition it was in before the problem arose that required fixing) is not an improvement.

Interestingly enough, certain changes to the land itself can be depreciated, including grading, clearing, excavations, and landscaping. However, the recovery period for these is 15 years.

Figuring out which work constitutes an improvement and which constitutes a repair can be tricky—and it's in your interest to classify as much as possible of the work as repairs, so that you can immediately deduct their costs. You can plausibly claim that some parts of a project are repairs and some are improvements. For example, you might have your kitchen floors redone after the dishwasher floods (a repair) and also install a new dishwasher (an improvement). See the list of examples of improvements below.

Depreciation exception: Section 179

A piece of the tax code called Section 179 lets business owners deduct the entire cost of certain long-term personal property in one year, rather than having to depreciate it. This allowance is subject to a maximum annual limit, which can change periodically. For 2013, the limit was $500,000. The $500,000 Section 179 limit expired at the end of 2013 and automatically went down to $25,000. However, as this book went to press, Congress was expected to extend the $500,000 annual limit at least through 2015. It's also limited to the total of your profit from all your businesses and your salary (if you have one).

Unfortunately, because of its various rules and exceptions, this section is nearly useless for landlords. You can use it only for personal property not contained in your rental property, such as computers, office equipment, office furniture, and business vehicles. On top of that, Section 179 property must be used for your business more than half the time, and you must have purchased the property in the year you claim the Section 179 deduction.

IRS List of Examples of Home Improvements

Additions
- Bedroom
- Bathroom
- Deck
- Garage
- Porch
- Patio

Heating & Air Conditioning
- Heating system
- Central air conditioning
- Furnace
- Duct work
- Central humidifier
- Filtration system

Plumbing
- Septic system
- Water heater
- Soft water system
- Filtration system

Lawn & Grounds
- Landscaping
- Driveway
- Walkway
- Fence
- Retaining wall
- Sprinkler system
- Swimming pool

Interior Improvements
- Built-in appliances
- Kitchen modernization
- Flooring
- Wall-to-wall carpeting

Insulation
- Attic
- Walls
- Floors
- Pipes and duct work

Miscellaneous
- Storm windows, doors
- New roof
- Central vacuum
- Wiring upgrades
- Satellite dish
- Security system

New IRS Regulations on Deducting Repairs and Improvements

Starting in 2014, complex new IRS regulations govern how to determine whether a business expense is a building repair that is currently deductible in a single year or an improvement that must be depreciated over many years (27.5 years to be precise, in the case of residential rental property).

Under the new regulations, an expense a landlord incurs for a rental building must be depreciated if it makes the building as a whole, or any one of eight separate building systems, materially better than before, adapts it to a new use, or restores it to "like new" condition.

The regulations also contain three "safe harbor" rules, enabling landlords to currently deduct rental building expenses even if they would have to be depreciated under the regular rules—the:

- small taxpayer safe harbor
- routine maintenance safe harbor, and
- "de minimis" safe harbor.

The small taxpayer safe harbor allows landlords who own rental buildings that cost less than $1 million (not counting the cost of the land) to currently deduct the total amount spent each year for repairs, maintenance, improvements, and similar expenses, provided that this amount doesn't exceed the lesser of $10,000 or 2% of the unadjusted basis of the building (usually, its cost).

The routine maintenance safe harbor permits a landlord to currently deduct expenses incurred to (1) inspect, clean, and test the building structure or each building system, and (2) replace damaged or worn parts with comparable and commercially available replacement parts. There is no annual dollar limit for this safe harbor. However, building maintenance is considered to be routine only if, when you placed the building into service, you reasonably expected to perform such maintenance more than once every ten years.

The de minimis safe harbor enables a landlord to currently deduct any item purchased for the business if it cost $500 or less. To qualify for this safe harbor, a landlord must establish an accounting procedure

New IRS Regulations on Deducting Repairs and Improvements (cont'd)

to treat such expenses as currently deductible and actually treat such amounts as such on its books and records.

For a detailed discussion of the IRS repair regulations, refer to *Every Landlord's Tax Deduction Guide*, by Stephen Fishman (Nolo).

Proving What You've Spent: Record Keeping

To save yourself from stress next April, track your income and expenses as they arise. That will give you a clear picture of your rental property's profitability, and help you claim the maximum in tax deductions. For example, without a paper trail, you won't be able to easily convince the IRS that the cleaning supplies you bought on a certain date were not for use in your home, but were used to prepare your vacant rental for an open house (and are, therefore, deductible).

> **TIP**
> **How long should you keep financial records?** The IRS expects you to keep any receipts and other records concerning a property's purchase and capital improvements for as long as you own the property. (And because repairs and improvements can be hard to distinguish, it's worth keeping repair records around, too.) The rest should be kept for three to five years, depending on local law. But, in case a child is ever injured on your property, keep those records permanently, because the claim could arise years later.

According to Kathy, who rents out a duplex in Seffner, Florida, "At first, when we bought our duplex, the mortgage payments wiped out all our rental income, so I didn't bother much with keeping track of expenses for tax purposes. But now, 28 years later, with the place paid off, you can bet I record everything—like my mileage when I go to the property, or my mileage to the bank when I make a deposit. It all goes into a ledger I keep."

Here's how to begin; and if at some point you own more than one rental property, follow the same system to separately track your expenses for each:

- **Buy a receipt book.** Some states require you to give tenants a receipt, but it's a good practice in any case, especially if they sometimes pay with cash. The receipts should list the tenant's name, amount paid, date paid, and mode of payment (including check number).

USA TODAY Snapshots®

How people lose track of cash
Percentage of adults who lose track of cash spending when doing the following:

Grocery shopping — 34%
Leisure shopping — 32%
Enjoying night out — 31%
Dining out — 26%
Buying snacks — 25%
Daily lunch — 22%

Note: Multiple responses allowed

By By Anne R. Carey and Sam Ward, USA TODAY 2010

- **Create files for expense receipts.** Each file should be labeled with one expense category, for example "Start-Up Expenses," "Operating Expenses," and "Depreciable Property Expenses." Also keep separate files for your bank and credit card statements, filed in chronological order.

- **Make sure your expense receipts make it into the files.** Receipts are important—the IRS won't necessarily accept, for example, a canceled check alone as proof of what you purchased, because it contains no independent verification of what you spent the money on. But you won't always be near your filing cabinet when making a purchase. Some landlords like to keep a separate envelope in their purses, wallets, or glove department, making it easy to slip the receipt in right after buying something. Write on the receipt what the item was, why you bought it, and, if you paid by check, the check number. Transfer these regularly to your file.

- **Track your cash spending.** A handful of quarters into the parking meter, a couple bucks for highway tolls, a few more dollars for cleaning fluid—it adds up. Your purse or glove compartment makes a handy place to keep a little notebook, in which you record every cash purchase, including the amount, date, and business purpose. If the cash came out of your personal account, repay yourself from your business account using a check, to create an automatic record. Like any normal human, you may sometimes forget to follow all these practices, so try to avoid using cash whenever possible.

- **Ask servicepeople for detailed and, in some cases, split-up invoices.** An invoice that states what was done, and preferably describes it in terms of "repairing, patching, replacing," and so forth, will help show whether the expense was for a repair or an improvement. Or if an electrician both repairs the wiring in your rental property and adds new wiring to a new porch on that property (an improvement), asking for separate invoices will allow you to deduct for the repair this year while depreciating the improvement cost. Invoices help in mixed-use situations, too. For example, if you're renting out one unit of the duplex you live in and a roofer redoes the shared roof, asking for separate invoices will allow you to pay one from your business account and one from your personal account.

- **Keep a log showing use of listed property.** As mentioned earlier, cars and other modes of transport, and various entertainment devices can be claimed as tax deductions only if you can show you used them for your business, not personal use. Whether you create a computer document or make notes in a folder, keep track of the dates and uses of these items.

- **Track long-distance phone calls on your personal phone.** If your property is far away, long-distance calls become part of your tax-deductible operating costs—in which case another notebook is in order. Keep track of the date, time, and purpose of your calls. (Or, you could just get a separate phone.)

- **Track use of your personal car on rental business.** As a first-time landlord, you're probably not going to invest in a new business car. That will probably mean logging a lot of miles in the family car. That expense notebook in the glove compartment? You can also use it to log the date, destination, before-and-after odometer readings, and purpose of your car trips (for example, to the rental property, the hardware store, or the bank). If you wish, you can stop doing this after 90 days (or after one week each month), call that your "sampling period," and use the results to extrapolate your rental mileage for the entire year. If a trip is for mixed purposes—for example, you drive from your home office to the dump with garbage from both your home and rental property, you can call it a business trip.

- **Keep business property separate or identifiable after you've bought it.** Whenever you buy things with your business account—perhaps new paint, a screwdriver, or office supplies, like postage stamps and a printer and paper—keep them in a separate place, label them as business property, or do whatever else will remind you not to convert them to personal use.

- **Keep notes on tenant complaints.** If a tenant raises an issue that leads to a repair, having a record will help establish that the work was indeed a regular operating expense, not part of a larger improvement.

- **Make calendar notations about your business activities.** Both when you're at home and if and when traveling for rental reasons, having notes in your calendar regarding what you did and who you met with will help support your expense deduction claims.

- **Save paperwork.** Don't throw away correspondence (including email) related to your rental property. Hang onto relevant business cards. Agendas from seminars or conventions you attend are also valuable pieces of your paper trail if you're ever audited.

Are You Rich Yet? Tracking Income and Expenses

Take another look at the projections you made regarding annual income and expenses in Chapter 1. You'll want to run the same type of numbers once you're in business, on a monthly basis—and using real, not projected numbers. The idea is to pull information from your bank and credit card statements and files of invoices and receipts, keep tabs on whether your income and expenses are balancing out as expected, and find out what's actually left in the till. If you're using a property management company, it should send you monthly financial reports—and you should review them carefully and raise any relevant questions.

You can do a bare-bones analysis the old-fashioned way, using the Monthly Income/Expense Worksheet below, a pencil, and a calculator. Of course, some months will be odd ones, for example if you paid your taxes or bought a large piece of equipment. The purpose is not to create an average, but to get regular snapshots of your expenses and your cash on hand. As you look back over these worksheets, you'll be able to spot which months you need to plan ahead for.

Unfortunately, a simple analysis like this one leaves out many factors, like the impact of tax deductions. And handmade worksheets are hard to work with at tax time. (We put more categories above than you'll find on Schedule E, to make sure you didn't forget anything.) That's why many landlords find it worthwhile to invest in an accounting software package, such as *QuickBooks* (for general small-business use).

You can also hire an accountant to put all your rental data together and produce financial reports. You'll have to decide whether the cost is worth the reduced effort on your part.

Monthly Income/Expense Worksheet	
Month: _____ Year: 20_____	
EXPENSES	
Advertising and tenant screening	$
Local transportation	$
Out-of-city travel, meals, and lodging	$
Cleaning and maintenance	$
Homeowners' insurance (if not included in mortgage payment)	$
Legal and other professional fees (accountant, property manager)	$
Mortgage payment (principal and interest, plus property taxes and insurance, if included)	$
Other loan payments	$
Repairs	$
Supplies (for office and rental property)	$
Income tax	$
Property tax (if not included in mortgage payment)	$
Utilities (if not covered by tenant)	$
Gifts and entertainment	$
Licenses	$
Homeowners' association dues (in condos and some developments)	$
Educational publications, subscriptions, and memberships	$
Tools and equipment	$
Construction and improvements	$
Other miscellaneous expenses	$
TOTAL EXPENSES	**$**
INCOME	
Rental income	$
Other income (such as late fees, interest on security deposit, or damage reimbursements; landlords of multiunit properties may also charge for items like laundry or parking)	$
TOTAL INCOME	**$**
RESULTS	
Net income this month (total income − total expenses)	$
Cash remaining from last month (get from last month's worksheet)	$
Total cash on hand this month	$

At the other end of the spectrum is the minimalist approach espoused by Phil, a landlord in Berkeley, California, who says, "We're somewhat accidental landlords, with only two units, and I just put all my records and receipts into one folder and use *TurboTax* at the end of the year. We don't even have an accountant—*TurboTax* has a premier version that addresses rental real estate." If you take Phil's approach, at least be scrupulous about running all expenses through your business checking account, and reviewing your monthly statements to make sure your balance is as expected.

How Much Cash to Keep in Reserve

As soon as you start turning a profit (which may take months or years), think about setting some of it aside for a rainy day. (We're assuming you're already setting aside enough to cover irregular expenses like property taxes and insurance.) It's simply bad business practice to spend everything in your business account and leave nothing to fall back on. That means resisting the temptation to either churn your profits back into property improvements or make them your weekend play fund.

USA TODAY Snapshots®

If you were to lose your job, how long would your savings last?

Median days:

December 2009
180 days

December 2008
120 days

Source: SnagAJob.com survey of 1,098 working adults 18 and older in 2008 and 1,045 working adults 18 and older in 2009

By Jae Yang and Sam Ward, USA TODAY 2010

Instead, take a portion of your business profits and transfer them to an interest-earning savings account. (This is comparable to the "emergency fund" that financial advisers suggest you keep for your family, with three to six months of living expenses, just in case of a job loss or another emergency.)

How much should you keep in your reserve fund? As with your main property, it's best to set aside enough to pay for unexpected events like the roof's starting to leak or a flood in the basement. Experts recommend saving the equivalent of 5% of a home's purchase price (or current value) each year to cover maintenance and repairs. Also keep enough to pay the mortgage and other monthly costs if the tenant unexpectedly moves out. This should cover as many months as are appropriate given the local average vacancy rate.

What to Do When Expenses Exceed Income

What if you're still not making any business profits and are perhaps struggling to cover the rental property's expenses? This can be both a short-term problem, in terms of how you pay the bills, and a long-term concern if your goal is to hold onto the property for a certain length of time. Here are the first steps toward dealing with the situation:

- **Figure out whether the problem is short or long term.** It's not uncommon to get into a temporary cash crunch—for example, because a tenant moves out unexpectedly and the place needs repainting before you rent it again. Your approach to that can involve temporary, stopgap measures—unlike situations where the monthly rent never covers monthly expenses. Also, if the tenant has simply stopped paying rent, see Chapter 9 for a discussion of how to restart the flow.

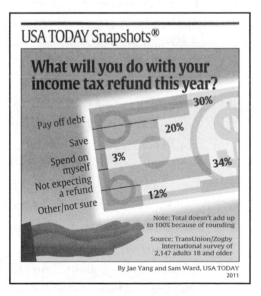

- **For short-term problems, look for sources of financing.** Can you loan cash to the business from your personal funds? That's a rational approach, as long as you can spare the money and you keep records of the transfer. However, it may mean shifting money that's currently held in stocks, bonds, or other investments. Talk to your financial adviser about whether, given the comparative rates of return between your real estate investment and others, this shift would be wise. If not, or if you don't have any personal sources of cash to draw upon, consider a home equity loan or line of credit from a bank; you'll be able to deduct the interest at tax time. Use credit cards only for minor expenses or as a last resort, due to their high interest rates.

- **Look at your largest outflows for areas to cut.** For example, can you cut expenses by refinancing your mortgage, shopping around for cheaper homeowners' insurance, or (if you're paying utilities) performing energy-saving repairs like sealing cracks?

TIP

Make sure you're in good communication with your tenant. Some cash crunches come about because the tenant isn't in the habit of calling you about minor maintenance issues before they turn into expensive emergencies. Such a situation often develops when landlords aren't responsive to tenants' early calls. And you need to stay on top of things like collecting late rents or terminating a tenancy for nonpayment.

- **Look into raising the rent.** Unfortunately, you can't do this every time cash is tight. If your tenant has a lease, you'll have to abide by its terms until the expiration date (though you could offer to buy the tenant out). And you'll have to comply with state and local laws governing rent increases, not to mention take into account local market conditions. See Chapter 1 for a full discussion of when and by how much you can raise the rent.

- **Prioritize your debts.** Put off paying your bills until close to their expiration date, and talk to creditors about accepting even later payments where possible. But whatever you do, don't miss a mortgage payment. If the problem is serious enough that you'll have trouble paying the mortgage, talk to your lender about workout options. For details, see the Foreclosure section of Nolo's website, at www.nolo.com.

- **For long-term problems, reexamine the numbers.** Go back to the analysis you did in Chapter 1 and reconsider whether the property is likely to sufficiently appreciate in value to make your current losses worthwhile. Also talk to your tax or financial adviser about whether the losses will help you shelter other income (a complex area requiring individual advice). If keeping the property no longer looks worthwhile, see Chapter 11 for advice on selling.

Finding Professionals to Help You

Plenty of first-time landlords get by without professional advice, relying instead on software programs for bookkeeping and tax preparation. But hiring a professional can make your life easier, and potentially help you save money in the long run. Below are the most likely categories of pros to help you. Notice that the list doesn't include so-called "tax preparers" of the sort you'll see in storefront offices during tax time. In most states, no licensing is required to be a tax preparer, so we don't advise taking your chances on them. Pros you might consult include:

USA TODAY Snapshots®

A good accountant is hard to find

What area is most challenging to find skilled financial professionals? Top areas:

Accounting 28%
Operational support 22%
Audit 18%
Finance 16%

Source: Robert Half International survey of 1,400 chief financial officers. Margin of error ±2 percentage points

By Jae Yang and Adrienne Lewis, USA TODAY 2008

- **Enrolled agents (EAs).** With at least five years of experience and licensing from the IRS, these are a reliable choice for tax advice and tax return preparation.
- **Certified public accountants (CPAs).** These provide sophisticated accounting and tax work, and are licensed and regulated in each state.

- **Licensed public accountants.** These are also reliable, though not as highly regarded as CPAs.

- **Tax attorneys.** If you get into serious trouble with the IRS or another tax agency, an attorney can provide legal representation. But for most tax advice, consulting a CPA will be more cost-effective.

Here are some tips for choosing a qualified professional:

- **Get recommendations.** Ask friends, business associates, or your local landlord association.

- **Look for experience in assisting landlords.** You're dealing with sometimes unique issues and tax considerations, so it helps to have an accountant or tax pro who's familiar with them.

- **Interview two or three prospects.** Choose the one who is not only reasonably priced, but seems knowledgeable and easy to communicate with. ●

Keeping Things Shipshape: Repairs and Maintenance

Everyone wants a nice place to call home, including your tenant. And while you're not required to turn the place into a palatial estate, you are responsible for keeping it in good repair and in a habitable condition. Besides, if someday you want to move back into this home, or retire in it, undoing years of poor maintenance will be a major bother.

To show you what maintenance entails, this chapter will cover:

- your legal responsibilities, and the tenant's responsibilities, for keeping the property livable
- how to prevent and respond to problems, and
- whether to hire the tenant or someone else to help you meet some of your repair and maintenance obligations.

Keeping your property in good repair requires some up-front work, but it will help keep your tenants happy—and a happy tenant will likely complain less and stay longer, reducing turnover and interruptions to your income stream. If you end up with a tenant whose repair demands are unreasonable (asking for cosmetic upgrades, not genuine repairs), having a fundamentally safe and sound rental will also let you confidently decline such requests.

Finally, regular attention to upkeep may prevent more major (and expensive!) problems later, because you'll catch the small repairs early. In the long run, that will save you money, reduce the chance of injuries, and ultimately translate into lower insurance premiums.

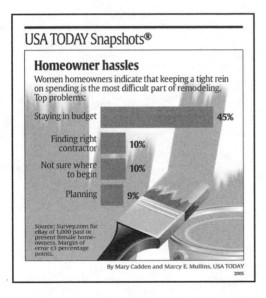

USA TODAY Snapshots®

Homeowner hassles

Women homeowners indicate that keeping a tight rein on spending is the most difficult part of remodeling. Top problems:

Staying in budget — 45%
Finding right contractor — 10%
Not sure where to begin — 10%
Planning — 9%

Source: Survey.com for eBay of 1,000 past or present female home-owners. Margin of error ±3 percentage points.

By Mary Cadden and Marcy E. Mullins, USA TODAY 2005

⚠ **CAUTION**

Don't invade the tenant's privacy just to make repairs.
Landlords in many states must give notice of entry when making repairs or doing inspections. You'll need to research and comply with your state's rules. Find yours in the "State Laws on Landlord's Access to Rental Property" chart in the Landlords section of Nolo.com. Then make sure your lease or rental agreement mentions these entry rules and your own policies, to minimize disputes with those tenants who feel landlords never have the right to enter their property.

Dealing With the Legalities: Your Repair and Maintenance Obligations

Your obligation to keep the property in good shape is imposed by law. But how do you know what's expected of you? And what does the tenant have to do? Here are some guidelines.

What are you responsible for?

Your responsibility to repair and maintain the property is based on several different legal principles. If you're worried about meeting all your obligations, start by learning and complying with the basics. First, figure out any repair and maintenance requirements imposed by your local housing codes. For example, many cities require landlords to install smoke and carbon monoxide detectors in residential units, or security items such as viewing devices in doors that open onto a hallway. Your local building or housing authority and health or fire department can provide this information.

Also get a copy of and carefully read your state's housing laws, which should lay out rules for repair, maintenance, and many other landlording responsibilities. Again, your local building or housing authority should be able to point you to the appropriate code sections, usually available online. To find a direct link to your state's statutes, visit www.nolo.com/legal-research and select State Law Resources.

Keeping your property habitable

According to a legal concept called the "implied warranty of habitability," you're required to offer and maintain livable premises. This means you must make sure the property meets minimum requirements (sometimes spelled out in local building codes), generally including:

- maintaining electrical, plumbing, sanitary, heating, ventilating, air-conditioning, and other facilities and systems
- supplying water, hot water, and heat in reasonable amounts at reasonable times
- providing trash receptacles and arranging for their removal, and
- maintaining any common areas in a safe and clean condition.

Every state but Arkansas has, by judicial decision or statute, adopted the implied warranty of habitability (and even in Arkansas, local laws may require that rental housing be habitable). Your state may specify additional requirements for making the place habitable, especially when features or services that might be essential in some places, like storm doors or shutters, might be virtually useless in other parts of the state.

The requirements won't always be listed somewhere obvious like in building codes, however. Often, it's the courts that decide what makes a place habitable. But you can assume that if an aspect of a dwelling (such as a weatherproof roof) makes it a fit place to live, you're probably responsible for maintaining it.

> **CAUTION**
> **Don't try to evade your responsibility to keep the place habitable.** Some landlords have tried advancing one of these two theories:
> - The tenants saw the place when they moved in, so it's no fair for them to complain now. In other words, by moving into an unfit rental, the tenant effectively agreed to accept those conditions, and waived the protections of the implied warranty.
> - The tenant signed a lease saying the landlord won't provide habitable housing, and is bound by that signature.
>
> Nice try, but courts almost always reject these theories. You're better off making sure your property is in good shape.

Common Myths About Repairs and Maintenance

Many landlords (and tenants) are under the mistaken impression that every time a rental property turns over, certain cosmetic changes, such as a new paint job, are required. But ugliness isn't a habitability problem—it's the actual condition of the rental property that determines what's needed in terms of repair and maintenance. Some changes may be called for during the tenancy, rather than at the end.

Paint. No state law requires you to repaint the interior every so often (local ordinances may, however), as long as the paint isn't creating a habitability problem—for example, it's so thick it seals a window shut. Lead-based paint, however, may create legal problems.

Drapes and carpets. So long as drapes and carpets aren't so damp or mildewed as to constitute a health hazard, and carpets don't have dangerous holes that could cause someone to trip, you aren't legally required to replace them.

Windows. A tenant is responsible for a broken window only if the tenant or a guest intentionally or carelessly broke it. If a burglar, vandal, or neighborhood child broke a window, however, you're responsible for fixing it.

Keys. You may need to change the locks and rekey the property for each new tenant. Even if it's not legally required, it's a good idea.

Keeping the property useable

Landlords have another legal responsibility with an obscure name: the "covenant of quiet enjoyment." As courts define it, this amounts to an implied promise that you won't act (or fail to act) in a way that interferes with or destroys the ability of the tenant to use the rental property and conversely, that you'll act in a way that enables peaceful use.

For example, if your failing to fix a leaky roof or taking care of a major rodent infestation means the tenant can't use the kitchen, you've failed to meet your obligations under the covenant. If the tenant can't live in your place, you have for all practical purposes evicted him or her (called "constructive eviction"). That lets the tenant wave goodbye to your property, without having to pay any rent as of the time you should have fixed the problem.

USA TODAY Snapshots®

Safety precautions at home
Percentage of adults in the USA who have:

Smoke alarms
96%   Fire extinguishers
            80%

                    Carbon monoxide
                    detectors
                    46%

Source: 2006 Fire Safety Census, a telephone survey of 1,005 adults 25 and older conducted in August 2006 by KRC Research for Liberty Mutual and International Association of Fire Fighters. Margin of error ±3.1 percentage points.

By Tracey Wong Briggs and Veronica Salazar, USA TODAY 2008

Keeping your promises

Beyond the basics, your property may have features like a washing machine, swimming pool, or dishwasher. Although keeping these things in working order may not affect the habitability of the place, you may still be legally required to repair and maintain them. Usually that's either because your lease or rental agreement says so expressly, or because it's implied, for example because you've repaired it in the past or advertised it as part of the property. After all, if you advertise a "hot tub in the backyard," the tenant can reasonably expect that the hot tub works under normal use, and that you'll keep it that way.

Minor repairs

Your most frequent tenant calls are likely to be about minor complaints —leaky faucets, temperamental appliances, worn carpets, or noisy heaters —not about major problems that make the house unlivable. Most of the time, these minor repairs are your responsibility.

But you can make an exception if the tenant or one of the tenant's guests caused a minor repair problem. In that case, the tenant either needs to take care of the repairs, or if your lease or rental agreement prohibits the tenant from doing so, pay you to do deal with them.

Relocating Your Tenants During Renovations or Repairs

Most repairs to your rental property will be quick and won't inconvenience your tenants much. For example, fixing the clogged toilet, replacing a lighting fixture, or even laying new carpets mostly require your tenants to stay out of the way and perhaps move belongings aside so workers can do their jobs. In these situations, you need not compensate tenants for the very temporary loss of the use of their home, and you certainly don't have to move them out (and pay for alternate lodging) while the work is being done.

Tenants may need to move out, however, if repairs are lengthy or involve chemicals that no one should be exposed to. Whether you or your tenants pay for the nights away depends on why the work is being done. If it's to maintain the rental in a fit and habitable condition, or you simply want to spiff the place up, you pay. But if you're doing cosmetic upgrades at the tenant's request, or the work is needed as a result of the tenant's negligence, the tenant can fairly be expected to cover the expense of temporarily moving out.

For instance, tenting and fumigating a termite infestation means that your tenants obviously cannot live there. Because maintaining a fit home is your responsibility, and tenants can't be blamed for the presence of termites, you'll need to pay for the cost of their temporary living quarters.

What if you decide to refinish the hardwood floors? Most contractors will advise occupants to remain away from the home for at least three days, both to allow the finish to dry and to avoid the very toxic odors. Whether you have to pay for alternate lodging depends on the reason for the work: If it's because a pipe burst and flooded the room, chances are it's not the tenant's fault, and you should pay for the hotel stay. But if the refinishing job is really a cosmetic upgrade requested by the tenant, or the flood was the result of the tenant's forgetting to turn off the bathtub faucet, the tenant should bear the expense of living elsewhere.

You can also draw the line at fixing up ordinary wear and tear. It's not your job to keep the rental premises looking just like new, just to stop deterioration. Nevertheless, if a tenant that you're happy with asks for a basic spruce up—replacing some shabby-looking but still functional blinds, for example—it may be worth doing. You'll probably have to make the changes if the tenant moves out, anyway.

> **TIP**
> **Best thing I ever did: Establish good communications with our tenants.** Phil, who owns a triplex, explains, "I work full time, and I probably could be more proactive about things like checking whether the rental units' roof needs fixing, or improving the landscaping. But we at least make sure to keep good dialogue going with our tenants, so that we know if something needs immediate attention, and they know we'll see to it quickly."

What is the tenant responsible for?

You aren't the only one with responsibilities—the tenant has some too. These include:

- **Keeping the rental unit in a reasonably clean and safe condition.** If the tenant doesn't do things like mop the tile floor in the kitchen every once in awhile, in which case you'd have to replace the caked grout before the next tenant moves in, you may legitimately deduct the costs from the security deposit. Before the end of the tenancy, if you discover that poor housekeeping has resulted in the need for repairs or property replacements, you may either cover the cost from the security deposit (and demand that the deposit be replenished to its original level), or simply bill the tenant for the cost.

- **Disposing of waste cleanly and safely.** Tenants are responsible for the consequences of unsanitary habits. For instance, if mice or ants invade the kitchen because your tenant forgot to wash the dishes before leaving on a two-week vacation, the tenant is responsible for paying the extermination and cleanup costs.

- **Keeping plumbing fixtures clean.** For example, bathtub caulking that has sprouted mold and mildew will render the tub unusable (or at least disgusting). Because it could have been prevented by proper cleaning, the tenant is responsible. On the other hand, if the bathroom has no fan and the window has been painted shut, the bathroom will be hard to air out, so the resulting mildew might be your responsibility.

- **Using electrical, plumbing, sanitary, heating, ventilating, air-conditioning, and other facilities and systems properly.** Examples of abuse by tenants include overloading electrical outlets and flushing large objects down the toilet. Catherine, who rents out a cottage behind her house, says: "After I had to call Roto Rooter out for the third time in six months, I had them put what they pulled out into a baggie, and told my tenant, 'If you put this stuff down one more time, you're paying the plumbing bill.' It was Clorox wipes, which say they're flushable, but not with our old Berkeley pipes. And I'd already warned the tenant about flushing anything other than toilet paper."

- **Fixing things the tenant breaks or damages.** If a tenant causes a serious habitability problem on your property—for example, carelessly breaking the heater—the tenant is responsible. You must make sure the repair happens, but you can bill the tenant for it. (The tenant can't just choose to forego heat, either.)

- **Reporting problems in the rental.** Some states require tenants to inform the landlord, as soon as practicable, of defective conditions on the premises that the tenant believes to be unknown to the landlord and believes are the landlord's duty to repair. As we'll explain further, below, your best bet is to ask the tenant to notify you of problems immediately, even if the law doesn't require it.

To protect yourself (and to notify your tenant of what's required), make sure your lease or rental agreement spells out these basic tenant obligations. And use common sense in dealing with tenant psychology.

For example, many tenants will ignore their maintenance obligations if they have to pay extra to comply. Gordon, a landlord with property in San Jose, California, says, "If the tenants have to pay for the water, they're not going to water the lawn. One way around this is to have an irrigation system on a timer. Another way is to keep the water in your name, and just raise the rent a bit."

TIP

Best thing I ever did: Learn to regularly remind tenants of key maintenance obligations. As Kathy explains, "I've found that the one thing my tenants are worst at remembering is to replace the filter on the air conditioner. Here in Florida, if you don't change the filter at least once a month, it starts freezing up, gets a drainage problem, and the pipes get moldy. By impressing upon my tenants that they must change the filter every time they pay their electric bill, and reminding them about it when we talk, I at least reduce the amount of money I'm spending repairing the AC."

If you don't meet your obligations: What the tenant can do

If you don't maintain your property in a fit and habitable condition, in compliance with legal requirements, your tenant may take action. The tenants' rightful responses may include one or more of the following:

- **Withholding rent.** In some states, if you don't keep the property livable, your tenant may be able to stop paying rent until necessary repairs are made. This is called rent withholding or rent "escrowing," because tenants often have to deposit the withheld rent in an escrow account until the repairs are done, at which point the money will be released to make the rent payment (maybe after some negotiations between you and the tenant on how you'll compensate the tenant for the inconvenience).

- **Repairing and deducting.** In states that allow this, a tenant can simply repair the problem and subtract the cost from the next month's rent. In most states there's a maximum dollar limit or a specific percentage of the month's rent the tenant can spend—for example, $300 or less than one half the monthly rent, whichever is greater. Also, states usually limit this to essential services, such as heat or water. And many states limit how often tenants may pursue this option, such as no more than twice in any 12-month period.

USA TODAY Snapshots®

Cool air a must-have

Americans who say home air conditioning is a necessity:

Today **54%**

1973 **26%**

Sources: The Roper Organization survey, December 1973; Pew Research Center survey, April 2009

By Anne R. Carey and Sam Ward, USA TODAY 2010

CAUTION
Don't drive tenants to repair and deduct. Though it will mean the repair gets done with little effort on your part, a repair that isn't done well could cost you in the long run. Moreover, when tenants use repair and deduct, you have no receipt (with your name on it) to prove the expense for tax purposes.

- **Reporting code violations to housing inspectors.** A tenant may complain to a local building, health, or fire department about problems such as inoperable plumbing, a leaky roof, or bad wiring. If an inspector comes out, you may be ordered to correct the problem—and subjected to a fine or penalty if you don't do so within a certain amount of time (often five to 30 business days).

- **Filing a lawsuit.** The tenant may sue and ask the court to order a rent refund for the period that housing conditions were substandard; payment of repair costs of property lost or damaged as a result of the problem (for example, furniture ruined by water leaking through the roof); compensation for personal injuries caused by the problem; and attorney fees. In some states, tenants may also get the court to order you to repair the defects, with rent reduced until you show the court proof that you've remedied the defects.

- **Moving out.** If you fail to make the rental property habitable, the tenant ultimately has the right to move out—either temporarily or permanently. These drastic measures are justified only in the case of truly serious problems; for example, where essential services are missing, or the place has been partly or totally destroyed. Tenants may move out if environmental health hazards such as lead paint dust make the place uninhabitable. Your state statute may have specific details, such as the type of notice tenants must give you before making their exit. You may have anywhere from five to 21 days to fix the problem, depending on the state and, sometimes, the seriousness of the situation.

Tenants can't use the first two options—withholding rent or repairing the problem and deducting it from the rent—just because they feel like it. Three conditions must be met:

- **The problem is serious, not just annoying, and imperils the tenant's health or safety.** Not every building code violation or annoying defect in a rental home is serious enough to justify such heavy action.

- **The tenant told you about and gave you a reasonable opportunity to fix the problem.** In some states, the law will tell you exactly how much time you have to make the repairs (ten days to three weeks is common); in others, you must respond within a reasonable time under the circumstances.

- **The tenant (or a guest) didn't cause the problem.** If they did, then you can't be expected or required to pay for it.

RESOURCE

More information on state rules on repairs and maintenance. The State Landlord-Tenant Laws area in the Landlords section of Nolo.com includes state-by-state charts of tenant rights to withhold rent or use the repair-and-deduct remedy. Also see the Rental Repairs and Maintenance section for useful articles.

Adopting a Good Maintenance and Repair System

Early attention to repair and maintenance issues will forestall many problems—but not all of them. And unexpected problems are in most cases your responsibility. You'll need a system that helps you prevent problems when you can and deal with them quickly when you can't. (At least maintenance and repair costs are tax deductible, as discussed in Chapter 6.)

Creating a maintenance and repair strategy

We suggest creating a systematic approach to maintenance and repairs, such as the one that follows.

When you have a new tenant:

- **Get everything shipshape before the tenant moves in.** Do a thorough evaluation and fix any problems. You'll want to repeat this every time there's tenant turnover, before the move-in. You may want to create a checklist, tailored to your property, to make sure you don't miss anything.

- **Clue the tenant in.** Set out the tenant's responsibilities for repair and maintenance in your lease or rental agreement, and point them out before the tenant signs.

- **Show new tenants how to handle routine maintenance.** Explain the basics, such as how to avoid overloading circuits, properly use the garbage disposal, and locate and use the fire extinguisher. Identify problems the tenant should definitely not try to handle, such as electrical repairs. Include a brief list of all these maintenance dos and don'ts as part of your move-in materials (discussed in Chapter 5).

Throughout the tenancy:

- **Be accessible.** Make sure the tenant can reach you to report any problems immediately. Have an answering machine, voicemail, or other service available at all times, and check your messages frequently. Also consider creating a form to take repair requests, then give the tenant a few copies at move-in and explain how to use the form.

- **Keep a written log of all complaints (including those made orally).** This should include a box to write your immediate and any follow-up responses (and subsequent tenant communications), as well as a space to enter the date and brief details of when the problem was fixed. Try to respond in writing to every tenant repair request (even if you also do so orally).

- **Respond quickly.** Handle repairs (especially urgent ones) as soon as possible, but definitely within the time your state law (if any) requires. Notify the tenant by phone and follow up in writing if repairs will take more than 48 hours, excluding weekends. Keep the tenant informed—for example, if you have problems scheduling a plumber, let your tenant know with a phone call or a note. We'll discuss responding to complaints further, below.

On a regular basis:

- **Have biannual tenant reviews.** Twice a year, give your tenants a checklist on which to report any potential safety hazards or maintenance problems, such as an entryway rug showing signs of fraying (replace it now, before it gets worse and someone trips). You might also want to create a form for this purpose, and give it to the tenant to fill out and return within a specified time period, such as a couple weeks. Respond promptly and in writing to all requests, keeping copies in your file.

RESOURCE

Looking for checklists, move-in letters, and more? Go to *Every Landlord's Legal Guide*, by Marcia Stewart, Ralph Warner, and Janet Portman (Nolo). It is full of helpful landlord forms and standard documents, which you can customize to your needs.

- **Use written reminders.** Remind your tenant of your policies and procedures to keep the property in good repair in every written communication, by printing it at the bottom of all routine notices, rent increases, and other communications. Tenants will be more likely to tell you about maintenance and repair problems if you remind them that you're truly interested.

- **Conduct an annual safety inspection.** Once a year, make time for a "safety and maintenance inspection," where you check that items such as smoke detectors, heating and plumbing systems, and major appliances are safe and in working order. These inspections are not required by law, but they're a good idea. Be sure not to overdo it—once a year is sufficient.

Your Right to Conduct a Safety Inspection

In many states, you have the right to enter a tenant's home to conduct a safety inspection, but you usually need to notify the tenant first. Some states specify 24 hours' notice, others simply state that it must be "reasonable notice." To be on the safe side, check your state's statutes and, if all that is required is "reasonable notice," allow 24 hours at least.

If a tenant objects and your state allows you to enter for this purpose (and if you've given adequate notice), the tenant's refusal is grounds for eviction. If your state doesn't allow the landlord to enter and inspect against the tenant's will, point out to the tenant that you take your responsibility to maintain the property very seriously. Remind the tenant that you'll be checking for problems that the tenant might not notice, which could develop into bigger problems later. If you still get a refusal, write a confirming letter to the tenant—it may protect you later if the tenant claims a safety hazard or that there's damage to the property (especially if the damage could have been prevented had you known about it).

Responding to tenant complaints

You should respond almost immediately to all complaints about defective conditions, by talking to the tenant and following up (preferably in writing). Explain when repairs can be made or, if you don't know yet, tell the tenant that you'll be back in touch promptly. Different problems require different levels of action:

- **Personal security and safety problems.** Respond and get work done immediately to fix problems that could result in tenant injury or property damage.

- **Major inconveniences to the tenant.** Respond and attempt to get work done as soon as possible, or within 24 hours if the problem is a major inconvenience to the tenant, such as a plumbing or heating problem. Otherwise, you risk a tenant's using one of the self-help remedies above, or simply feeling dissatisfied and moving out.

- **Minor problems.** Respond within 48 hours (on business days) if the problem is not too serious. You'll avoid a tenant's major dissatisfaction, and you won't have to worry that your inaction will trigger the tenant's inappropriate but highly annoying use of remedies such as withholding rent or making repairs and deducting their cost from the rent.

If you can't take care of a repair right away, let the tenant know your timeline. For the sake of speed, do this orally (a voice mail on the tenant's phone should serve), and then follow up in writing. If there's a delay, maybe because the part you need to fix the oven has to be specially ordered, explain this.

As important as these repairs are, you can't just march onto the property to make them until you've taken steps to protect the tenant's rights. You can enter the rental premises only with the tenant's consent, or after having given the amount of notice required by state law, usually 24 hours. Try to pick a reasonable time of day, to keep the peace (and potentially follow the law), except in cases of emergency, or where it's impractical to do so.

Can Tenants Alter the Property?

Your tenant may want to personalize the place—paint the living room, install a closet system, or put in a dishwasher, for example. If it's a tenant whom you like and would hate to lose, think about allowing it, after considering:

- **Is the improvement or alteration easily undone?** Repainting is easy to redo, while knocking out a wall to install a wine closet is more permanent.
- **Does the improvement or alteration enhance your property?** For example, resurfaced kitchen cabinets might actually add value.
- **Does the law protect the tenant's right to make the particular improvement or alteration?** For example, in some cases, the law might protect a tenant's rights to install a satellite dish, and you'll need to comply with such laws. See Chapter 5, "Step Aside: Tenants May Be Allowed to Make These Repairs or Alterations," for more on the subject.

If you and the tenant reach an understanding, put it in writing, carefully describing the project and materials, including whether the improvement or alteration is permanent or portable, the terms of the reimbursement, if any, and how and when you'll pay the tenant, if at all, for labor and materials.

Anything your tenant attaches to a building, fence, deck, or the ground itself (called "fixtures") belongs to you, unless you agree that it's the tenant's. Either way, it's wise to spell out in your lease or rental agreement who will own the improvement. And make it clear that if the tenant later fails to properly restore the premises, or removes an alteration that was meant to be permanent, you'll deduct the resulting costs from the security deposit or take further legal action if necessary.

Responding to problems at a distance

If your property is in another state and you haven't hired a property manager, you face additional challenges in getting repairs done. Laura, who lives in Washington state, describes how she handles this for her Nevada and Florida properties: "My tenants know enough not to call me at 3:00 in the morning. Of course, their timing can still be horrible—just before my son's wedding, I got about 50 phone calls concerning the water heater in one of my houses. Still, I've found that I can accomplish a lot by phone. I view dealing with repair issues as a partnership with my tenants. Sometimes I'll have them call the repairperson to make an appointment, which makes more sense given that they're going to have to be the one to let the person in. I tell them to have the repairperson call me after arriving at the house. Then we'll plan the job and I'll usually pay for it over the phone, and ask the repairperson to send me the receipt. This system tends to go smoothly."

It's also smart to line up a list of potential repairpeople while you're in town visiting the property, rather than waiting until an urgent situation arises. We'll discuss how to find good people later in this chapter.

No Thanks! Hiring Someone Else to Do the Work

If you live far from your rental property, don't have time to deal with the hassle of repairs or maintenance, or are simply too busy or not very handy, you may want to hire someone to take care of maintenance and repairs for you. Your primary options are to hire a property manager, a handyperson, or the tenant.

> **TIP**
> **Learning some maintenance and repair skills may be smart.** "I do a lot of my own maintenance," says John, who has owned multiple properties since 1975. "It gets me on the property and shows a presence; it shows that I care. Besides, you have to learn to do some repairs yourself, because you can't afford to hire someone for every little thing."

Hiring a property manager

If you hire a property manager, that person's package of services will probably include overseeing maintenance. This can have its advantages, especially since many property management companies have professionals on staff to deal with maintenance problems, and have vetted a host of other specialized professionals like plumbers, electricians, and general contractors.

But watch out for a few potential bumpy spots, too. For example:

- **Make sure the property manager will respond immediately.** Ask for a commitment to a specific turnaround time. You don't want your property damaged, or your tenant injured, because the property manager didn't get around to acting promptly.

- **Confirm that the property manager is available 24 hours a day, 365 days a year.** That will avoid issues like a desperate call from a tenant on Christmas morning, complaining that the heater is broken and the manager is nowhere to be found.

- **Find out whether you'll be charged extra for maintenance calls.** Some property management companies make money by tacking on administrative fees when hiring outside contractors or vendors.

- **Know whether the property manager is authorized to conduct repairs without your prior approval.** Your contract should specify what level of repairs may be done without getting an okay from you first. You want your property manager to be able to act quickly if there's an emergency, especially if you're on vacation or otherwise unavailable. On the other hand, you don't want to give a manager authority to undertake a major or expensive repair or replacement, such as replacing the stove without consulting you first.

Also, keep in mind that the property manager will probably not conduct annual inspections or periodically ask the tenant whether any repairs are needed. This is something you'll either have to do yourself, negotiate with the property management firm to include in your agreement, or pay extra for.

For more information on hiring a property manager, see Chapter 10.

Hiring a handyperson

As a middle-ground option between doing the work yourself and paying for the deluxe services of a property manager, you can hire others. Your best bet is to find a reliable handyperson for basic repairs, and hire a contractor (discussed below) for more specific or skill-intensive tasks.

A good handyperson will have an extensive background in home repair. Many are even trained and licensed contractors. You'll want someone who is available 24 hours, in case of emergencies. Choose someone who's been in business for awhile, and thus will be likely to stick around and become familiar with your property.

To find a competent handyperson, ask other rental property owners or real estate professionals for recommendations, as well as friends and colleagues. It's best to find one who carries primary health insurance and liability insurance, which will protect you if the handyperson is injured on the job, causes any property damage, or injures others. A reputable worker will be willing to provide this proof. An insured handyperson will probably charge more than an uninsured one might—but it's worth it for the extra security of knowing you or your insurance company won't end up paying for the consequences of any accidents.

Also, for the sake of both your project and your financial risk, make sure the person you hire has complied with any state rules and licensing requirements. In some states, for example, it's illegal to hire unlicensed contractors for certain kinds of work.

Hiring a contractor

In some cases, you, your handyperson, or your property manager may not have the skills needed for the task at hand. In that case, you'll probably hire a contractor, such as a plumber or an electrician. Again, you're looking for someone who's available quickly when you're in a jam—especially if you're not nearby.

Ask other rental property owners or real estate professionals for recommendations. Look for someone who is properly licensed and insured. You can often find this information on your state's contractor

Don't Become an Accidental Employer

When you hire someone to fix a leaky faucet, mow the lawn, or retile the bathroom, you probably don't think of that person as your "employee." But the IRS or other governmental agencies may feel differently if that person becomes a regular worker who takes orders from you—unlikely in a single-family rental, but something to bear in mind if you expand into multiunit properties.

Once the government considers you an employer, and not simply someone who hires an independent contractor for a specific job, your obligations to the worker (and the government) will change dramatically. For example, you'd need to secure proof of the worker's authorization to work in the United States, to withhold and pay Social Security and Medicare taxes, and maybe also pay workers' compensation insurance and state unemployment taxes.

For IRS purposes, the more control you exercise over the tasks a worker does and how he or she does them, the more likely the IRS is to consider the person an employee. Workers are more likely independent contractors if they:

- can earn a profit or suffer a loss from the work
- furnish the tools and materials needed to do the work
- are paid by the job, not by the hour
- work for more than one place at a time
- invest in equipment and facilities
- pay their own business and traveling expenses
- hire and pay any assistants, and
- set their own working hours.

For more information, see IRS Publication 15-A, *Employer's Supplemental Tax Guide*, and the "Using Independent Contractors and Freelancers" articles in the Employment Law section of Nolo.com.

licensing board website, but get confirmation from the contractor in case anything has changed.

Hiring the tenant

You may want to delegate some of the responsibility of managing the property to your tenant. It's not always a bad idea. After all, the tenant is aware of the problems, and is highly motivated to fix them. On the other hand, because tenants aren't normally interested in the long-term condition of the property, many won't attend to repairs with the same concern that owners bring to the job.

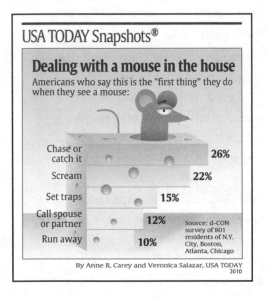

USA TODAY Snapshots®

Dealing with a mouse in the house

Americans who say this is the "first thing" they do when they see a mouse:

Chase or catch it — 26%
Scream — 22%
Set traps — 15%
Call spouse or partner — 12%
Run away — 10%

Source: d-CON survey of 801 residents of N.Y. City, Boston, Atlanta, Chicago

By Anne R. Carey and Veronica Salazar, USA TODAY
2010

But first, make sure the tenant has the necessary expertise, which will probably depend on both the task and the tenant. Second, make sure hiring the tenant is cost-effective. While it's certainly convenient—you don't have to find a professional to handle it—it isn't necessarily cheaper. If you credit or pay the tenant hourly, but it takes twice as long (or causes further damage), you won't save money.

Compensating the tenant for repairs

If you decide to allow the tenant to make repairs from time to time, you have two options for how to pay the tenant. You can:

- **Reduce the rent.** This will probably be your tenant's preference. Of course, you'll want to agree to this practice ahead of time, agree to the payment terms, and lay out your agreement in writing, within the rental agreement.
- **Pay directly for the work.** Paying an on-site tenant to do repair and maintenance is preferable to giving the tenant a reduction in

rent for work performed, because if the job isn't done right, you can simply cancel the work arrangement rather than amend the lease or rental agreement. Plus, there will be no question that the tenant is still obligated to pay the full rent as usual. If you choose this route, be sure to write down what you expect your tenant to do, and for how much money.

TIP

In a multifamily property, beware of turning a tenant into an employee. No matter which method of compensation you choose, if your tenant will be performing regular maintenance duties in a multi-family rental situation (such as dealing with minor plumbing repairs and sweeping the lobby and front steps), your tenant will be your employee. As an employer, you'll need to comply with the requirements described in "Don't Become an Accidental Employer," above. (In a single-family situation, it's unlikely that making a tenant responsible for yard upkeep, and including that provision in your lease, would carry the same risk.)

Types of repairs a tenant can't do

Even though it may be cheapest to buy a book at a local hardware store, throw some parts into your cart, and hire the tenant to replace the water heater or repair faulty wiring, it's not a good idea for such major repairs, because:

- **The quality of the repair may be low.** Unless your tenant just happens to be a skilled contractor, you risk the repairs being inadequate, so that you end up redoing them (or worse).

- **You're legally responsible if the tenant gets injured or injures someone else.** A tenant who doesn't know what he or she is doing can easily cause injuries, especially if dealing with sensitive systems like heating or wiring. Hiring the tenant means you'll be responsible for these injuries—even if they occur later (for example, when the newly installed light fixture comes crashing down during a dinner party). Of course, you could always try to recoup your losses by suing that tenant (called "seeking indemnity" in legalese),

Let Your College Kid Be the Landlord? Maybe.

St. Cloud State University sophomore Parker Lahti is majoring in real estate. At 19, he's also a homeowner.

Other students, too—with a little help from Mom and Dad—are combining academics with the real-world responsibilities of mortgage payments and home repair. The houses—sometimes called "kiddie condos"—are turning college students into landlords who collect rent rather than pay it.

Lahti's house has four bedrooms, two bathrooms, a laundry room, a two-car garage, and a basement he'll use for entertaining. And with his roommates sharing the $1,200 monthly note, Lahti says, they're getting a pretty good deal. Each will pay $300 a month, once he finds someone to fill the fourth bedroom. On-campus apartments in St. Cloud rent for about $319 a month.

Full-time students without a job or credit history can, with their parents' support, get a condo loan from the Federal Housing Authority. Many expenses, such as repairs, may be tax deductible.

Lahti's father agreed to buy the house but told Lahti the payments would be his responsibility. "It teaches him a little bit about working with tenants and paying utility bills," Tom Lahti says.

Students may find being a homeowner harder than it sounds, Jan Baldry, a real estate broker in Waukesha, Wisconsin, says. For one, they have to be careful about whom they accept as renters. Students "have a reputation for being wild and messy and moving out without giving any notice," she says.

The situation also could cause headaches for parents. "When your child calls at midnight and says the bathroom shower doesn't work, you're the one who has to fix that," Baldry says.

 USA TODAY "Homeownership 101; College kids are landlords, Thanks to Mom and Dad," by Scott Brooks, September 8, 2003.

but your chances of recovery will be slim unless your tenant has significant assets. On the other hand, a maintenance or repair service will generally carry its own insurance (confirm this before you engage its services).

- **The law may not permit you to delegate major repairs to the tenant.** Judges and legislators fear that the tenant will rarely be in the position, either practically or financially, to do the kinds of repairs that are often needed to bring a structure up to par—and it's still your duty to make the place habitable. A few states allow the landlord and tenant of a single-family dwelling to agree in writing that the tenant is to perform some of the landlord's statutory duties, but generally landlords retain the duties imposed by health and safety codes and the implied warranty of habitability.

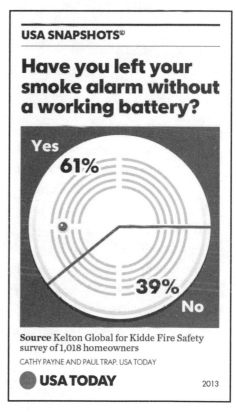

USA SNAPSHOTS©

Have you left your smoke alarm without a working battery?

Yes
61%

39%
No

Source Kelton Global for Kidde Fire Safety survey of 1,018 homeowners

CATHY PAYNE AND PAUL TRAP, USA TODAY

USA TODAY   2013

Avoiding problems

Repair and maintenance arrangements between landlords and tenants often lead to dissatisfaction—the landlord feels that the tenant has neglected certain tasks, or the tenant feels that there's too much work for the money. To keep things flowing smoothly:

- **Put it in writing.** Any agreement as to repairs or maintenance should be written and signed, either as part of the lease or rental agreement or as a separate employment agreement. This will avoid mutual misunderstandings about who's responsible for what.

- **Provide enough detail so that the tenant knows exactly what's expected.** Whether it's repairing a broken window, dealing with a routine plumbing problem, or landscaping, give specific descriptions and limits to the tasks. And make sure the tenant is qualified to do these tasks.

- **Pay fairly.** If you don't, you'll increase the tenant's resentment, while decreasing motivation to get the job done. If you ever have a dispute with the tenant, a judge won't look kindly on an unreasonably low payment for the tenant's hard work, especially if it doesn't even add up to minimum wage.

- **Treat the delegation of duties as separate from your other duties as landlord.** Your agreement with your tenant has nothing to do with your other responsibilities. For example, if you and your tenant agree that the tenant will do gardening work in exchange for a reduction in rent, and you're watching the shrubs die or take over the sidewalk, you may not respond by shutting off the water or retaliating in other ways. The proper recourse is to discuss the problem with the tenant and, if it persists, to cancel the arrangement. ●

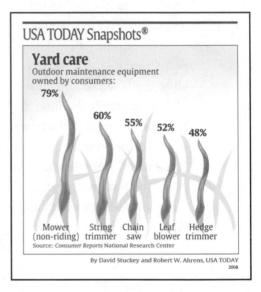

USA TODAY Snapshots®

Yard care
Outdoor maintenance equipment owned by consumers:

79% Mower (non-riding)
60% String trimmer
55% Chain saw
52% Leaf blower
48% Hedge trimmer

Source: *Consumer Reports* National Research Center

By David Stuckey and Robert W. Ahrens, USA TODAY
2008

Landlord Liability for Injuries, Crimes, and More

As a landlord, you have some level of legal responsibility for your tenant's safety. In addition to providing a well-maintained place to live, you're legally required to create an environment that protects your tenant from certain dangers. In this chapter, we'll cover those dangers and how to avoid them, including:

- your responsibility for tenant injuries
- dealing with environmental problems like mold and lead
- protecting tenants from crime, and
- buying insurance to protect yourself.

Fortunately, the likelihood of having problems that will result in serious legal or financial liability is low, especially if you follow the preventative measures we recommend throughout this book. And with a good insurance policy, even if you're confronted with some surprises, you'll be covered.

Ouch, That Smarts: Liability for Tenant Injuries

It's probably no surprise that you must keep your property safe for your tenant and any guests—and it's a responsibility to take seriously. After all, an injured tenant can seek financial recovery for medical bills, lost earnings, pain and other physical suffering, permanent physical disability and disfigurement, and emotional distress. Tenants can also look to you for the costs of property damage that resulted from faulty or unsafe conditions. As Jason, a landlord in Texas, remembers, "The tree in front of our rental house was overgrown and overdue for a trimming, but I put it off. Last winter, a storm broke a major branch, crushing my tenant's car, which was parked in the driveway. My insurance carrier paid for it, because I'd been remiss in not taking care of the tree, but my premiums went up."

Consistently practicing good maintenance serves a double purpose: It will not only help prevent tenants from getting injured (or having their property damaged) in the first place, but will help you defend yourself if a tenant claims you're responsible for an injury or damage.

You're not responsible for everything

It isn't always easy to determine whether you're legally responsible for a tenant's injury. Basically, you may be liable for injuries resulting from:

- **Negligence.** An injured tenant may claim you acted negligently—that is, carelessly, in a way that wasn't reasonable under the circumstances—and thus caused the injury. Landlords have been found negligent after a tenant fell down a staircase due to a defective handrail, a tenant's child was scalded by water from a water heater with a broken thermostat, and a tenant received electrical burns when attempting to insert a stove's damaged plug into the wall outlet.

- **Violation of a health or safety law.** Many state and local laws require smoke detectors, sprinklers, inside-release security bars on windows, childproof fences around swimming pools, and so on. Some states say that a landlord who doesn't take reasonable steps to follow the laws will be considered negligent, and responsible for any resulting tenant injuries. Additionally, your violation of a health or safety law may indirectly cause an injury and lead to liability. For example, if you let the furnace deteriorate in violation of local law and a tenant is injured trying to repair it, you may be liable, unless the tenant's repair efforts were extremely careless themselves.

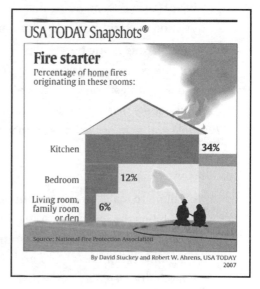

USA TODAY Snapshots®

Fire starter
Percentage of home fires originating in these rooms:

Kitchen 34%

Bedroom 12%

Living room, family room or den 6%

Source: National Fire Protection Association

By David Stuckey and Robert W. Ahrens, USA TODAY
2007

Dog Bites and Other Animal Attacks

Hard to believe, but you may be liable for injuries caused by your tenants' animals, be they common household pets or more exotic, wild animals.

Dangerous domestic pets. If a person injured by a vicious animal can prove to an insurance adjuster (or a jury) that the landlord knew (or should have known) that the animal had dangerous tendencies, and failed to take reasonable steps to prevent the injury (such as demanding that the animal leave the property or evicting the tenant), the landlord may be held liable.

Dangerous exotic pets. Keeping wild animals is generally considered an "ultrahazardous activity." So if your tenant keeps a monkey or tiger and you know about it (or should have), a court will assume that you understood the dangers presented, and may hold you responsible if the animal injures someone.

- **Failure to make certain repairs.** If your lease or rental agreement prohibits the tenant from making repairs or alterations without your consent, you can get into trouble if you're told about such a problem but don't fix it, and then the tenant gets injured as a result. The legal reason is that you breached the contract (the lease) by not making the repairs. (You may be found negligent, as well.)

- **Failure to keep the premises habitable.** If a problem is so serious that the rental unit becomes unfit for human habitation—and you knew of the problem and had a reasonable amount of time to fix it—you could get into trouble for any resulting tenant injuries. What type of problem makes a house uninhabitable may vary by circumstance, however. For example, a large, jagged broken window would make the premises unfit for habitation in North Dakota in winter, but a torn screen door during summertime in southern California would not.

- **Reckless or intentional acts.** If you harm a tenant on purpose or "recklessly," you may be in hot water. In the legal sense, "recklessness" usually means extreme carelessness regarding an obvious defect or problem (like ignoring a fire hazard for months). Acting recklessly can be very expensive, making you potentially liable for "punitive" damages: extra damages, beyond the cost of the injury, to punish you for bad behavior.

Me? I'd Never Hurt a Fly!

If you hit a tenant during an argument, that's an intentional act. But so are emotional or psychological injuries inflicted intentionally, such as:

- **Sexual harassment,** or repeated, disturbing attentions of a sexual nature (or a single outrageous act) that leave a tenant fearful, humiliated, and upset

- **Assault,** even if it's nonphysical—for example, threatening or menacing someone, and

- **Repeated invasions of privacy,** such as by unauthorized entries into the tenant's living space.

- **Other duties imposed by law.** In rare instances, courts or state legislatures have decided that landlords are automatically liable for certain kinds of injuries. This legal principle is called "strict liability," or liability without fault. It's usually imposed only when a hidden defect poses an unreasonably great risk of harm to people who can't detect or avoid the danger. For example, Massachusetts landlords are strictly liable if their tenants are poisoned by lead-based paint.

Liability for injuries to guests and trespassers

If you act negligently and a tenant's guest or even a trespasser (who wasn't invited by you or the tenant onto the property) is injured, will you be responsible? In a few states, you're liable without regard to why the injured person was there in the first place. As a general rule, however, you don't owe the same "duty of care" to a nontenant as you do to your tenant, especially if it's a trespasser. For example, a tenant who gets hurt by falling from an unfenced porch can make a fairly strong argument that you were negligent; but a trespasser, even an innocent one who has come to the wrong address, and falls off the same porch, might have a harder time recovering from you.

If a tenant is at fault, too

If the tenant is partially to blame for getting injured, your picture isn't so grim. For example, a drunk tenant who, while stumbling around, trips on a loose brick on the front steps may not be able to collect as much, or at all, from the landlord.

If a tenant knows of a danger and takes a chance anyway, thus causing or worsening the injury, the law will say that the tenant has "assumed the risk" of injury. In some states, such a tenant may not be entitled to recover anything, regardless of any negligence by the landlord. In other states, a tenant's recovery will be lowered based on how much the tenant appreciated (but ignored) the danger involved.

While a tenant's own carelessness may decrease the hit to your wallet (or your insurance policy), it won't decrease the time you'll spend dealing with the incident. For example, Walt, with a single-family rental in Miami explains, "My tenant, Dorothy, definitely knew that the bedroom casement window had become hard to lift and secure, but she didn't say a word about it. The first I heard was one night when she called from the hospital, after the window had come crashing down on her arm and hurt her wrist, real bad. She sued me. At least the jury got the picture that Dorothy was partly at fault, so she got only a portion of the damages she'd asked for. (My insurance company paid.) Still, I had to spend days going to the lawyers' offices and preparing for and attending the trial."

How to prevent liability problems

Here are some great ways to protect yourself from lawsuits and hefty insurance settlements and at the same time make your tenants' lives safer and happier:

- **Follow the maintenance plan in the last chapter.** Look for dangerous conditions and fix them promptly; comply with all health, safety, and building codes; conduct regular safety inspections; ask tenants to report problems; and document problems and resolutions.

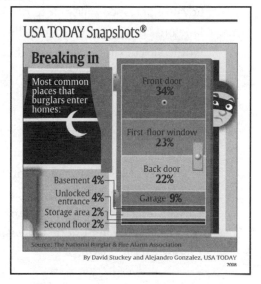

USA TODAY Snapshots®

Breaking in

Most common places that burglars enter homes:

Front door **34%**
First-floor window **23%**
Back door **22%**
Garage **9%**
Basement **4%**
Unlocked entrance **4%**
Storage area **2%**
Second floor **2%**

Source: The National Burglar & Fire Alarm Association

By David Stuckey and Alejandro Gonzalez, USA TODAY 2008

- **Warn of dangers you can't fix.** You won't always be able to do much about some dangers like a steep driveway or winding stairs. But if you know, or should know, about such defects, you have a duty to tell the tenant about them. The best way is to mention them in your lease, rental agreement, or move-in letter. If appropriate, also post warning signs near the hazard.

- **Look for tenant security issues.** Install and maintain basic security features such as dead bolt locks, smoke detectors, fire extinguishers, window locks, outside lighting, and any other features appropriate for your property.

- **Be vigilant about dangers to children.** If children are drawn onto your property by an irresistibly interesting (to children) but dangerous feature, such as a stack of building materials or an abandoned refrigerator (known in legal jargon as an "attractive nuisance"), you must exercise special care. Because young children can't read, or tend to ignore warnings, you should place physical barriers between the children and the attractive feature. And if the danger is of the type that can be cleaned up or removed (like the refrigerator), you should do so.

> **CAUTION**
> **Tenants can't sign away rights to be compensated for injuries.**
> Landlords used to protect themselves from most tenant lawsuits with an "exculpatory clause"—lease language absolving the landlord in advance of responsibility for tenant injuries, even those caused by the landlord's negligence. There may be unusual situations when a narrowly worded exculpatory clause would be appropriate—for example, if you've delegated appropriate repair and maintenance duties to a tenant (described in Chapter 8)—but in general, they're rarely enforced by courts, so our advice is not to use them.

- **Supervise contractors.** If construction is being done on your property, make sure the person in charge secures the site and removes or locks up dangerous tools or equipment when the site is left unattended. Consider sending your tenant written notice of the intended project, suggesting extra precautions during the construction period.

Liability for Environmental Health Hazards

If your property poses any environmental health hazards to tenants and you know about them, you've got to tell tenants, and most of the time, you must remedy the problem—even if you didn't cause it. (This is a relatively new duty, imposed in the last few decades.) This liability is based on many of the same legal theories described above, such as negligence and negligence *per se* (negligence that's automatic when a statute is broken).

Asbestos

Exposure to asbestos is linked to an increased risk of cancer. Homes built before the mid-1970s often contain asbestos insulation around heating systems, in ceilings, and in other areas. Until 1981, asbestos was also widely used in many other building materials, such as vinyl flooring and tiles. Asbestos that breaks down and enters the air—for example, when it's disturbed during maintenance or renovation work—can give rise to significant health problems.

OSHA Regulations and Asbestos

The U.S. Occupational Safety and Health Administration (OSHA) requires rental property owners of homes built before 1981 who employ maintenance employees (including outside contractors for repair and maintenance jobs) to notify these people that a property may contain asbestos, and in some cases, test for it. You can avoid the responsibility only by having a licensed inspector test and confirm no asbestos is present in the home.

OSHA regulations also require custodial workers (such as the handyperson who installs smoke detectors in the acoustic tile ceilings) to have gone through specialized training and use particular work procedures. The procedural rules get extra strict after any intentional disturbance of asbestos or asbestos-containing materials.

If you hire a contractor to perform major renovations or repairs that involve asbestos, the contractor must comply with OSHA's education and prevention rules. But if your own employees do the work, the burden falls on you to learn and implement the rules (see our resource suggestions later in this chapter).

If you learn there's asbestos on your property (perhaps when complying with OSHA's testing and maintenance requirements, above), you can't pretend not to know about it. It becomes an undisclosed and dangerous defect that you must tell tenants about and take steps to remedy. Some states may also say you've breached the implied warranty of habitability when, despite knowing about the problem, you do nothing, potentially giving the tenant the right to break the lease and move out without notice, pay less rent, withhold the entire rent, or sue to force you to make the place habitable.

Unless the asbestos material has begun to break down and enter the air, it's usually best to leave it alone and monitor it. You can do this as part of your regular safety inspection, discussed in Chapter 7, and you can also require your tenant to report any deterioration to you. If you must disturb asbestos, warn the tenants first, giving them an opportunity to avoid the area. You might even consider temporarily relocating your tenant. The costs of a few days or weeks in alternate housing will pale compared to the expense of a personal injury lawsuit.

If you learn that asbestos material is airborne (or is about to be), seek an expert's advice on remedies. When removal is necessary, hire trained asbestos removal specialists, and check to make sure the debris is legally disposed of in approved hazardous waste disposal sites. Don't allow tenants to make repairs to or otherwise invade any spaces containing asbestos, for example, by drilling holes in the ceiling to hang plants.

RESOURCE
Asbestos resources. For more on asbestos rules, inspections, and control, see OSHA's website at www.osha.gov or call 800-321-OSHA. Also check into OSHA's interactive computer software, called "Asbestos Advisor" (available free at www.osha.gov), which will help identify asbestos on your property and suggest the most sensible solution.

Lead

As we all know, exposure to lead-based paint and lead water pipes may lead to serious health problems, particularly in children. Buildings constructed pre-1978 are likely to contain some lead, whether it's in the paint, pipes, or solder used on copper pipes.

You must, under federal law, inform the tenant, even before signing or renewing a lease or rental agreement, of any information you have on lead paint hazards on the property. If you've had your property tested, that includes showing tenants a copy of the report, or a summary written by the inspector. It also includes giving the tenant the lead hazard information booklet *Protect Your Family From Lead in Your Home*, by the Environmental Protection Agency (EPA) and available at www.epa.gov/lead/pubs/leadprot.htm. Agencies in many states have developed their own pamphlets, which you can use instead of the EPA version if the EPA has approved them.

With a few limited exceptions, every lease and rental agreement must include a disclosure page, even if you haven't tested for lead. You can use the one developed by the EPA, "Disclosure of Information on Lead-Based Paint and/or Lead-Based Paint Hazards," available at www.epa. gov. The form has a place for tenants to initial, indicating that they've received it. Note the date they received it, and if you and the tenant are also signing the lease or rental agreement on the same day, enter the time you signed it, too. If you're ever challenged, or investigated by a government agency, you'll be able to prove that the tenant received the disclosure form before signing the rental documents.

> CAUTION
> **You have additional obligations if you renovate the property.**
> When you renovate a building constructed before 1978, EPA regulations require that current tenants receive lead hazard information before any renovation work begins. A copy of the EPA pamphlet *Renovate Right: Important Lead Hazard Information for Families, Child Care Providers, and Schools* will do.

Most states also require landlords to carefully maintain any existing lead paint and lead-based building materials, and they mandate who may work on lead paint abatement. If you're subject to a state statute, you must comply with it as well as the federal law.

There's no federal legal requirement that you be proactive and test for the presence of lead. But you may want to anyway, for these reasons:

- **Controlling lead is much easier than going through a lawsuit.** Besides, do you really want to live with the knowledge that a child's health has been damaged?

- **Ignorance may not shield you from liability.** At some point, a court will no doubt rule that the danger of lead paint in older housing is so well known that owners of older housing can be presumed to know of the danger.

- **You can't simply refuse to rent to tenants with children.** Though you may feel this protects them, this is illegal discrimination in all states.

- **You can't shift responsibility with a clause in your lease or rental agreement.** An exculpatory clause, which attempts to absolve you from any responsibility for lead-based injuries, won't protect you. In fact, it may work against you, showing that you knew of the lead problem.

- **Any refinance or sale will probably bring the problem to light.** Your lender may require lead testing before approving a loan.

- **Your insurance company may soon require lead testing as a condition of issuing a policy.** Claims based on lead-based injuries are very expensive—expect the insurance company to require testing before issuing a homeowners' policy, or to exclude claims based on lead. Review your coverage with your insurance broker.

> **RESOURCE**
> **Lead hazard resources.** Information on the evaluation and control of lead-based paint and other hazards, disclosure forms, copies of the *Protect Your Family From Lead in Your Home* and *Renovate Right* pamphlets, lists of EPA-certified lead paint professionals, and more may be obtained from the National Lead Information Center at 800-424-LEAD or www.epa.gov/lead. The EPA website (www.epa.gov) also includes a map with links to state and local websites, where you can find information on related lead hazard laws.

Lead is relatively easy to detect—you can buy home-use kits that contain a simple swab, which turns color when drawn over a lead-based surface. Knowing how much lead is present, and how to best clean it up, however, are subjects for a certified lead abatement specialist. Plan on speaking with one if a lead test, done professionally or with an at-home kit, comes up positive.

Radon

Radon is a naturally occurring radioactive gas associated with lung cancer. It can enter and contaminate a house built on soil and rock containing uranium deposits or through water from private wells drilled in uranium-rich soil. Radon can become lethal when trapped in tightly sealed homes (well insulated or with poor ventilation), when escaping from building materials that have incorporated uranium-filled rocks and soils, or when released from aerated, contaminated household water. Problems occur most frequently in areas where rocky soil is relatively rich in uranium and in climates where occupants keep their windows tightly shut.

You're not legally required to test for radon, but you should do so if levels are known to be high in your area (ask your city planning department or insurance broker). For the best results, hire an EPA-certified inspector. Testing takes at least three days, and sometimes months. Do-it-yourself radon testing kits are also available; make sure the kit says "Meets EPA Requirements."

If testing indicates high radon levels, be sure to warn tenants and correct the problem. Start by giving them the EPA booklet *A Radon Guide for Tenants* (see "Radon resources," below). Ventilation measures will effectively disperse the gas in most situations. These measures range from the obvious (open the windows and provide cross-ventilation) to the somewhat complex (sealing cracks in the foundation or sucking radon out of the soil before it enters the foundation). According to the EPA, a typical household radon problem can be solved for $500 to $2,500.

> **RESOURCE**
>
> **Radon resources.** Contact the EPA Radon Hotline at 800-767-7236, or visit the EPA website (www.epa.gov/radon). The site has links to state agencies that regulate radon, gives information on finding a qualified radon reduction provider, and includes a map of radon zones by state. You can also download a copy of *A Radon Guide for Tenants* and other publications.

Carbon monoxide

Carbon monoxide (CO) is a colorless, odorless, lethal gas; a byproduct of fuel combustion produced by nonelectric home appliances, such as gas dryers, refrigerators, ranges, water heaters or space heaters, oil furnaces, fireplaces, charcoal grills, and wood stoves. If appliances or fireplaces aren't vented properly, CO can build up within a home and poison the occupants. Unlike radon, whose deadly effects work over time, CO can build up and kill within a matter of hours. And, unlike any of the environmental hazards discussed so far, CO cannot be covered up or managed.

If you have a regular maintenance program, discussed in Chapter 7, you should be able to spot and fix the common malfunctions that cause CO buildup. Here's how to avoid problems:

- Install carbon monoxide detection devices in the home (many states require these already).
- Check chimneys and appliance vents for blockages.
- Prohibit tenants from using indoor, portable gas or charcoal grills.
- Warn tenants never to use a gas range, clothes dryer, or oven for heating.
- Prohibit nonelectric space heaters, or specify that they must be inspected annually. Tenants can get recommendations from fuel suppliers.
- Check the pilot lights of gas appliances regularly. They should show a clear blue flame; a yellow or orange flame may indicate a problem.

RESOURCE
Carbon monoxide resources. The EPA website offers useful instructional material, including downloadable educational pamphlets, at www.epa.gov/iaq/co.html. Local natural gas utility companies often offer consumer information. Also contact the American Gas Association for consumer pamphlets on carbon monoxide; it's at 202-824-7000 or www.aga.org.

Mold

Across the country, tenants have won multimillion dollar cases against landlords for significant health problems—such as rashes, chronic fatigue, nausea, cognitive losses, hemorrhaging, and asthma—allegedly caused by exposure to "toxic molds." But not all mold produces toxins, and most mold is not otherwise harmful—for example, the mold that grows on shower tiles isn't dangerous. The trouble is, it takes an expert to know whether a particular mold is harmful or just unsightly and annoying.

Mold often grows on water-soaked materials, such as wall paneling, paint, fabric, ceiling tiles, newspapers, or cardboard boxes. However, all that's really needed is an organic food source, water, and time. Throw in a little warmth, and the organism will grow quickly, sometimes spreading within 24 hours. Humidity sets up prime growing conditions. Floods, leaking pipes, windows, or roofs may lead to mold growth in any structure.

No federal law sets permissible mold exposure limits or building tolerance standards for residences, and only a few states have taken steps toward establishing permissible mold standards. Some local ordinances identify mold as a legal nuisance or a property condition that the landlord must clean up. Check with your city building, health, or environmental health departments to find out whether your city or state has passed any relevant laws.

Law or no law, your legal duty to provide and maintain habitable premises naturally extends to fixing leaking pipes, windows, and roofs—the causes of most mold. If you're lax, and mold grows as a result, you may be held responsible for a tenant's resulting health problems.

But instead of worrying about unlikely lawsuits, focus on preventing the conditions that lead to mold growth. The following steps are especially important if your rental house is in a humid environment or has had past mold problems:

- **Check for and fix moisture or mold problems before new tenants move in.** This will help prevent problems before they start.
- **Make sure every tenant understands how to help prevent mold growth.** Use your lease or house rules to educate tenants about

sensible housekeeping practices and how to fix problems should they arise. Give tenants specific advice, such as how to ventilate the rental unit, avoid creating areas of standing water, and clean vulnerable areas, such as bathrooms, with cleaning solutions that will discourage mold growth.

- **Encourage tenants to immediately report signs of mold.** This includes reporting conditions that may lead to mold, such as plumbing leaks and weatherproofing problems.

- **Do all necessary repairs and maintenance to clean up or reduce mold.** For example, consider installing exhaust fans in rooms with high humidity (bathrooms, kitchens, and service porches) or provide tenants with dehumidifiers in chronically damp climates.

Should You Test for Mold?

Properly testing for mold will cost you more than you want to pay. Although over-the-counter kits can be bought for around $30, their results are questionable. A professional's basic investigation for a single-family home will run you $1,000 or more. To further complicate matters, there are relatively few competent professionals in this new field, and no state or federal certification programs to govern them.

If you have visible signs of mold, you're much better off simply getting rid of it, using the procedures described below. The procedures are the same no matter what kind of mold it is.

Most mold is relatively harmless and easy to deal with. A weak bleach solution (one cup of bleach per gallon of water) will remove mold from nonporous materials. Use gloves and avoid exposing eyes and lungs to airborne mold dust (use a mask). Allow for frequent work breaks with plenty of fresh air.

Clean or remove all infested areas, beginning on a small patch to make sure you don't develop adverse health reactions such as nausea or headaches. (If you do, call in an experienced professional.) Contain the work space with plastic sheeting and enclose debris in plastic bags. Don't try removing mold from fabrics such as towels, linens, drapes, carpets, and clothing—you'll have to dispose of these already ruined items.

If the mold is extensive, consider hiring an experienced mold remediation company with excellent references. For more information, check out the sites noted in "Mold resources," below.

> **CAUTION**
> **Check your insurance policy.** You may be dismayed to find that it excludes mold damage from coverage (or will on the next renewal). Even if mold is covered, many insurers try to wiggle out by claiming that it falls within the "pollution exclusion." Most policies won't cover you if you commit or allow pollution, the classic example being deliberately dumping solvents onto the property. Talk to your insurance broker if you're concerned about mold coverage.

> **RESOURCE**
> **Mold resources.** For information on mold detection, removal, and prevention, visit the EPA website at www.epa.gov/mold.

Bedbugs

Bedbugs are biting, obnoxious pests that nest in mattresses, bed frames, and beyond. In fact, they can infest an entire room or house, spreading via cracks in the walls, heating ducts, and other openings. They're also excellent stowaways, crawling into luggage, clothing, pillows, boxes, and furniture as these are moved from an infested home or hotel to another location. Secondhand furniture is a common source of infestation.

You'll learn that bedbugs have infested your property when the tenant complains of widespread, annoying bites that appear during the night (fortunately, bedbugs don't carry disease-causing germs). To minimize the outbreak, take the following steps immediately:

- **Confirm the infestation.** Make sure you're not dealing with some other pest, such as fleas. Because several kinds of insects resemble bedbugs, you'll need to capture a critter or two and study them. Go online for pictures, and compare your samples. If it looks like a bedbug, call an experienced pest control operator, pronto.

> **TIP**
>
> **Bring in the pros.** A can of Raid isn't going to do the job, and will end up costing you more in the long run. Depending on the size of the rental, expect to pay from $100–$750 for the initial service, and $75–$300 for follow-up treatments. If you find a company that offers to control bedbugs for a lowball amount like $50 per unit, get another bid. For more information, see www.epa.gov/bedbugs.

- **Declutter, move the tenant out, exterminate, vacuum—and do it again.** Bedbugs thrive in clutter, so tenants must remove all items from closets, shelves, and drawers and wash all bedding and clothing in hot water. As University of Kentucky professor of entomology Michael F. Potter told *USA TODAY*'s Donna Freydkin, "As little as five or ten minutes kills everything on high heat. Cold will not kill the eggs and not all the adults." Put washed items in sealed plastic bags, then move the tenant out during treatment. Most of the time, tenants can return the same day. Upon return, the tenant—or you—must thoroughly vacuum. Exterminators may recommend a second and even a third treatment, with exhaustive cleaning and clutter removing in between.

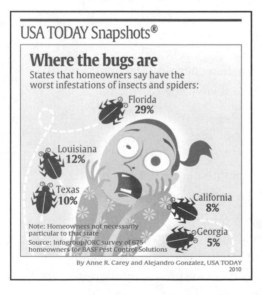

USA TODAY Snapshots®

Where the bugs are

States that homeowners say have the worst infestations of insects and spiders:

Florida 29%
Louisiana 12%
Texas 10%
California 8%
Georgia 5%

Note: Homeowners not necessarily particular to that state

Source: Infogroup/ORC survey of 675 homeowners for BASF Pest Control Solutions

By Anne R. Carey and Alejandro Gonzalez, USA TODAY 2010

Don't Let the Bedbugs Bite

First come the bites, amazingly itchy, raised red welts that appear literally overnight. Then, you might notice scarlet spots on your sheets from smashed bugs or perhaps clusters of little black dots that you assume are dirt but are in fact constellations of fecal matter.

And one day, you might wake up in the wee hours of the morning, flip on the lights and find red bugs, slightly bigger than ticks, crawling on your sheets, pillows, and legs.

Welcome to the most retro pest of the 21st century, the bedbug. The bugs, which were thought to be wiped out by powerful pesticides such as DDT 30 years ago, are back and infesting major urban areas, suburbia, and the heartland.

Debbie Wunder and her husband, Rusty Pistachio, picked up the insects from a hotel in Curacao in the Netherlands Antilles. They didn't realize until later that they were bringing them home to Manhattan. He was eaten up all over; she didn't get a single bite, which isn't unusual, experts say. Bugs often feast on one person and ignore another.

The bedbug problem, says Michael Raupp, professor of entomology at the University of Maryland, "is across the board. This is a general problem and is on the upswing in all of our states."

Once you pick them up in a hotel, a subway, or a rental car and they invade your living space, it's difficult to get rid of them. They're becoming ever more resistant to the few sprays that are approved to fight them after DDT was banned in 1972.

Wunder, who now lives in Los Angeles with her husband, bought covers for her new mattress and box spring, washed or dry-cleaned all her clothing, and says she's become a bedbug vigilante.

"I will never ever sleep in a hotel bed without doing a thorough check of the mattress and linens," she says.

 USA TODAY "They're ba-a-ack for a snack; It's easy to say 'Don't let the bedbugs bite'—until the paranoia-inducing, bloodsucking parasites shake you awake," by Donna Freydkin, November 7, 2007.

Your insurance will probably not cover the cost of hiring a pest control company for bedbugs (nor for any other vermin or insect infestation). However, insurance may cover you for the tenant's claims for lost or damaged belongings, medical expenses, and related moving and living expenses, as well as your loss of rent. If your tenant has renters' insurance, suggest referring the matter to the insurance company.

No tenant is going to be happy to hear that you've had a past bedbug problem, and no statute or court decision directs you to reveal a rental's bedbug history. Nevertheless, if a prospect questions you directly about bedbugs, especially if the issue is clearly of critical importance to the person, you must answer truthfully. Otherwise you risk the tenant's breaking the lease or suing you for damages. Even if you don't disclose, if you had a problem and it reappears, the tenant may still pursue these options, creating quite a headache for you.

RESOURCE

Bedbug resources. Useful information on identifying and eradicating bedbugs is available on the EPA website at www.epa.gov/bedbugs and on www.techletter.com (maintained by a pest management consulting firm).

Keeping Tenants Safe: Liability for Crime

Even the safest neighborhoods have occasional incidents of crime, and depending on the circumstances, you may be held at least partially responsible for resulting tenant injuries and losses. For example, if you know about drug dealing on the sidewalk right in front of your rental property, you may have a duty to take steps to deal with it (starting with involving the police). Once again, preventive measures are your best response. Thankfully, the most successful prevention techniques— proper lighting and good locks, for example—are inexpensive. And they'll help you avoid the greater costs produced by actual incidents of crime, including increased insurance premiums and lost income due to rapid turnover.

Here are some suggestions to effectively and reasonably protect your tenants:

- **Meet or exceed basic legal requirements for safety devices.** Buy and maintain dead bolt locks, good lighting, and window locks, especially when they're required by state and local housing codes. (Ask your state or local housing agency or rental property owners' association.)

- **Respond to the environment.** Examine and research the vulnerability of your property and neighborhood. If your tenants will pay more rent if you make the building safer, you'd be foolish not to do it.

- **Tighten up management practices.** For example, strictly control who has a key to the property.

- **Educate your tenants about crime problems and prevention strategies.** Make it clear that they—not you—are primarily responsible for their protection. Explain what they can do to minimize the chances of assault or theft (avoid being alone on the street or in outside parking lots late at night). Also warn tenants of the limitations of the security measures you've put in place.

- **Don't hype your security measures.** You don't want to inadvertently promise a higher level of security than you're prepared to provide. Derek, who rents out a house in Atlanta that he inherited from his mother, learned this lesson the hard way: "I'd described the neighborhood as 'safe and secure,' and basically promised my new tenant that the security service hired by the homeowners' association was on duty 24/7. Guess what: The tenant got mugged at about 7 p.m. while walking his dog. Then I found out that the 'security service' consisted of an off-duty policeman making the rounds now and then. The tenant's lawyers argued that my tenant would never have ventured out if he'd known the true state of security, and I lost the case."

- **Deal with common security problems.** At the top of your list should be fixing burned-out exterior floodlights and broken locks (the top way landlords are found liable for tenant injuries caused by criminals) and cutting back overgrown shrubbery that provides a convenient lurking spot for criminals. Also ask tenants for their suggestions, and quickly respond. If an important component of your security systems breaks, be prepared to fix it on an emergency basis and provide appropriate alternative security.

- **Purchase adequate liability insurance.** This will protect you from lawsuits related to crime on your rental property.

These steps will not only limit the likelihood of criminal activity on your property, but will also reduce the risk that you'll be found responsible if an assault or robbery does take place.

> **TIP**
>
> **Protect yourself, too.** Take precautions for your own personal safety:
>
> - **Promptly deposit rent checks and money orders.** If possible, do not accept cash.
> - **When showing your property, bring someone with you.** If you must show the property alone, at least let someone know, and say when you expect to be done.
> - **Go high tech.** Especially if the property is in a high-crime area, carry a cell phone and small alarm device (such as beeper-sized box that emits a piercing alarm when its pin is removed).

> **RESOURCE**
>
> **More information on liability issues.** The Landlord's Liability area of the Landlords section of Nolo.com includes useful articles on a landlord's liability for tenant injuries, environmental hazards, criminal activity on the rental property, and injuries caused by a tenant's dog.

Protecting Neighbors From Illegal Tenant Activities

It shouldn't be your fault when tenants break the law. Yet, increasingly over the last decade, stricter laws and court decisions have made landlords liable when they fail to sufficiently respond to tenants' activities, especially ongoing illegal activities such as drug dealing. You might face:

- **Nuisance lawsuits.** A legal "nuisance" is a pervasive, continuing, and serious condition—like a pile of garbage or group of drug dealers—that threatens public health, safety, or morals. Every state has a nuisance abatement law, which allows the government, and sometimes the neighbors, to fight back, often by court order and fines against the landlord. In some states, neighbors can sue in small claims court, seeking monetary compensation (each neighbor may sue for the maximum limit) and an order requiring the landlord to evict the troublemakers, install security, and repair the premises.

- **Forfeiting the property.** Federal and state forfeiture proceedings—where the government takes your property because of the illegal activities of one or more tenants—are the most dramatic and devastating consequence of owning crime-ridden rental property. Forfeitures are relatively rare, but may be accomplished on the basis of a single incident.

If you suspect that a tenant or potential tenant may be up to something illegal—or that you're being paid rent from ill-gotten gains—check out *Every Landlord's Legal Guide*, by Marcia Stewart, Ralph Warner, and Janet Portman (Nolo) for advice on dealing with these situations.

Insurance Coverage for Property and Liability

After scaring you with everything you can be sued or otherwise held responsible for, here's a reason to breathe a sigh of relief: You can protect yourself from many problems by buying adequate insurance. A well-designed insurance program can cover your rental property for both physical losses and people's injuries.

Getting adequate liability coverage

Commercial general liability coverage will reimburse for injuries or losses suffered by others as the result of defective conditions on your property or your carelessness, up to the limits of the policy. Equally important, it covers the cost of settling personal injury claims, including lawyers' bills for your defense.

For example, if your tenant gets injured falling down a defective staircase that you knew about, had a chance to fix, but failed to repair, your insurance company would handle any lawsuit or claim brought by the tenant and pay any settlement or award (again, within your policy limits). The same would be true if your tenant's child's playmate, over for the afternoon, drowned in the backyard pool that you'd failed to equip with a legally required antisuction device.

Liability policies usually state a dollar limit per occurrence and an aggregate dollar limit for the policy year. For example, your policy may say that it will pay $300,000 per occurrence for personal injury or a total of $1 million in any one policy year.

Depending on the value of your property and of your personal assets, buying even more coverage (called an "umbrella policy") is an excellent idea, especially if you're in a large metropolitan area, where personal injury damage awards are likely to be very high. Umbrella policies are not expensive. Don't put your property at risk of being sold to pay a court judgment!

When choosing liability coverage, consider buying a policy that provides protection for not only physical injury claims, but also claims of libel, slander, discrimination, unlawful and retaliatory eviction, and invasion of privacy suffered by tenants and guests.

You can also suggest, and in most states you can require, that your tenant buy liability insurance as part of a renters' policy. Having a renters' policy in place will protect your own insurance. Here's how it works: Suppose the tenant starts a fire on the stove and burns the kitchen. Your own property insurance would cover the damage—but so would the tenants' insurance. If you require that the tenant's policy be "primary," (that is, applied first to any claim), you can insist that the tenant's carrier, not yours, cover the damage. You're always better off when you don't have to go to your carrier with a claim.

Getting adequate property coverage

Your property insurance should cover losses from a whole host of perils, such as damage from fire, storms, burglary, and vandalism. In negotiating coverage, there are five main questions to consider:

- **What features of the rental property are insured?** Be sure your insurance covers all the property you want protected, be it outdoor fixtures, appliances like washing machines, property used to maintain the house (such as gardening equipment and tools), personal property you're leaving in the house (for example, if it will be partially furnished), and personal business property such as computers.

> Ⓠ **TIP**
> **Make sure your tenants know that your insurance doesn't cover loss or damage to their personal property.** If a thief steals your tenants' jewelry or a fire damages their clothing and electronics, they're on their own. Your tenants will need to purchase their own renters' insurance to cover personal property losses—it's relatively affordable, at around $150 to $300 per year.

- **What perils will be insured against?** Coverage for damage caused by fire and smoke is common in the most basic policies. Standard policies also cover damage from wind, hail, lightning, explosions, volcanoes, riots and vandalism, theft, water damage (from burst pipes, for example), and similar events.

- **What perils will be excluded from coverage?** Damage from mudslides, windstorms, the weight of snow, police activity, power outages, sewer backups, dry rot, vermin, war, nuclear perils, losses if your house is vacant for 60 days or more, or losses caused by your own—or your tenant's—intentional or criminal actions, poor maintenance, or failure to preserve or protect the property after it's been damaged, may all be excluded from your policy. Earthquake insurance on the house itself and flood insurance are typically separate. (They're usually expensive and have very high deductibles, but are still worthwhile if your building is highly susceptible to earthquake or flood damage.)

> **TIP**
> **Check out "loss of rents" insurance.** This will reimburse you for the lost rental income if your property is sidelined—for example, due to a fire or other calamity.

- **How much insurance should you buy?** "Inadequate insurance coverage plagues homeowners across the USA," say *USA TODAY*'s Kathy Chu and Elizabeth Weise. Be sure to carry enough insurance on the building to rebuild it if it's destroyed. That doesn't usually mean you'll get a blank check—most policies cover "replacement cost," or a preset dollar amount that was calculated when you first got the policy. (That's better than "actual cash value coverage," which pays only the property's replacement cost minus any depreciation or wear and tear since it was built.) The problem with replacement cost coverage, as Chu and Weise found, is that the cost of building materials has climbed "far above overall inflation. Prices of construction materials can rise even more after natural disasters." Increased demand for home contractors after a disaster may also drive up prices. For a reality check, ask a local contractor how much a structure like yours would cost to build today. If it's more than the amount offered by your insurance, work with your insurance rep to raise your replacement cost figure. Another worthwhile option is buying an "inflation guard," which raises the stated value of your house by a set percentage each year. At least there's no need to insure the total value of your real property (the legal term that includes land and buildings), because land doesn't burn or get knocked over.

- **Is your house old enough that it will need code upgrades during reconstruction?** Building codes normally require that an older building be rebuilt to modern standards and codes, which is often much pricier than simply replacing it as it was. Ask for "ordinance or law coverage." It's almost never included in standard policies, but is worth paying a little extra for.

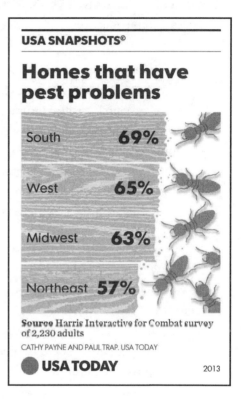

USA SNAPSHOTS©

Homes that have pest problems

South	**69%**
West	**65%**
Midwest	**63%**
Northeast	**57%**

Source Harris Interactive for Combat survey of 2,230 adults

CATHY PAYNE AND PAUL TRAP, USA TODAY

USA TODAY   2013

> 💡 **TIP**
> **Tell your insurance company about remodels or upgrades.** *USA TODAY*'s Sandra Block discovered (in 2006) that many Americans "who have made significant home improvements, such as adding a room or deck said they hadn't updated their homeowners' insurance, or weren't sure if they had. If your policy is based on the value of your home before you remodeled, you may not recoup the money you spent to add a bathroom or update your kitchen."

Converting your existing homeowners' policy

If you're an accidental landlord converting your own house to a rental, you may want to continue with your current insurance company. However, you can't just sit back and expect your homeowners' policy to remain in effect. Contact the insurer and ask that the policy be rewritten to fit your new role as a landlord. (In fact, current industry practice is to actually split rental property insurance into two separate policies, one for property and one for liability.) If you don't change your coverage, your insurer could simply deny any of your later claims. Of course, you don't have to stick with your existing insurer—comparing prices is a fine idea, too.

> **TIP**
> **Buying a new home to live in?** You can save money, according to Mike Mansel, certified insurance counselor, by "looking into using the same insurance company for both your rental property and your new home. That way the insurer can simply extend the liability portion of your homeowners' policy to the rental property—which will be less expensive than buying two separate liability policies. After that, you'll just need to buy a separate fire policy for the rental, also with the same company."

During the conversion, your insurer will reassess the level of risk regarding the fire portion of the policy. It may say that your property is now at higher risk of damage because of possible vacancies and because tenants tend to be harder on a property than a homeowner. Your rates may go up a bit for this part of the policy. However, your overall rates will probably go down, because you'll no longer need coverage for personal possessions (unless you're leaving a lot behind).

Do a careful comparison between your new and old policies before signing. You may discover that coverage you assumed would still be included is no longer there, but can be added in.

> **CAUTION**
> **Don't let your house sit empty for 60 to 90 days or more.** If you have a typical homeowners' policy, this will result in its being canceled. Check your policy to be sure, and talk to your insurance agent if you think this might become an issue.

If Your Home Is Uninhabited or Rented, Insurance Coverage Changes

In many neighborhoods around the country, "for sale" signs outnumber telephone poles, and some of those signs are looking awfully weather-beaten.

One way around this problem is to stay put until the economy turns around and the housing market recovers. In the interim, it's not enough to ask your next-door neighbor to keep an eye on your property until the new owners move in.

You should also contact your insurance agent, or the company that provides your homeowners' insurance. Standard homeowners' policies are designed to cover homes that are occupied. If you leave your home uninhabited for a month or longer, your policy may not cover damage or losses, says Michael McRaith, director of the Illinois Department of Insurance.

You could also expose yourself to lawsuits, McRaith says. If a child gets hurt while playing on your property, your insurance may not protect you from liability, he says.

The amount of time you can leave your home unoccupied before it affects your coverage varies, depending on your insurer. Some insurance policies exclude coverage for fire-related damage if the property has been vacant or unoccupied for 30 days, says Richard McGrath, chief executive officer of McGrath Insurance Group, in Sturbridge, Massachusetts. For others, it's 60 days, he says.

Other types of claims may also be excluded if your home has been left unattended. For example, State Farm's homeowners' policy won't cover damage caused by vandalism after a home has been vacant for 30 days, spokesman Dick Luedke says.

Damage caused by frozen pipes may also be excluded if the home was vacant when the pipes burst, he says.

Once you notify your insurer that you're leaving, a couple of things could happen:

If Your Home Is Uninhabited or Rented, Insurance Coverage Changes (cont'd)

- Your insurer will adjust your policy to one that covers vacant properties. If you know how long your home will be vacant, you may be able to buy a policy that will cover that period of time. You'll pay a higher premium for vacancy coverage, but without it, you could be on the hook for the cost of repairing or replacing your home.

- You'll have to get a new policy. Some insurers won't cover vacant homes. In that case, you'll need to find a company that will. Some insurers specialize in covering higher-risk properties, such as vacant homes, says Jeanne Salvatore, spokeswoman for the Insurance Information Institute, an industry-funded education organization.

An independent insurance agent can help you search for policies that will fit your circumstances.

Insuring rental property

If you manage to rent your home, you'll be able to cover at least some of the cost of the mortgage. But here, too, you'll probably have to pay more for homeowners' insurance.

Insurers consider a rented home a higher risk than one that's occupied by its owners because renters have less interest in caring for a property. "When you're a homeowner, your care and upkeep is probably going to be a lot better," McGrath says.

If you rent your home, you're going to need a landlord policy, Salvatore says. Premiums for these policies are higher than premiums for owner-occupied homes. But it will reimburse you for lost rental income if the house burns down or becomes otherwise uninhabitable, she says. A landlord policy will also increase your liability coverage, protecting you in the event that your tenant sues you, Salvatore says.

USA TODAY "If your home is uninhabited or rented, insurance coverage changes," by Sandra Block, August 10, 2010.

Working with your agent to get the best coverage

Not all insurance agents are created equal. Get recommendations from other landlords, or from real estate people with several years' experience. A good agent will listen to your needs and help you find a policy that addresses them, and will:

- **Analyze your business operations.** Steer clear of any agent who, without learning the specifics of your property and business, whips out a package policy and claims it will solve all your problems.

- **Make you feel comfortable discussing your needs.** While some policy buyers try to keep their rates down by downplaying areas of unusual risk, this is a bad idea. If you don't disclose all the facts, you may not get the coverage you need, or the insurance company may later try to deny you coverage because you misrepresented the nature of your operation.

- **Explain what's excluded.** Does the policy exclude damage from a leaking sprinkler system? From dog bites? From an earthquake? If so, and these are risks you face, find out whether they can be covered, and at what cost.

- **Represent only highly rated carriers.** Insurance companies are rated according to their financial condition and size. The most recognized rater is the A.M. Best Company, which assigns letter ratings according to financial stability (A++ is the highest) and Roman numeral ratings reflecting the size of a company's surplus (XV is the best). Because 80% of American companies receive an A rating or higher, there's no reason to choose a company rated anything less. As to surplus, you'll be on solid ground requiring an "X." Your local public library will likely have the *Best's Key Rating Guide*, or you can find it online at www.ambest.com.

Saving money on insurance

Few landlords can afford to adequately insure themselves against every possible risk. Here are some guidelines to help you keep costs down:

- **Set priorities.** Ask yourself: What types of property losses would threaten the viability of my business? What kinds of liability lawsuits might wipe me out? Tailor your coverage to protect against these potentially disastrous losses. Get enough property and liability coverage to protect yourself from the most common claims, adding coverage for serious risks where it's reasonably priced.

- **Select a high deductible.** The deductible is the amount you must pay out of pocket before insurance coverage kicks in. The cost difference between a policy with a $250 deductible and one with a $500 or $1,000 or even higher deductible is significant— particularly if you add up the premium savings for five or ten years. Consider using the money you save to buy coverage you would have otherwise gone without, such as for loss of rents.

- **Reduce your risk.** Good safety and security measures, such as regular property inspections, special fire prevention measures, adding dead-bolt locks, or requiring that tenants buy renters' insurance, may eliminate the need for some types of insurance or lead to lower rates or discounts. Also ask your insurance agent what you can do to get a better rate.

- **Comparison shop.** No two companies charge exactly the same rates. But be wary of an unusually low price, which may be a sign of a shaky company. Or it may be that you're unfairly comparing policies that provide very different types of coverage. Make sure you know what you're buying, and review your coverage and rates periodically.

RESOURCE
For more information on choosing business insurance: See the Insurance Information Institute's website at www.iii.org.

Living in Perfect Harmony?
Dealing With Difficult Tenants

D espite your careful screening, you're bound someday to have a less-than-perfect tenant. It may be one who's chronically late with the rent, disturbs the neighbors with loud parties or a constant stream of visitors, or brings in a dog without your permission. Whatever the problem, you'll want to know how to resolve it quickly, with minimum hassle or expense.

In this chapter, we'll help you figure out how to deal with difficult tenants and enforce the terms of your lease or rental agreement. We'll cover:

- common tenant problems and what to do about them
- different methods for resolving disputes, and
- how to evict a tenant, if that becomes necessary.

> **TIP**
> **Lesson learned the hard way: It's not my house anymore.**
> Amy, who rents out her former home in Austin, Texas, while she attends graduate school out of state, says, "After my first set of tenants left, I discovered that they'd painted all the rooms different colors and that their dogs, which I hadn't known about, had destroyed the backyard and the storm door. That was crushing—I still felt like it was my house."

Common Tenant Problems—And What to Do About Them

While tenants come in all shapes and sizes, most tenant problems boil down to a few common and recurring themes. Here, we'll cover some of the problems you're likely to encounter, and how you may wish to approach them. Later in the chapter, we'll explain specific negotiating strategies, as well as how to legally get a tenant to leave.

Late rent

While being a day or two late every once in awhile shouldn't be a reason to evict—especially if it's an otherwise reliable tenant—you probably do want to enforce on-time payments. This will help show that you're serious about this business relationship and avoid reinforcing late-payment habits.

The first time your tenant is late, simply call and make sure the payment didn't get lost, forgotten, or misplaced. If the tenant apologizes profusely and pays you immediately—especially a tenant with a history of on-time payments—you may have nothing more to worry about. The next time it happens, however, you should probably invoke the late-fee clause in your lease or rental agreement.

> **TIP**
> **Enforce your right to the late fee.** Your tenant may decide to pay the rent, but not the fee. If you're thinking, "I'll take it out of the security deposit," check your state's laws first—many forbid that. Instead, if your lease or rental agreement says that the fee is considered "additional rent," you'll be able to use a "Pay or Quit" notice to demand the late fee, and you can begin eviction proceedings if the tenant doesn't pay the fee (or move). If your rental document doesn't describe the fee as additional rent, you'll have to sue in small claims court to get it—hardly worthwhile for such a small amount.

If the tenant promises to send a check soon but doesn't, fails to respond to your call, or says "Sorry, I can't make the payment," your next step will probably be to send a termination notice (often called a Pay or Quit notice). This notice should explain that the tenant must pay rent within a designated time or move out. If the tenant doesn't comply, you can file an eviction lawsuit. (Proper termination notices and evictions are covered later in this chapter.)

Breaking the lease early

A lease obligates you and the tenant for its entire term. But tenants' life circumstances don't always cooperate, and you may well encounter times when a tenant needs or wants to break the lease and move out early. Sometimes, the reason for their leave-taking is legally recognized (as when the landlord refuses to repair a problem that makes the rental unfit). But more often, it's love, a job, school, or the prospect of a better deal somewhere else.

What can you do about it? If you suspect that the tenant is about to split, have a conversation. Together, you may be able to address an underlying issue, such as the tenant's fear that you won't change your no-pets rule to make room for a new puppy. Or maybe the tenant is leaving because you haven't held up your end of a bargain—have failed to repair a leaky roof, for example—in which case, you might negotiate a last chance to do your part. (By the way, if that tenant leaves for such a reason, you won't be able to ask for rent on the balance of the lease.)

USA TODAY Snapshots®

Something stinks!

Nearly all adults (96%) say they have noticed an offensive odor in someone else's home at some time, but only 36% admit noticing such a smell in their own home.
Most commonly cited odors:
Cigar/cigarette smoke
81%
Pet smell
80%
Food
63%
Musty odor
57%
Overpowering air fresheners
50%

Source: Harris Interactive online survey for Dutch Boy of 2,056 adults

By Michelle Healy and Alejandro Gonzalez, USA TODAY 2008

But suppose the tenant is departing for purely personal reasons, and you can't work something out. Now, you're faced with a vacancy you weren't prepared for. The tenant is still responsible for the balance of the rent left on the lease, but that's not the end of the story. In most states, you must take reasonably prompt steps to rent the unit again. Once it's rented, your former tenant's liability for the balance ends.

Nip Security Deposit Deductions in the Bud

At the end of your tenant's lease, you'll get inside the rental to assess its condition. You can fairly deduct from the security deposit those sums needed to remedy damage beyond normal wear and tear and necessary cleaning.

But don't wait until then to take a look around. You might want to have a look mid-lease, to make sure minor problems don't develop into big ones, and to educate your tenants as to what to expect when they move out. As Stuart, with property in Davis, California, says, "No matter how clearly we try to explain security deposits in advance, each time the lease is up and I inspect the place, the tenants' mouths drop at the deductions. They always seem to think the security deposit is just for rent, not for cleaning."

If you want to do a mid-lease inspection, follow your state's rules regarding landlord entry, giving the required amount of notice and scheduling the visit on an agreed-upon day and time. When you find a problem—a hole in the wall, stained carpets—decide whether to fix it now or later (maybe it will be just as efficient to clean the carpets in six months, when the tenants leave).

Who pays? As long as the problem is one for which you could legitimately use the security deposit, you can demand that the tenants pay directly, or you may use the deposit. If you use the deposit, be sure to demand, in writing, that the tenants replenish the deposit. Their failure to do so would be grounds for terminating the lease.

Other violations of the lease or rental agreement

Even rent-paying tenants are frequently known to violate important terms of the lease or rental agreement. Here are some of the most common violations, and what steps to take before terminating the agreement:

- **Moving in a pet.** If your agreement specifically forbids pets, or limits them to a certain type of pet, but your tenant moves one in anyway, you must decide whether you're willing to allow it.

USA TODAY Snapshots®

Watch where you lay things
Top five possessions dog owners said their dogs damaged because of chewing habits:

Shoes — 39%
Furniture — 38%
Clothing — 26%
Kids' toys — 20%
Electronic equipment — 15%

Source: TheHealthyChew.com   By David Stuckey and Dave Merrill, USA TODAY 2006

You may decide to ignore your rule if the tenant is reliable, the pet appears well-behaved, and you have not promised other tenants in a multifamily building that the property will be pet free. Sometimes, it's not worth the bother of forcing the tenant to get rid of the animal or move out. However, if you decide to let the pet stay, you should amend your rental agreement to reflect it, and may want to increase the security deposit or require an additional "pet deposit" (check your state's security deposit law to find out whether you may charge additional sums or separate pet deposits). Also remember that certain types of animals—namely nondomestic pets, such as monkeys and certain dog breeds—may heighten your legal liability. Talk to your insurance company to find out, and for more information on liability, see Chapter 8.

> 💡 **TIP**
>
> **Best thing I ever did: Build a fence.** Stuart thought his tenant was bringing only one dog—a small, sweet pit bull. But, he says, "Then a friend joined them, who had other pit bulls—which were not so sweet or friendly. The neighbor, who has some small dogs, started complaining, afraid that the tenants' dogs would eat hers. But the pit bulls hadn't actually done anything wrong, and if I kicked out the tenants I wasn't likely to get replacement ones for a few months. So I went up and built a reinforced chain-link fence. That kept the neighbor satisfied."

- **Moving in other occupants.** A new boyfriend or girlfriend, an out-of-town buddy who's job hunting—any of these people might have the tenant saying, "Sure, stay as long as you like," without remembering your rental terms. But your lease or rental agreement should prohibit tenants from moving in additional occupants without your consent—other than the occasional short-term personal (that is, not Airbnb) guest, or a new spouse or child, whom you probably can't legally refuse. If you suspect that someone has moved in, talk with the tenant. If you're inclined to allow the new occupant to stay, you still need to go through the same formal screening steps you took when selecting your original tenant. If you don't want to accept the newcomer, or your screening turns up red flags, you can demand that the person leave. If necessary, give your original tenant a Cure or Quit termination notice, which offers two choices: either get rid of the unauthorized occupant or move out.

TIP

You can terminate any month-to-month tenancy with proper notice (30 days in most states). You needn't give a reason, as long as your motives aren't discriminatory or retaliatory. Note, however, that tenants in rent control cities with "just-cause" eviction protection, and all tenants in New Hampshire and New Jersey (which have statewide just-cause protections) may be able to resist a termination where the landlord can't provide a justifiable reason.

- **Illegal subleasing.** Instead of moving others in, the tenant might simply move out, either permanently or temporarily, and have a newcomer (a "subtenant") move in without asking your consent. You might find out what's happening when you see a new name on the rent checks. If you're willing to allow the arrangement, you can do so—but should first do careful screening, and create a direct legal relationship with the subtenant. With a permanent subtenant, terminate the original lease and sign a new one (the subtenant now becomes your tenant). With a temporary subtenant, you can write a sublease signed by all three of you, which will expire on the agreed-upon date. If you prefer not to consider the subtenant at all, or you find the subtenant unacceptable, you can refuse your consent and, if the newcomer moves in anyway, begin eviction procedures.

- **Excessive noise.** Some degree of noise is normal, but a tenant's loud parties, blaring music, or early morning carpentry projects can disturb neighbors and others. You'll want to act immediately to put a stop to the problem, first by pointing out any clauses in your lease or rental agreement prohibiting excessive noise. Even without a written provision, talk to the tenant immediately if you hear a complaint, then follow up with a warning letter if it isn't resolved. Not taking action could lead to legal troubles like code citations or a small claims lawsuit. In fact, if your rental property has other tenants, they have a right to quiet enjoyment of the premises.

RESOURCE
For more information on state and local noise laws, visit the Noise Pollution Clearinghouse's website, at www.nonoise.org/lawlib.htm.

Of course, there are plenty of other lease or rental agreement terms that your tenant may violate. Your state's law will most likely insist that you give the tenant a few days (anywhere from three to ten days is common) to correct, or "cure," a lease or rental agreement violation. You would do this using a Cure or Quit notice—that is, telling the tenant to fix the problem or leave. However, there are two important "but ifs" that would allow you to use the less generous "Unconditional Quit" notice:

- **Repeated violations.** In some states, if the tenant has violated the same lease clause two or more times within a certain period of time, the tenant may lose the right to a second chance.

- **A violation that can't be corrected.** Some lease violations have a permanent—and therefore incurable—effect. For instance, if your lease prohibits tenant alterations without your consent, and your tenant nevertheless removes the living room wallpaper, you can hardly demand that the tenant cease violating the lease clause. It's simply too late to save the wallpaper.

Past criminal convictions

Although you're generally free to reject prospective tenants with criminal records, you won't necessarily find out about these convictions until you've already rented the unit. At that point, your first impulse might be to look for a way to get the tenant out of your building, particularly if the conviction is for a recent, violent crime. With a month-to-month tenant, it's easiest to just give the regular, required amount of notice to move out. (But there's an exception if the conviction was for drug use, and the tenant is currently not using illegal drugs. Such a tenant is protected from termination under federal fair housing laws.)

> **TIP**
> **Your tenant-screening report may not have told you everything.** "I ordered a background report on a prospective tenant," said Alex, a landlord in Cleveland. "It came back clean—but luckily I didn't stop there. When talking to a prior landlord, I learned that this guy had been convicted of a drug sale, though he didn't end up serving time. That's probably why the report didn't include the conviction. But with that information, I denied the application."

If your tenant has a lease, and is otherwise law- and rule-abiding, you won't be able to terminate the agreement just because you now know about the criminal record, no matter how unsavory or alarming. But it's a different story if your lease or rental agreement states that false and material information on the rental application will be grounds for termination. In that case, you can take steps to terminate the tenancy and evict.

Violations of a tenant's basic legal responsibilities

Virtually every state allows you to end the tenancy of a tenant who has violated basic responsibilities imposed by law. Violations might include grossly deficient housekeeping practices that cause an unhealthy situation, like allowing garbage to pile up; seriously misusing appliances, like defrosting the freezer with an ice pick; or substantially damaging the property, perhaps by knocking holes in the walls.

USA TODAY Snapshots®

Garbage time

Top five foods thrown away by U.S. consumers because of spoilage:

Fresh vegetables and bagged salad — 58%
Fresh fruit — 49%
Bread — 48%
Milk, yogurt and cheese — 29%
Pre-packaged sandwich meat, hot dogs, bacon — 19%

Source: DuPont Ipsos Public Affairs

Note: Margin of error ±3% percentage points.

By David Stuckey and Marcy E. Mullins, USA TODAY 2005

The obligations to keep the property liveable and to refrain from damaging it should already be set out in your leases or rental agreements. But even if they're not, tenants are still legally bound to observe them.

If a tenant or guest substantially damages the premises, you'll be within your rights to use an Unconditional Quit notice. The law does not require you to give tenants accused of serious misbehavior a second chance. Tenants who have earned this type of termination notice generally get only five to ten days (it varies by state) to move out.

Tenant's illegal activity on the premises

In recent years, many states have responded aggressively to drug dealing in residential neighborhoods by making it easier for landlords to evict based on these or other illegal activities. You don't always have to wait until the tenant is convicted of a crime or even arrested—you may be able to evict based on your fact-based suspicion that illegal activity is afoot. But first, check your state's law to learn what level of proof you'll need to support this termination.

Evictions based on criminal activity are often called "expedited evictions," because they take less time than a normal eviction. Expedited evictions are preceded by an Unconditional Quit notice that tells the tenant to move out (and do it quickly). If the tenant stays, you can go to court and file for eviction. The court hearing on the eviction is typically held within a few days, and, if you win, the tenant is given very little time to move.

Resolving Disputes

If you have a problem tenant who won't listen to reason, but eviction doesn't seem like your best option (or perhaps you don't have solid legal grounds for it), there are other means for settling your dispute. Here are some ideas.

Try to negotiate a settlement

Because fighting a court battle costs time and money, you're almost always better off trying to settle any dispute first—whether it's over the acceptable noise level at your tenant's next party (some concrete guidelines specifying days, times, and decibel levels would help), or whether the tenant was justified in repainting the living room without your approval. Your goal should be to achieve the best result at the lowest cost. If instead you act on conviction or principle (whether right or wrong), chances are you'll spend far too much time and money.

Your first step in working toward a compromise with a problem tenant is to call and arrange a time to meet. Dropping over unannounced to talk may work in some circumstances, but is generally not a good idea, because the tenant may feel threatened and react defensively. Writing a letter first, offering to meet with the tenant to work something out, is a good way to let the tenant know you want to settle the matter. Here are some negotiating pointers:

- **Ask to hear the tenant's point of view.** Once the tenant starts talking, listen closely and don't interrupt.
- **Acknowledge hearing key points, even if you disagree with them.** Sometimes it's even a good idea to repeat the tenant's concerns, to demonstrate that you know what they are.
- **Avoid personal attacks.** This only raises the level of hostility and makes settlement more difficult.

- **Be courteous, but not weak.** Let the tenant know you have the resources and evidence to fight and win if you can't reach a settlement.

- **If possible, try to structure the negotiation as a mutual attempt to solve a problem.** For example, if a tenant's guests have been disturbing the neighbors, seek solutions that recognize the interests of both parties.

- **Put yourself in the tenant's shoes.** What would you want to get out of the settlement? Let the tenant have at least a partial sense of victory.

- **When you propose settlement terms, make it clear that you're compromising.** Offers of settlement (clearly labeled as such) can't be introduced against you if you ever end up in court.

- **For a powerful incentive, try money.** To avoid later costs, be willing to pay—perhaps by reducing rent for a short period, lowering the amount owed for damages to the premises, or offering an outright cash settlement for the tenant to leave (with payment made only when the tenant hands you the keys). Many tenants may settle at a surprisingly low figure if they can walk away from the bargaining table a little richer.

- **If you reach an understanding, promptly write it down and have all parties sign it.** You or your lawyer should volunteer to prepare the first draft. If you're paying the tenant some money as part of your agreement, make sure the tenant acknowledges in writing that your payment fully satisfies the claim.

Send a warning notice

Giving the tenant a written notice to cease the disruptive activity can be effective. Even if your oral warning or attempts to negotiate have been unsuccessful, people tend to take written notices a bit more seriously.

Your letter should include:

- details of the problem behavior, including dates and times of the occurrence

- what exactly you want the tenant to do (such as stop having noisy parties, pay for damage to the rental unit, or get rid of a long-term guest)

- the specific lease or rental agreement provision that prohibits this behavior, such as a clause requiring tenants to repair damaged property, or a lease restriction on guests, and

- the consequences for the tenant's failure to comply (such as termination or eviction proceedings).

> **TIP**
> **Involve the cosigner when you send your warning notice.**
> Jim, who rented to three college students in Boston, insisted that each student's parents cosign the lease. When Jim learned that the students had brought in two unauthorized occupants, he wrote to them, pointing out that their lease forbade unapproved residents; and he cc'd their parents. That did the trick. "Once the parents realized that they could be financially responsible for damage caused by these newcomers, they apparently got on the phone, and the newcomers were gone within a couple of days."

What if the tenant doesn't reform, despite your reminder? If you want to get the tenant out, you certainly have grounds for terminating. However, in a sense, you'll have to start over, by giving the tenant a formal termination notice that meets your state's requirements. (Termination notices are explained further, below.)

Try mediating

If your settlement efforts don't work out, you may wish to try bringing in a neutral third party to mediate. Mediation is often available at little or no cost from a publicly funded program. A mediator has no power to impose a decision, but simply helps both sides work out a mutually acceptable solution.

Mediation can make good sense, especially if any of the following are true:

- You've had otherwise positive experiences with the tenant, who seems worth dealing with in the future.
- The tenant agrees to split the cost (if any) of mediation.
- The tenant wants to avoid eviction and the expense and delay of litigation.
- The tenant is up to date on rent (or has cooperated by putting the rent money into some type of escrow account).

Mediation in landlord-tenant disputes is usually fairly informal. The mediator will ordinarily have everyone sit down and express all their issues—even emotional ones. This often cools people off and results in a quick compromise. If not, however, the mediator may talk to each person sequentially to try and determine his or her bottom line. Then, shuttling back and forth, the mediator helps the parties structure an acceptable solution. At some point, everyone has to get back together to sign off.

RESOURCE
Need information on local mediation programs? Call your mayor's or city manager's office, and ask for the staff member who handles "landlord-tenant mediation matters" or "housing disputes." That person should refer you to the public office or business or community group that attempts to resolve these disputes informally, and at little or no cost. Most local courts also provide referrals to community mediation services. For lists of professional mediators and extensive information on mediation, see www.mediate.com.

Represent yourself in small claims court

If your attempts at settling a dispute fail, you may end up having to sue. Fortunately, if the dispute is over a relatively small amount of money (less than $10,000 in most states), you can cost-efficiently represent yourself in small claims court. A few states call small claims courts by other names (such as landlord-tenant court), but the purpose is the same: to provide a speedy, inexpensive resolution of disputes. In a few states, eviction suits can be filed in small claims court.

Avoiding Retaliation Charges

Tenants have a number of legal rights, such as the right to complain to governmental authorities about health or safety problems or the right to be free from illegal discrimination. To ensure that these rights protect tenants, most states forbid a landlord from retaliating against a tenant who asserts them.

A tenant who is avoiding eviction or legal liability may claim your legitimate actions are retaliatory. To counter such claims:

- Establish a paper trail to document important facts of your relationship. For example, set up clear, easy-to-follow procedures for tenants to ask for repairs, and respond promptly.

- Demonstrate that you have a good reason to end the tenancy. In other words, be prepared to prove that your reasons were valid and not retaliatory.

- Have legitimate business reasons for any rent increase or other change in the conditions of the tenancy, and make the changes reasonable. In theory, you may not need a reason to increase the rent (unless you live in a rent-controlled area), but if you have no plausible business reason—such as evidence that local rents have risen—you'll have a harder time countering a tenant's claim that the increase was illegal.

- If a tenant files a complaint with a government agency just before you were going to raise the rent or give the month-to-month tenant a termination notice anyway, wait. In some states, if a landlord's negative act occurs within a certain time from the date of a tenant's complaint, the landlord will have a harder time countering the claim of retaliation. Wait until that time period is up.

Small claims court procedures are relatively simple and don't normally require a lawyer's help. You pay a small fee, file your lawsuit with the court clerk, have the papers served on your opponent, show up on the appointed day, tell the judge your story, and present any witnesses and other evidence. The evidence you bring with you is usually the most important part of your case—for example, a photograph of a damaged house and the convincing testimony of someone who helped you fix it are usually all you need to prevail and recover money over and above the tenant's deposit.

Don't immediately head for small claims court just because it's relatively easy and you're sure you have a good case. If you suspect you won't be able to collect the money owed—from your tenant's paycheck, bank account, or other financial resource—small claims court will be a waste of time. A judgment you can't collect is worthless.

RESOURCE
For more information on small claims court, see the Small Claims Court & Lawsuits section of Nolo.com, which includes a chart of small claims court limits and rules for all 50 states, plus useful articles on preparing your case and testifying in court.

When All Else Fails: Terminations and Evictions

Unfortunately, even the most sincere and professional attempts at conscientious landlording sometimes fail, and you need to get rid of a troublesome tenant. The key to winning an eviction lawsuit (sometimes called an unlawful detainer, or UD, lawsuit) is properly terminating the tenancy before you go to court. Otherwise, you can't proceed with your lawsuit, let alone get a judgment for possession of your property or for unpaid rent. In order to properly terminate, you must give your tenant adequate written notice, in a specified way and form. If after that the tenant doesn't move (or reform), you can file a lawsuit to evict.

Because an eviction judgment means the tenant won't have a roof over his or her head, state laws are usually very demanding of landlords. Each state, and even some localities, such as those with rent control, have their own procedures as to how termination notices and eviction papers must be written and delivered ("served"). Different types of notices are often required for different situations. You must follow the rules and procedures exactly. Otherwise, you'll run into delays in evicting the tenant—and maybe even lose your lawsuit—even if your tenant has bounced rent checks from here to Mandalay.

No matter how solid your reasons for evicting, get ready for the tenant to mount a defense—and possibly win. For one thing, the way that you've conducted business with the tenant may affect the outcome. If the tenant can point a finger at you, such as for acting in retaliation, it may shift attention away from the tenant's wrongdoing and sour your chances of victory.

Eviction itself—that is, physically removing the tenant and possessions from your property—can't be done until you've gone to court and proven that the tenant did something wrong that justifies ending the tenancy. And even then, you can't just move the tenant's stuff out onto the sidewalk and say goodbye. In most states, you must hire the sheriff or marshal to perform that task.

Sending termination notices

For a month-to-month tenancy, termination is theoretically easy: Simply give the proper amount of notice (30 days in most states). You don't usually need to give a reason (unless your property is covered by rent control). For a tenancy governed by a lease, you'll have to wait until it expires on its own at the end of the lease term. You generally aren't required to renew a lease.

But if your tenant has done something wrong, you may not want to wait the 30 days or until the lease expires. State laws allow you to terminate by serving the tenant with one of three different types of notices. Although terminology varies somewhat from state to state, the substance of these notices is remarkably the same. Most states set standards for the content and look of a termination notice, requiring certain language and specifying the size and appearance of type:

- Pay Rent or Quit notices are typically used when the tenant hasn't paid the rent. They give the tenant a few days to pay or move out ("quit").

- Cure or Quit notices are typically given after a violation of a term or condition of the lease or rental agreement, such as a no-pets clause or the promise to refrain from making excessive noise. Typically, the tenant has a set amount of time in which to correct, or "cure," the violation; a tenant who fails to do so must move or face an eviction lawsuit.

- Unconditional Quit notices are the harshest of all. They order the tenant to vacate the premises with no chance to pay the rent or correct the lease or rental agreement violation. In most states, Unconditional Quit notices are allowed only when the tenant has repeatedly violated a lease or rental agreement clause, has been chronically late with the rent, has seriously damaged the premises, or has engaged in illegal activity.

Many states have all three types of notices on the books. But in some states, Unconditional Quit notices are the only notice statutes on the books. This means that you are free to give your tenants a number of days to pay up, fix the problem, or cease the violation, but you don't have to—you can demand that they just leave.

Terminating for late rent payments

Not surprisingly, the top reason landlords terminate a tenancy is nonpayment of rent. In most states, this is grounds for immediately sending a termination notice, giving the tenant a few days—usually three to five—to pay up. The exact number of days varies from state to state. In some states, you don't even need to give the tenant a chance to pay up, but can go straight to using an Unconditional Quit notice.

> **CAUTION**
> **Make sure you know your state rules as to the earliest date you can serve a termination notice.** Some states won't let you send a termination notice (either a Pay Rent or Quit notice or an

Unconditional Quit notice) until the rent is a certain number of days late. Instead, tenants enjoy a statutory "grace period," plus the time specified in the Pay Rent or Quit notice, in which to come up with the rent. (In other states, you may provide for a grace period in your lease.)

If the tenant is late with the rent and you deliver a termination notice—whether or not it gives the tenant a few days to pay the rent—expect a phone call, an email, or a visit from your tenant, hoping to work something out. If you accept rent for the entire rental term, you have canceled the termination notice for that period. In most states, it's as if the tenant had paid on time in the first place.

After all this, what if the tenant is late again with the rent? Check your state's law. In several states, you don't have to give such tenants a second chance—or at least not a third chance, within a certain time period.

If you accept even a partial amount of rent a tenant owes—whether for past months or even just the current month—you will, in most states, cancel the effect of a Pay Rent or Quit notice. But you can still go ahead with your attempts to get the tenant out—just pocket your tenant's payment with one hand and hand over a new termination notice with the other, demanding that the tenant pay the new balance or leave.

> CAUTION
> **If your tenant is in the military or the activated reserves, special rules apply.** Federal law (the War and National Defense Servicemembers Civil Relief Act) requires a court to stay (postpone) an eviction for up to three months unless the judge decides that military service does not materially affect the tenant's ability to pay the rent. The law applies only to evictions for nonpayment of rent, not for other reasons, such as keeping pets in violation of the lease. Nor does it apply if you've terminated a rental agreement with a 30-day notice.

How eviction lawsuits work

When the deadline in the termination notice passes, your tenant is supposed to pack up and leave. Unfortunately, that doesn't always happen. Nor can you just call the police and have them escort the person out. Instead, you must file and win an eviction lawsuit. The resulting court order will give you the right to call a sheriff or marshal and arrange to physically evict a tenant who refuses to leave. The whole process may take weeks—or months—depending on whether the tenant contests the eviction in court.

Eviction lawsuits are filed in a formal trial court (called "municipal," "county," or "justice") or in small claims court. A few states have separate landlord-tenant courts in larger cities, specifically set up to handle evictions. Some states give landlords a choice of where to file; others confine eviction lawsuits to one court or the other. Call the clerk of your local small claims court to find out whether it handles evictions.

If small claims is an option, it's usually best for an eviction, because of its speed and simple procedures. And you can, if you really want to (or if the court won't allow attorneys there anyway) go without a lawyer and save on those fees. Your main job will be to gather evidence to persuade the court to believe your side of the story. But if lawyers are allowed in small claims court in your state, you might want to use one. As described just below, eviction lawsuits are rather tricky, and it may be more effective to hire a pro. (By the way, you can always consult with an attorney; what some states don't allow is for litigants to actually bring lawyers to small claims court to present their cases for them.)

If small claims court isn't an option, you'll have even more reason to hire a lawyer. Regular court is far more complex, with more rules about what kind of evidence can be submitted, and more procedural steps to get to a resolution.

RESOURCE
Nolo's Lawyer Directory can help you find an attorney who's right for you. All participating attorneys promise respectful service, and Nolo's profiles provide more in-depth information than any other lawyer directory about each attorney's experience, qualifications, and personal approach to practicing law.

To get an eviction lawsuit going (in any court), you'll have to follow these steps:

- **File a complaint.** This legal document lists the facts that you think justify the eviction. It also asks the court to order the tenant to leave the property and pay any back rent, any damages directly caused by having unlawfully remained on the property, court costs, and possibly attorney fees. Your complaint doesn't need to be long or complex—in fact, in some states, landlords use a preprinted complaint form, prepared by the court.

- **Serve the tenant.** When you file a complaint, the clerk will assign a date on which the case will be heard by the court. That date is entered on the "summons," a piece of paper that tells the tenant he or she is being sued and must answer your charges in writing and appear in court within a specified number of days or lose the lawsuit. You must then arrange for the tenant to be given the complaint and the summons. In legal jargon, this is called "service of process." State laws are quite detailed as to the proper way to deliver, or "serve," court papers. Most critically, neither you (including anyone who has an ownership interest in your business) nor your employees (if you have any) can serve these papers. The method of delivery is specified as well: Normally, the preferred way is "personal" service, which means that a law enforcement officer or professional process server personally hands the tenant the papers. Failure to properly serve the tenant is one of the most common errors landlords make, and may result in court dismissal of your lawsuit even before trial. Even a seemingly minor mistake—such as forgetting to check a box, checking one you shouldn't, or filling in contradictory information—will increase the chances of your tenant's successfully contesting the lawsuit.

- **The tenant answers.** The tenant must file a document called an "answer" on or before the date printed on the summons. (If the tenant doesn't, and then doesn't show up in court, you'll usually win the lawsuit automatically.) Like your complaint, the answer need not be a complex document, and may be a preprinted form.

The tenant may dispute that what you say is true. Alternatively, the tenant may try to put forth a good legal reason (such as discrimination or retaliation) to excuse what would otherwise be grounds for eviction. This is called an affirmative defense.

Tips on Dealing With a Tenant During an Eviction

To keep things businesslike:

- Avoid all unnecessary personal contact with the tenant during the eviction process unless it occurs in a structured setting, such as a mediation.
- Keep your written communications to the point and as neutral as you can.
- Treat the tenant like he or she has a right to remain on the premises, even though you're trying to prove the opposite. Until the day the sheriff or marshal shows up to evict, the tenant's home is legally his or her castle.

Once you're done with these preliminaries, you'll proceed with your lawsuit. Many eviction cases never end up in trial—for example, because the tenant moves out or negotiates a settlement with the landlord. But each case that does go to trial will have its own unpredictable twists and turns, which can greatly affect trial preparation and tactics. For this reason, you'll probably need to hire a lawyer, if you haven't done so already.

CAUTION

Complete your lawsuit, even if you think you've won already. Never walk away from a lawsuit without formally ending it, even if the tenant moves out or pays what's owed without going to court. Doing so preserves your reputation as someone who uses the courts with respect. If you're simply a no-show, expect a chilly reception the next time you appear in court. In addition, if you don't appear for trial but the tenant does, the tenant may win and be entitled to move back in and collect court costs and attorney fees.

How Tenants May Stop or Postpone an Eviction

In rare instances, a tenant may be able to get a judge to stop an eviction that's already been ordered, but only by convincing the court of two things:

- Eviction would cause a severe hardship for the tenant or family.
- The tenant is willing and able to pay any back rent owed (and your costs to bring the lawsuit) and future rent, as well.

It's very unusual for a judge to stop an eviction—after all, if the tenant's sympathetic predicament (and sufficient monetary reserves) weren't persuasive enough to win the case in the first place, these arguments probably won't be given new weight after the trial.

The tenant may instead ask for a postponement of the eviction. Typically, evictions are postponed in three situations:

- **Pending an appeal.** A tenant who files an appeal may ask the trial judge to postpone ("stay") the eviction until a higher court decides the case.
- **Until the tenant's circumstances improve.** A tenant may be able to persuade a judge to allow a little more time to find a new home.
- **Until the weather improves.** In most states, judges are not required to postpone an eviction on frigid days, but there's nothing to stop a tenant from asking.

Eviction lawsuits are typically decided on the spot or very soon thereafter, after the judge has heard the witnesses and reviewed any relevant laws. If you win, you get an order from the judge (a "judgment") declaring that you're entitled to possession of the property. You may get a money judgment for back rent and court costs and attorney fees, too.

You'll need to take the order to the local law enforcement official, along with the appropriate fee, which the tenant will be expected to pay back as part of your costs. The sheriff or marshal will give the tenant a notice saying that the official will be back, sometimes within just a few days, to physically remove the tenant if necessary.

USA TODAY Snapshots®

Open to misinterpretation
Communication modes that adults find easy to misinterpret the tone:

E-mail 80%

Text message 78%

Letter/written 71%

Telephone 53%

Face-to-face 37%

Source: Harris Interactive survey for Whitepages.com of 2,395 adults Jan. 3–Jan. 5. Margin of error, ±3 percentage points. Respondents could answer more than one

By Mary Cadden and Suzy Parker, USA TODAY 2007

Unfortunately, having a judgment for the payment of money isn't the same as having the money itself. Your tenant may be unable (or unwilling) to pay you, despite the fact that you have a formal court order. Unless the tenant voluntarily pays up, you will have to collect the debt—for example, by using the tenant's security deposit or hiring a collection agency.

If you lose the eviction case, your tenant can stay, and you'll likely end up paying for your tenant's court costs and fees. You may also be hit with money damages if the judge decides you acted illegally, as in the case of discrimination or retaliation.

How not to evict: Illegal "self-help"

As any experienced landlord will attest, there are occasional tenants who do things so outrageous that the landlord is tempted to bypass normal legal protections and take direct and immediate action to protect the property. For example, one landlord with whom we spoke said, "Out of desperation, I asked two tough-looking, armed friends of mine to come over and tell the tenant it was long past time to go."

Don't do anything like this. Shortcuts such as threats, intimidation, utility shutoffs, or attempts to physically remove a tenant are illegal and dangerous.

Today, virtually every state forbids these "self-help" evictions. If you resort to them, you may well find yourself on the other end of a lawsuit.

Even if your state hasn't legislated against self-help evictions, throwing your tenant out on your own is highly risky and likely to land you in more legal entanglements than if you had gone to court for an eviction judgment in the first place. The potential for nastiness and violence is great; the last thing you want is a patrol car at the curb while you and your tenant wrestle on the lawn. And you can almost count on a lawsuit over the "disappearance" of your tenant's valuable possessions, which the tenant will claim were lost or taken when you removed them. Using a neutral law enforcement officer to enforce a judge's eviction order will avoid these potential problems.

RESOURCE

Finding your state's laws and resources on terminations, evictions, mediation, and lawsuits. The Landlords section of Nolo. com includes many state-by-state charts on topics covered in this chapter, including state rules on termination for nonpayment of rent or violation of a lease term, tenants' rights to break a lease, illegal eviction procedures, notice requirements to terminate a month-to-month tenancy, and security deposit disputes in small claims court. The Small Claims Court and Lawsuits section of the Nolo site includes useful articles on mediation, filing a lawsuit, and working with a lawyer. You can also find a list of experienced landlord-tenant lawyers in your state in Nolo's online Lawyer Directory. ●

Don't Want to Do It Alone?
Hiring a Property Manager

B eing a landlord can, at times, turn into a busy job. In the words of Sarah, a San Francisco landlord who rents out half her duplex, "You don't get something for nothing." If your time is already stretched super-thin, you might consider getting help. Fortunately, lots of people make it their business to work as a stand-in rental property owner—they're property managers, and if you find the right one, your rental business will get a lot simpler.

A property manager focuses on renting and maintaining property, by handling tasks from finding and screening tenants to maintaining the property to cleaning it up after a tenant moves out. Of course, there's a catch: Property managers normally charge about 10% of your monthly rental income for their services. And that doesn't count any additional tasks, such as handling terminations or evictions, for which you'll pay extra.

In this chapter, we'll help you decide whether paying to hire a property manager is right for you, by explaining:

- what a property manager does
- when hiring a property manager makes the most financial sense
- how to find and choose a property manager, and
- what to include in your signed agreement with a property manager.

What a Professional Property Manager Does

If managing a rental property sounds like a lot of hassle, hiring a property manager may be just the ticket. Here are some tasks you'll be able to offload:

- **Setting the rental price.** Although the final figure will be up to you, a good property manager should research the going rate for local rentals like yours. Setting a realistic rental price will help keep vacancies low and your income stable.
- **Advertising the property.** A good property manager will know how to best advertise your rental, and will make the most of

different methods (Internet, local papers, or flyers) to distribute the information.

- **Preparing the property.** When you're between tenants, the property manager will clean the place up and arrange for any necessary maintenance work like painting, replacing fixtures, and more. Instead of you trying to cram these tasks into your after-work and weekend schedule, the property manager will bring in professionals to handle them all at once. That means faster results and shorter vacancy periods.

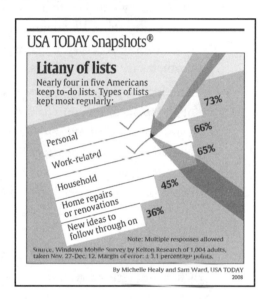

USA TODAY Snapshots®

Litany of lists

Nearly four in five Americans keep to-do lists. Types of lists kept most regularly:

Personal **73%**
Work-related **66%**
Household **65%**
Home repairs or renovations **45%**
New ideas to follow through on **36%**

Note: Multiple responses allowed

Source, Windows Mobile Survey by Kelton Research of 1,004 adults, taken Nov. 27-Dec. 12. Margin of error: ± 3.1 percentage points.

By Michelle Healy and Sam Ward, USA TODAY 2008

- **Screening tenants.** Your property manager may take phone calls from applicants, show them the property, have them fill out applications, interview them, run credit or criminal background checks, and verify employment and rental history. The property manager uses this information to find the best tenant (though you may have a say in the final selection).

- **Moving tenants in.** Once you find an appropriate tenant, the property manager will negotiate the lease or rental agreement, coordinate the tenant's move and provide keys, give the tenant a move-in checklist, and handle any other move-in responsibilities.

- **Collecting rent.** The property manager will collect monthly rent and, depending on the terms of your contract with the manager, deal with problems if a tenant doesn't pay. In most cases, managers will be motivated to collect the rent because their pay is a percentage of the rental income—if there's no income, they don't get a penny.

- **Handling tenant problems.** Late rent isn't the only tenant problem that may crop up (as discussed in Chapter 9). Your property manager will work on resolving all manner of problems and deal with tenant complaints or concerns (though they will not handle an eviction for you). As Rosario, a landlord in El Paso, Texas, says, "I've found that tenants feel more comfortable approaching the property manager than me about issues with the property—maybe they think I'll take it personally if they complain. Anyway, it all works out, because that way they don't wait until the small problems turn into big ones."

- **Keeping the property in good condition.** This means taking care of all repairs and maintenance (described in Chapter 8), as well as regular, general upkeep like mowing and pruning the yard. Usually, a property manager has someone on staff or on call—such as a handyperson—to handle immediate problems, and a list of seasoned professionals to call for more serious issues.

> **CAUTION**
> **Your maintenance and repair costs may go up.** The fees you pay to a property manager probably mean any maintenance problems will be identified quickly—and you'll end up paying someone for even simple tasks (like fixing a broken door lock or tightening a loose hinge), which you might otherwise have been able to handle on your own. When a property manager hires someone to fix a problem, you'll pay not only that worker, but also the manager, for setting up (and possibly supervising) the job.

- **Performing inspections.** A property manager can handle the regular inspections that every property requires, to make sure there's no major damage or problem that needs repair.

- **Managing finances.** Your property manager should also perform certain financial tasks, including collecting, holding, and returning deposits; tracking income and expenses; and sending you regular (monthly or quarterly) reports on these items.

- **Complying with laws and regulations.** A good property management company will know applicable federal, state, and local laws and regulations, like those governing security deposits, rent control, and evictions. This will save your having to study and figure out how to comply with these laws—although you (the property owner) will still retain the ultimate liability for the property and tenants.

> **CAUTION**
> **Lesson learned the hard way: Don't expect regular monitoring from the property manager.** As Darla, who rented out her former home in Seattle, explains: "Because I lived several hours away, I relied on the property managers for regular maintenance. Mostly, I was happy with them, but they didn't catch the fact that my tenants were keeping dogs—and that the dogs were ruining the carpets. Worse yet, before I sold the place and asked the tenants to move, they sprayed the carpets with some oily substance—perhaps to mask the dog odors—which cost me $400 to remove and clean. If I'd lived locally, I could have driven by occasionally, and probably would have spotted the dogs."

Should You Hire a Property Manager?

If you're not sure whether you're ready to pay someone a relatively large amount of cash to manage your property, consider two things: whether you're in a good position to manage the property yourself, and whether property management makes financial sense.

Are you ready to take care of the property yourself?

Having just read about the process of managing a property, you know the basics of what's involved—selecting and managing tenants, keeping the property in good repair, making sure your tenants don't cause trouble in the neighborhood, and handling tenants' departures and the return of their deposits, for example.

Even if you think you're able to handle the serious tasks, there are situations in which hiring a property manager makes good sense. Here are some of them:

- **You live far away.** Maybe you're renting out a vacation home in a remote part of the state, or maybe it's an investment property across the country. Whatever the case, if you can't be right there to handle management tasks, you'll waste a lot of time trying to do so remotely—and your property will probably suffer without someone there to see how the tenants are treating it, handle emergencies, and so forth.

- **You don't want to study the ins and outs.** If you're not interested in learning about and complying with federal and state laws, understanding how to find and screen tenants, or figuring out at least the basics of home repair and maintenance, hiring a property manager is a good idea.

- **You don't have time to spare.** Maybe your successful career is more lucrative than your time spent managing a property could ever be, or maybe you've got your hands full caring for children or an elderly parent. If your life is already jam-packed, adding the stress of managing a rental property may simply be too much to deal with.

- **You own multiple properties.** If you own a multiunit property or several different properties, the amount of time you'll spend being a landlord will go up—but so will the income you'll get from the rent, so hiring a property manager may become more affordable. Even if you aren't at that sweet spot yet, if you plan to be, it's worth keeping in the back of your mind.

> **TIP**
> **You can hire a property manager for a short period of time.** That's what Laura, a landlord with properties in Washington, Nevada, and Florida, did in preparing for a month-long trip to Europe. It allowed her some stress-free travel. On the other hand, she discovered that, "I'd rather work with tenants myself, especially when it comes to choosing

new tenants. I think I'm more concerned than the property manager about finding someone who's easy to deal with. I ended up with an angry tenant (chosen by the company) who tried to get out of paying for damage."

How much does property management cost?

Typically, you'll pay between 6% and 12% of the rental income to the manager. Single-family homes are almost always on the higher end of this percentage scale, because it's more costly to deal with them, per unit, than multifamily properties. To get an idea of what property managers in your area cost, call a few and ask.

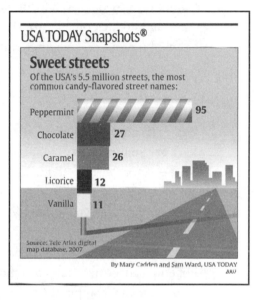

USA TODAY Snapshots®

Sweet streets
Of the USA's 5.5 million streets, the most common candy-flavored street names:

Peppermint 95
Chocolate 27
Caramel 26
Licorice 12
Vanilla 11

Source: Tele Atlas digital map database, 2007

By Mary Cadden and Sam Ward, USA TODAY 2007

! CAUTION
High-maintenance properties mean higher management fees. If your property isn't in good shape, expect to pay more—not only in repairs, but in the property manager's fee. A manager will rightfully assume that it's going to take more time and effort to manage your property than it would to handle a similar property in good condition.

Of course, an advantage to paying a percentage-based fee out of your monthly income is that the property manager will be highly motivated to keep the place occupied. Still, you might also need to factor in various add-on costs, such as:

- **Extra fees to find a new tenant.** Some property managers charge an extra fee to advertise, screen, and move a new tenant in, such as one half the first month's rent. While your initial reaction might be, "Whoa, I'm not paying for that!" take a closer look at the numbers first: The manager might negotiate by setting your monthly fee comparatively lower. And if the manager helps you find a stable tenant who stays several years, wouldn't it be better to pay 8% per month plus a leasing fee rather than 10% a month without a leasing fee? (Then again, if you don't see an adjustment in the manager's prices to account for this fee, this argument loses its luster.)

- **Administrative fees for repairs and maintenance.** You'll need the property manager to hire outsiders—plumbers, electricians, and other repairpeople. What you don't need or want is for your manager to tack on a fee for doing this, so negotiate that ahead of time. Find out also whether you'll have to pay any extra fees if the company buys supplies on your behalf, like paint or carpeting.

⊙ **TIP**

If your homeowners' association maintains the property, don't pay your property manager to do it. If you live in a condominium or other common interest development, your homeowners' association may take care of communal areas, such as garden areas and shared hallways. Make sure your property manager knows what the association is responsible for: You don't want the manager to handle and charge you for repairs you weren't responsible for in the first place. Instead, the property management company should notify the association when it receives a tenant complaint concerning a common area. You may be able to negotiate a lower fee with your property manager because there's less to manage.

- **Minimum monthly fees for unoccupied property.** Some property managers set a baseline monthly fee that they'll get paid even if the property isn't occupied—or if it's occupied by a deadbeat tenant who doesn't pay the rent. This decreases the manager's impetus to find you a tenant, not to mention to choose a good, reliable one who'll pay on time.

- **Full fees regardless of whether the tenant pays the rent.** Allowing the management company to collect its fee even if the tenant hasn't paid on time is a bad idea. You want the property manager as motivated as you are to collect the rent, which means you'll want them to have a financial stake in the tenant's timely payment.

- **Late fees going to the property manager.** Some property managers specify that they get to keep any late fees. Again, this isn't ideal, because it reduces their motivation to make sure the rent is collected on time. You'll also want to be certain late fees don't exceed legal maximums—if they do, look for another property manager.

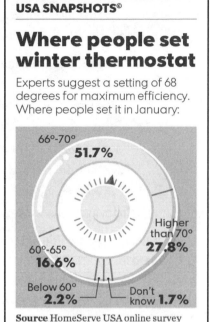

USA SNAPSHOTS®

Where people set winter thermostat

Experts suggest a setting of 68 degrees for maximum efficiency. Where people set it in January:

66°-70°
51.7%

Higher than 70°
27.8%

60°-65°
16.6%

Below 60°
2.2%

Don't know **1.7%**

Source HomeServe USA online survey of 1,891 U.S. adults in February

ANNE R. CAREY AND PAUL TRAP, USA TODAY

● **USA TODAY**   2014

Will the costs undo your profits?

A 6%–12% fee can seem pretty steep if you're just trying to eke out a small profit. To decide whether it makes financial sense, add it to the expense portion of your Monthly Property Expense Estimate, in Chapter 1, and then rerun the numbers to show your expected profits.

Also adjust the other expenses on your worksheet, where appropriate—a slight bump upward in your repair and maintenance costs, but (unless the property manager charges you extra), removal of the costs to market your property. Take a close look at what's included in any prospective property manager's fees, and make additional expense adjustments—for example, if lawn care is part of the package, remove your expected weekly payment to the mowing service.

Comparing Pros and Cons

Use this checklist to help you decide whether the benefits of hiring a property manager outweigh the costs. The more boxes you check in each category, the more you should lean toward that choice.

On the plus side of hiring a manager (check every box that describes you):

☐ I have very little free time to take care of maintenance, tenant communications, and other tasks.

☐ I don't relish the idea of interacting with tenants personally.

☐ I live far from the property.

☐ I can earn enough from rents to comfortably pay the property manager's fees, leaving me free to spend my time elsewhere.

On the minus side of hiring a manager (check every box that describes you):

☐ I have enough free time to spend managing the property, or it's so close to my current house that the time requirements will be reduced.

☐ I'm handy myself, or know a lot of good repairpeople, so there wouldn't be much point in delegating those tasks.

☐ I enjoy the idea of earning money by taking an active role as a landlord.

☐ The fees for high-quality local property managers would all but obliterate my profits anyway.

TIP

The property manager's fee is tax deductible. We discussed various tax deductions in Chapter 6—and this is one of them.

Even if the fees for property management will wipe out all or much of your rental income, you don't have to rule it out entirely. You may find a property manager who will provide limited services for a lower fee— for example, agree that you'll find your own tenants, but the manager will collect the rent and coordinate repairs. The expense may be worth it if it frees you of whichever parts of your responsibilities are hardest to juggle or handle at a distance.

As you study your adjusted numbers, keep in mind that a property is usually its least profitable in the early years. If you wait a couple years more—either paying for property management and losing money, or managing the property yourself until you turn a profit—you may be in a better financial position. At that time, paying for a management company may fit more comfortably within your budget, especially if you can increase rents.

How to Find the Best Property Manager

Anyone can manage a property for you—but that doesn't mean you should let them. Instead, you're looking for a professional manager who knows the business. Many professional property managers are licensed real estate brokers or work for them (as some states require). But it's better if the company is dedicated to property management, not buying and selling real estate. The skills required are very different, and you want someone who is focused on management, not doing it as a side business in the hopes that you, the landlord, will decide to sell the property and use the broker as your selling agent.

Several trade organizations offer education and training leading to designations such as "Certified Property Manager." (These designations are not, however, legal licenses.) What's probably the best program is offered by the Institute of Real Estate Management (IREM), which offers three designations: Certified Property Manager (CPM), Accredited Residential Manager (ARM), and Accredited Management Organization (AMO—and for the management firm, not the individual manager).

To find out more about what these designations mean, visit the IREM's website, at www.irem.org.

Getting recommendations

You may already know of several reputable property managers in your area, but if not, you'll need to start looking for one. Here are some likely resources:

- **Ask friends and family.** Of course, you want to talk to people who are familiar with the rental property market in the area you're looking to hire. Neighbors can be another good resource, especially if you're in an area with a lot of rentals, such as a condo complex.

- **Talk to colleagues and your local apartment association.** Other owners of properties similar to yours are probably your best bet— your needs won't have much in common with those of a landlord for a 50-unit building, for example. However, you might find out whether those large owners belong to an apartment owners' association, and ask whether the association has a "small owners" group.

- **Search professional directories on the Internet.** Visit the website of the Institute of Real Estate Management (IREM) at www.irem.org and click "Find a Professional." Or visit the National Association of Residential Property Managers' (NARPM) website at www.narpm.org and under "search for," click "Property Managers." To find a local or state member of the National Apartment Association, visit the NAA website at www.naahq.org.

With a list of a handful of names, do a quick Internet search to find out whether these managers have websites. If so, you might find out whether a firm specializes in any particular area of residential property management, or whether it's located in close enough proximity to handle your property.

Meeting and choosing among potential managers

Once you've narrowed down your list of potential hires, call three or four of them and arrange to meet and discuss working together. Be prepared to ask some targeted questions, such as:

- **Do you hold any licenses?** Find out whether the agent is a licensed real estate agent (required in some states), and whether he or she has earned any special certifications, like the Certified Property Manager designation through the Institute of Real Estate Management (IREM).

- **How long have you been in the property management business?** You're looking for someone with at least several years' experience.

- **Who will handle my property?** Make sure you meet with the person who will actually be responsible for managing your property (if it's one person). Then find out that particular person's experience level, and make sure you get along—remember, you could be working together quite a bit. Finally, make sure you know who's going to help you out if that person isn't available.

- **How many (and what types of) properties do you manage?** You're looking for someone who's not too busy to comfortably deal with you. If you're working with an individual manager, find out not only how many clients the company has, but how many properties that individual is responsible for. Someone in charge of several multifamily complexes will have little time or incentive to spend on your lowly single-family home (larger contracts are more lucrative). Also find out what type of properties the company deals with—be sure they have experience with properties similar to yours.

- **What are the fees?** You want to know all fees—your monthly fees and any add-ons, for things like finding a new tenant, cleaning a property after a tenant moves out, or delivering a termination notice. Also ask whether you'll be charged, and how much, if the place is vacant.

- **How will you advertise the property?** You want to know that your property manager is using effective advertising methods, especially ones you might not have access to (anyone can put a posting on Craigslist).

- **How do you screen tenants?** Take a look at the written application form (and ensure it doesn't violate any laws on its face, such as those prohibiting discrimination) and find out what background checks the company will conduct and how. Make sure the company is as focused on finding a reliable tenant as you are—despite the fact that the company might be all too happy to receive extra payments for late fees or tenant turnover.

- **How do you handle repairs and maintenance?** Make sure someone will be available to handle any problems, 24 hours a day, seven days a week. Refer to Chapter 8 for a full list of repair and maintenance issues to discuss with your property manager.

- **Do you have a standard property management agreement?** Most management companies do, and as we'll explain below, they're written to benefit the company, not you. Make sure the standard agreement can be altered if necessary. Most companies will resist this, but it's not impossible to find one that will make reasonable adjustments.

- **Do you have a standard lease?** Most property management companies do, and you want to take a look before signing on. As with a property management agreement, a lease agreement will be written to benefit the company first, not you or the tenant. Make sure the lease is fair and legal. In particular, check that the late fees don't exceed the maximum allowed in your state.

- **How will you send financial information?** Your property manager should provide you a regular report that details income and expenses. You'll want to know how often you can expect to receive the report and what format it will be in. Ask for a sample.

- **What kind of insurance do you carry?** It's important that the company carry comprehensive general liability insurance, workers' compensation insurance (to pay for any injuries sustained by employees), automobile insurance, and errors and omissions insurance (in less legal terms, malpractice insurance). Ask to see proof (a "certificate of insurance," on an "ACORD" standard form).

- **Do you have a fidelity bond?** Property managers handle a lot of money—and it isn't unheard of for a less-than-honest employee to skim some off the top. A fidelity bond (in the $1,000,000 range) will protect you if someone makes off with some of your rent money.

- **Do you have references?** Get and call two or three, and make sure they own properties similar to yours. Find out whether they're satisfied with the service they've received, how long they've been working together, and specifics like how long it takes the property manager to respond to inquires, requests, or complaints—both the owner's and the tenant's.

Once your questions have been answered satisfactorily, drive by the properties owned by the references of any manager you're considering hiring, and any other properties you know the manager handles. Take a close look at how well they're maintained. If you have a chance, talk to the tenants—they're likely to give you an unbiased answer on what it's like to deal with the management company. Once you've made your decision, get ready for the next step: signing a property management agreement.

Put It in Writing: Drafting an Agreement With Your Property Manager

For convenience' sake, your property manager's company doubtless has a standard agreement that it will ask you to sign. Every agreement will include some basic provisions, which you'll want to review carefully. Make sure the agreement:

- **Identifies the parties.** This should be fairly straightforward—you and any co-owners should be named, as should the property management company. However, if it's important to you to work with a specific employee, you might want that spelled out in the agreement.
- **Specifies the property.** Make sure the property is sufficiently identified, particularly if it's in a multiunit building or complex.
- **Details the fees you'll pay.** You want the fees very clearly spelled out—the regular fee ("10% of the monthly rent") as well as any add-on fees, or minimum monthly fees paid even if the property is vacant. How often you'll have to pay the fees is also important to see spelled out—often, they're deducted from the rent

payment, with the rest of the payment forwarded to you (be sure the agreement specifies how quickly the company must forward the rent to you, minus its fee). Also be sure you know where and how your rent money is held before it's divvied up—ideally, in an individual trust account.

- **Explains the manager's responsibilities.** Look back to the list of responsibilities at the beginning of this chapter. Are they all covered in the agreement? If not, you'll have a hard time getting the manager to take care of them.

- **Explains your responsibilities.** Your list of responsibilities should be short—making timely reimbursements to the management company for repair expenditures is probably the most important one. But if you've agreed to hire a property manager for limited services only, it will be important to clearly list what you'll still be responsible for handling.

- **Includes the contract's duration.** You don't want a management agreement with an end date in the far future—it decreases the manager's motivation to make sure you're a satisfied customer. On the other hand, you shouldn't expect the contract to be significantly shorter than the tenant's lease period—it wouldn't be fair to the property manager to bring a tenant in, only to have you take over managing the property. No matter how long you agree to continue the management relationship, make sure it's spelled out in the agreement, as well as how much notice will be needed if you or the management company want to end the relationship early (for example, 30 days' written notice). Avoid an agreement that allows you to terminate only for specified reasons.

- **Addresses how much the manager can spend without your authorization.** You'll probably create a reserve account into which you'll deposit money that the manager can use for necessary expenses like repairs. Make sure your agreement specifies how much the manager can spend without prior approval—as well as where and how the money will be held.

- **Doesn't disclaim responsibility.** In many contracts, you'll find a provision in which the property management company attempts to hold itself harmless if its own errors and those of its employees cause you harm or injury. You may also see a related clause, called an indemnity clause, in which you promise to reimburse the company for any losses it suffers as a result of its negligence. Obviously, these are onerous clauses and you should get rid of them if you can. If you can't, you can take some solace if both you and the company have adequate insurance—with insurance properly in place, these clauses will seldom come into play.

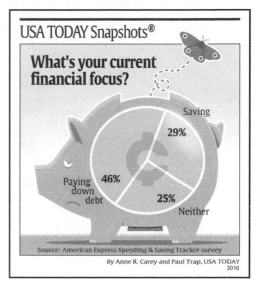

USA TODAY Snapshots®

What's your current financial focus?

Saving 29%

Paying down debt 46%

25% Neither

Source: American Express Spending & Saving Tracker survey

By Anne R. Carey and Paul Trap, USA TODAY 2010

- **Is signed.** Both you and a representative of the property management company should sign and date the agreement.

> **CAUTION**
>
> **What happens if there's a dispute between you and the property manager?** Your agreement should specify whether you must resolve any legal disputes through specific avenues, like mediation or arbitration.

If you find that any of the provisions of an agreement are unacceptable, you'll have to decide whether to challenge them or sign anyway. A property management company should agree to alter an agreement, if your request is reasonable. If not, you may want to consider going elsewhere.

Ready to Quit? Exiting the Rental Property Business

No matter how much you enjoy being a landlord or how profitable it is, at some point, you may be ready to give it up. Maybe you're ready to spend your time on other projects, or spend your money on other investments. Or perhaps you're simply ready to enjoy the benefits of selling the property—the appreciation that's accumulated, in part thanks to your conscientious maintenance.

In this chapter, we'll discuss the decision to stop being a landlord. We'll cover:

- identifying your objectives so you can develop an exit plan that meets them
- deciding when the time is right to get out
- exploring different ways to exit the business, and
- getting the property ready to sell.

What's the Driving Force? Identifying Your Exit Plan Objectives

People have lots of different objectives when they decide it's time to stop being a landlord. Here are some of the most common ones:

- **Realizing profit.** Over the years, you may have watched the value of your property rise. While that looks good on paper, it won't pay your son's college tuition or buy you the sailboat you've always wanted. You may be interested in cashing in on that gain.
- **Avoiding taxes.** The downside to ongoing increases in your property's value is that the taxes you'll owe on profits when you sell are going up, too. Many landlords are hoping to avoid, or at least limit, this tax liability—and, if they previously lived in the property, to preserve their eligibility for the capital gains tax exclusion.
- **Reducing workload.** For some, dealing with a rental property simply gets to be too much bother, or interferes too much with their day job.

- **Passing money to heirs.** Lots of landlords want to make sure they have adequate assets to pass on. They may worry that leaving property to their heirs is more complicated and stressful for these heirs than leaving money.

- **Keeping a property that you want to use yourself.** Some landlords may be done with the business—but not the property. For example, you may have inherited a cottage that you're now ready to retire in.

As you read through this chapter, keep your own objectives in mind, and see which of the options here best meets them.

What Are Your Options? Exploring Opportunities

There are many ways you can stop being a landlord. It may be as simple as putting the house on the market, or as complex as executing a tax-deferred exchange to buy another investment property. We'll explain the details of these and other strategies, below. Chapter 12 explores a "soft" exit strategy: rent to own. Chapter 13 discusses yet another variation—moving into the house yourself and renting out a room.

Sell the property

The most straightforward way to get out of the rental property business is to sell the property. Selling your property has the advantage of being relatively simple to do—you may have done it before with a personal residence—and it gives you an immediate (and often large) amount of cash to spend any way you please.

But selling your home has some disadvantages, too. First of all, it involves high transaction costs. If you hire a real estate agent, you'll pay a commission (usually 5%–6%). That doesn't count the cost of getting the property ready for sale, or any of the other transaction costs that are commonly paid by the seller (which customarily vary by geographic area). Altogether, you could spend up to 10% of the sale price just on these costs.

But the transaction costs won't be your biggest expenses—they'll probably pale in comparison to your capital gains tax bill. For example, if you bought a house four years ago for $200,000 and you sell it now for $300,000, you'll pay taxes on approximately $100,000 (though probably a bit less after adjusting the basis, which we'll explain further below). Assuming a long-term federal capital gains tax rate of 15%, that's $15,000 to the federal government alone. States also collect capital gains taxes.

What's Your Long-Term Capital Gains Tax Rate?

Prior to 2013, long-term capital gains were taxed at 15%. But the picture became more complicated after Congress passed the "fiscal cliff tax deal" on January 1, 2013. As of that date, the rates became:

- 20% for married couples filing jointly with income of $450,000 or more and singles whose income is $400,000 or more
- 15% for earners in the 35%, 33%, 28%, and 25% brackets, and
- 0% for earners in the 15% and 10% brackets.

This leaves most people subject to the 15% capital gains rate. We will, therefore, use this figure for purposes of illustration in the discussions below. But if you fall into one of the other categories, be sure to adjust the examples' outcomes accordingly.

CAUTION

Short-term capital gains are taxed at ordinary income tax rates. If you've owned your property for a year or less and are selling it at a gain, you'll be taxed at your ordinary income tax rate—probably much higher than 15%! You might be better off waiting to sell until you've held the property for more than one year.

How to Estimate Your Capital Gains Tax

Worried about how much you're going to pay in capital gains taxes? Do some rough calculations first. Your capital gains tax liability is based on your purchase price, but you're allowed to increase that amount (called the "basis") to account for certain expenses, thereby decreasing your taxable gain. Include these adjustments when you calculate your tax liability.

Step 1: Start with your purchase price. Then add your closing costs, such as title fees, escrow fees, and recording fees. Add only the costs you paid, and don't count any amounts in escrow for future payment, like taxes or insurance premiums. (If you're not sure whether an expense qualifies, look at IRS Publication 551, *Basis of Assets*, available at www.irs.gov.)

Step 2: Did you make any improvements to the property? If they have a useful life of more than one year, you can add those costs to the basis. There are a few other expenses that can adjust your basis, but they won't apply to most people. These include things like zoning fees and legal fees—for example, for defending a challenge to title. See Publication 551, above, if you think one of these exceptions may apply to you.

Step 3: Estimate how much you think you can sell your home for, based on an honest assessment of its fair market value.

Step 4: Reduce the sale price by the cost of your sale expenses, such as broker fees, title fees, and escrow fees.

Step 5: Subtract the Step 2 figure—the adjusted purchase price—from the Step 4 figure—the adjusted sales price. This is the amount you will be taxed on as a capital gain, not counting the depreciation you must recapture (at a higher tax rate).

In addition to taxes on your gain, you'll have to pay taxes on the "recapture" of depreciation you took over the years. As explained in Chapter 6, the IRS requires you to take annual deductions to account for the decreased value of your rental building (but not the land it sits on) caused by normal wear and tear.

On residential property, the IRS arbitrarily set the "life" of the property at 27.5 years. That means that over 27.5 years, you're allowed to deduct the purchase price of the property (minus the land) in equal amounts. So if you bought a property with a house on it worth $100,000, each year you probably deducted around $2,750.

This works great while you're a landlord and are taking the deduction, but when you're ready to sell, you must pay tax on any profits that essentially paid you back for the depreciation deductions you took. The tax rate depends on when you bought the property, but if it was after May 6, 1997, it's fairly safe to say you'll pay a 25% capital gains tax.

As you can see, selling the property can be expensive. But although these tax rates seem high, they're considerably lower than most of us pay on our regular income.

Avoid taxes with a 1031 exchange

If you read the information above and are horrified at the tax bill that might accompany a sale, you might be interested in the "1031," "like-kind," or "Starker" exchange. In a 1031 exchange, you can defer paying taxes on the sale of a business or investment property when you reinvest your gain in other business or investment property.

Despite the name, you don't literally swap one property for another— you can sell your property to any buyer and find a property you want to purchase from any seller. But to qualify as an exchange, you must meet certain requirements. Most importantly, you have 45 days from the sale of the first property to find and identify potential properties to purchase. Within 180 days of the sale, you must actually purchase one or more of those properties. During that time, the sale proceeds can never be in your hands, or the transaction won't be considered an exchange. Instead, all the cash from the sale must be held in an escrow account. (You'll usually hire a third party, called a qualified intermediary, to hold the cash for you—your transaction costs will be a little bit higher as a result.)

Although this arrangement allows you to defer capital gains taxes from the sale, you'll have to pay tax eventually, when you sell the property bought in the exchange. (The exception would be if you do another exchange, in which case your taxes will be deferred again.) However, to fully defer your taxes, the new property you buy has to be worth the same as or more than the old property you are selling. You can also defer the taxes on the recapture of depreciation you've taken on your current property, discussed above.

Exchanging property provides other advantages, too. For example:

USA SNAPSHOTS®

Who does your income taxes?

● 2009 ● 2014

A professional
54%
49%

Me
30%
37%

Another family member
13%
11%

Not sure
4%
3%

Source Rasmussen Reports in February 2009 and February 2014

ANNE R. CAREY AND PAUL TRAP, USA TODAY

● **USA TODAY**   2014

- **You can leverage your investment into a higher value property.** If the value of the property you currently own increases significantly, you may want to trade up to a more expensive property or properties that yield higher rents. For example, if the rental house you bought for $100,000 is now worth $500,000, you may use your gain to purchase an eight-unit building that costs $900,000. Because you aren't paying taxes, you have more cash available for such a leveraged investment.

- **If you're tired of the day-to-day management of being a landlord, you can buy a lower-maintenance property or buy into an exchange company.** For example, you can exchange an active rental property for undeveloped land you think will appreciate soon. Or you can purchase a fractional share in an investment property (known as a tenancy in common). In the most sophisticated arrangements, you own a part of a large commercial property, with a professional company managing it and distributing rent payments to you, with very little other responsibility. Be aware, however, that exchange companies charge fees, and you'll pay capital gains on the dividends as they're paid each year. Additionally, the buy-in price is high—often several hundred thousand dollars.

- **You can buy multiple properties.** While there are some rules about the number and types of properties you can buy, you can exchange a single property for several different investment properties.

- **You can continue to depreciate property.** If you have depreciated your current property to or near the maximum amount allowed, a 1031 exchange gives you the opportunity to start fresh with a new property. However, the adjusted basis of the current property transfers to the replacement property. That means you can take depreciation deductions only on the new property reduced by the depreciation you've already taken on the old one.

Because 1031 exchanges have very technical requirements, see your tax or legal adviser if you're considering one. Also, if you pass away during the exchange period, your heirs could face adverse tax consequences.

Offer seller financing to home buyers

If you're ready to sell your property but aren't interested in reinvesting in another business or investment property, you have another option to help soften the tax blow: an installment sale, sometimes called "seller financing." With an installment sale, you act as a lender as well as a seller, letting the buyer pay you over time. You may be the primary mortgage holder or a secondary mortgage holder.

Buyers are attracted to installment sales because they avoid the expense or hassle of dealing with a traditional lender, and because installment sales offer flexibility.

For example, a buyer who is self-employed—and can't show regular income despite a profitable business—may have a hard time getting a traditional loan. Or maybe the buyer needs a lower monthly payment than the bank will offer, and you're able to offer more creative financing.

But installment sales aren't just good for buyers—you may benefit, too. First of all, you'll earn interest on the money lent to the buyer, receiving a stable, steady return on your investment. Additionally, you can spread out payment of your capital gains taxes, which need to be paid only in the year you receive the actual gain. And your gain will be partly the loan principal, so in the early years, when most of each payment is usually interest, your capital gains tax bill will be low. (You will still be taxed on the interest income, at ordinary income tax rates.) This frees more money for other investments or uses.

Of course, there are drawbacks to the installment sale. Perhaps the biggest risk is the possibility that the buyer won't make its payments. As a secured lender (one who has filed a mortgage or deed of trust), you'd have the right to seek payment through a foreclosure, but that's an expensive and time-consuming process. And if you were the second mortgage holder, you'd be paid only after the first mortgage holder is paid.

The other major drawback is the risk that the buyer will pay the loan off early. If this happens, you'd have all the remaining taxable gain due in that year, which could wreak havoc on a well-planned tax strategy. Although you might be able to limit this possibility by including prepayment penalties on the loan, many states limit the amount of any prepayment penalty.

TIP
You can combine a 1031 exchange with an installment sale. This topic is beyond the scope of this book, but if you're interested, speak with a financial or tax adviser.

Move into the property yourself

Perhaps you've been holding onto your property so that you can someday retire or move into it. This approach offers certain tax benefits.

If you convert a property you have owned for at least two years to your main home and live there for two out of the five years before its sale, you don't have to pay tax on the portion of your gain that's attributable to your personal use. The maximum exclusion under this provision is $250,000, or $500,000 if you're married and filing jointly. (If that sounds different from the way you thought the capital gains tax exclusion worked, you're right: In 2008, Congress changed the calculation method in order to collect more taxes.) If you own and live in a multiunit property, you can use the exclusion on a fractional basis, excluding gain on the portion of the property that was your principal residence.

For example, if you buy a house in 2009 and rent it out for four years, then live in it for an additional six years, you can exclude 60% of your gain, and will have to pay taxes on only 40%. But this won't help you avoid taxes on your recaptured depreciation deductions.

For more information, see IRS Publication 523, *Selling Your Home*, available at www.irs.gov.

> CAUTION
> **Did you acquire your property in a 1031 exchange?** If so, you must live in it for five years, not two, before you can take the primary residence exclusion.

Bring in a co-owner

If you're tired of being the sole owner and caretaker of your property, you could ask someone to buy in. Legally speaking, you'd turn the ownership into a tenancy in common—a form of joint ownership that allows you and co-owners to hold property in unequal shares. Neither of you needs the other's permission to sell your interest, and you can decide how to divide up, use, and care for the property.

You may be able to find a buyer who's interested in this arrangement, and is willing to manage the property. If you also act as the mortgage holder, you'll have monthly income at the same time. See a legal or tax adviser for details.

Donate the property to a charitable remainder trust

Though donating your property to a charity may seem like a money-losing proposition, it can have significant tax advantages. You can name yourself and your spouse as beneficiaries of the trust, creating an income stream for the rest of your life, then donate the remainder (the property) to a charity of your choice.

You can also take a significant tax deduction, based on the projected value of the benefit the charity will receive (after your death) and the type of charity you donate the property to. For more information on this and other estate planning strategies, see *Plan Your Estate*, by Denis Clifford (Nolo).

What Rights Does the Tenant Have If You Sell?

If you have tenants living on your property at the time you decide to put it on the market, you'll need to understand their rights (and yours) during the selling process and beyond. (If the property is vacant, you can skip this section.) Dealing with current tenants can be a challenge (and a possible hindrance to a sale), which is why many owners wait until the property is vacant before selling.

Tenants with leases will continue to have the right to live on the property until the lease ends, despite the change in ownership. In other words, the new owner will step into your shoes, and must honor the lease just as you did. This doesn't mean, however, that you or a prospective owner can't approach tenants and ask to buy them out of their leases. Tenants have no obligation to negotiate with you or the buyer, but many will, seeing an opportunity to make some money.

USA TODAY Snapshots®

Why people move

46% Housing-related
27% Family-related
18% Work-related
8% Other reasons

Source: Census Bureau, 2005-06 data

By David Stuckey and Veronica Salazar, USA TODAY 2008

What Does a Buy-Out Cost?

When deciding how much rent to charge, you looked at the state of the market—was it hot or cold, and what were the rents for properties like yours? You'll use the same approach, and add in some individual factors, if you decide to try to end a current tenancy early by buying out your lease-holding tenants.

First, understand that the tenants will have to find another place to live. What rent will they have to pay to find a comparable unit? If they are long-term, good tenants, whom you've wisely kept around by making modest rent increases over the years, if the market is hot (and rents for comparable rentals are high), and there are few comparable rentals available, your tenants will be facing a steep uptick in rent per month. Expect to pay at least the difference between their current rent and the expected new rent, times the number of months left on the lease. On the other hand, if the market is soft and the cost of a similar rental is close to their current rent, your offer could be much lower.

Next, determine whether you'll include help on moving costs. You might be inclined to skip this—after all, you wouldn't be helping them move at the end of the lease. But here is where you need to think creatively and keep your goal—a vacant property—in mind. Suppose you're asking them to leave six months early. Your tenants will be losing interest on the moving money when they spend it six months early. Offer at least to cover this sum. Throw in a bit more to compensate them for the inconvenience this sudden move entails—and keep in mind that disruptions that involve kids' schooling, commuting, and loss of a familiar neighborhood are hard to quantify but mighty important to the people involved.

Before concluding that existing tenants will enjoy continued residence under a lease that exists at the time of the sale, check the lease itself.

A few, especially those custom-drafted by attorneys familiar with the property and the current owner/landlord, include a clause providing for early termination in the event that the property is sold before the lease termination date. Such a clause might say, for example, that the lease will terminate 60 days after escrow once a sale has closed. In a lawsuit, courts tend to uphold these clauses, especially if they provide tenants with a reasonable notice period.

Tenants who rent on a month-to-month basis present you and the new owner much more flexibility. As you know, you can terminate month-to-month tenants with proper notice, 30 days in most states. While you may not terminate for an illegal (retaliatory or discriminatory) reason, ending a tenancy in order to prepare and show the property (which you would do), or to live in it once it's purchased (which the new owner would do) is legal in every state. Some long-term monthly tenants are entitled to slightly more notice in some states, but the general rule is the same—you can end their tenancies with relative ease.

If You Decide to Sell: Getting Ready

If you decide to sell the property, even in a 1031 exchange or installment sale, you'll have to deal with putting your house on the market and finding a buyer. A little advance planning will help you maximize your return.

Is now a good time to sell?

Many factors affect whether it's a good time to sell your rental property. Unless you have no choice in the matter—for example, you need the cash, or a life change has made managing a property impossible—it's worth considering whether now is the best time to put your place on the market. Consider these factors:

- **Your local real estate market.** Real estate markets fluctuate—and they're often intensely local. What's happening can vary by city, neighborhood, block, or even street, so make sure you understand what's being sold nearby and at what price. If you know the market is cold—that there are more houses on the market than there are buyers—you can't expect to command the same price for your property as you would if the market were hot (if there were more buyers than available houses). In a cold market, consider whether you'd rather wait to see if prices increase. (But keep in mind—if the property isn't producing income, this could end up costing you more in the long run, as you continue to pay for taxes, maintenance, insurance, and to make regular monthly mortgage payments.)

- **The condition of the property.** Over the years, you've worked to conscientiously maintain the property. But you can't necessarily say the same for your tenants. And if you have long-term tenants, you may not have made a lot of improvements or accounted for regular wear and tear, either. You might need to wait until you can invest some cash up front before putting the property on the market.

- **Whether the property is currently occupied.** Whether you want to offer an occupied property when you sell may depend on who you expect your buyer to be—an individual looking for a home, or an investor looking for an income-producing property. Either way, it may be easiest to show the property when it's empty, so if you are between tenants, this may be a good time to make a sale. (On the other hand, some buyers will be happy to find a property with a stable, income-producing tenant—particularly if they themselves are first-time landlords, perhaps buying your duplex.)

- **The effect that selling will have on your tax liability.** As discussed above, when you sell can significantly impact your tax liability. Make sure you understand the consequences—for example, if you sell at a gain after owning a property less than a year, any gain will be a short-term capital gain, taxed at your current income tax rate. If that's higher than the current long-term capital gains rate of 15% (for most people), you might want to hold off to qualify for the lower rate.

Hire an agent or sell it yourself?

The vast majority of property owners enlist real estate agents to help them sell. Real estate agents serve many functions: They help set a realistic price for the property, prepare it for sale, advertise it, find and show it to prospective buyers, negotiate and close the sale, and handle paperwork to make sure the whole process goes smoothly.

Of course, these services come at a cost—typically 5% to 6% of the sale price. And you, as the seller, will normally be expected to pay the full cost, with your agent splitting the commission with the buyer's agent.

Some sellers instead choose to sell the property themselves. They reason that they can handle a lot of the basic tasks an agent takes care of, and that the biggest challenge—marketing the property—should be no problem, because many buyers look at properties on the Internet. Having saved the cost of the commission, they can easily afford to hire an attorney or title officer to help with the closing. Other expenses may include the cost of online listing services, like www.forsalebyowner.com or www.fsbo.com, which help increase exposure and traffic to the property.

But selling a property yourself can be harder than it looks. First, you've got to do enough research to set your starting price just right— too high, and you may drive away potential buyers, who are unlikely to return after your house goes stale on the market. Also expect to spend large amounts of time on tasks like coordinating visits by prospective buyers, evaluating offers and deciding whether to accept or counteroffer, and making sure all the formalities that lead to a closing—title insurance, removing contingencies, and more—are properly handled.

If you instead decide to work with an agent, you'll want to choose the best (especially because you won't pay a premium to do so—the standard commission remains the same). You're looking for someone who is experienced, trustworthy, and professional. Ideally, this means someone who's been operating in the area where you're selling for at least three years, has handled many transactions involving rental properties, and promptly returns calls and schedules appointments with interested buyers. If you're doing a 1031 exchange or an installment sale, find an agent experienced in that field.

Ask other rental property owners in the area for recommendations, and interview at least three potential agents. Below are some questions you can ask.

Real Estate Agent Interview Questions

☐ Do you work full-time as a real estate agent? (Best answer: Yes.)

☐ How long have you been in the real estate business? (The longer the better, but at least three years.)

☐ Do you have additional certifications beyond your general real estate license? If so, what are they? (More certifications show a commitment by the agent to professional development.)

☐ How many residential investment real estate transactions have you been a part of in the past year? (Should be a minimum of ten.)

☐ In how many of those did you represent the seller? (Best answer is "all of them"; should be at least half.)

☐ What was the price range of homes you sold in the last year? What was the average price? (Should be about your price range.)

☐ Do you specialize in certain types of property? (Should be the type of property you're selling, like a single-family house or condo.)

☐ Do you specialize in a certain geographic area? (Should be the geographic area where you're looking to sell.)

☐ Do you partner with other agents or use assistants? (If so, find out whom you'll be working with, what their real estate experience is, and what they'll be doing.)

☐ How will I reach you? Are there days or times you're unavailable, or do you have vacations planned? (Make sure you can reach the agent when you need to. If you plan to sell soon, make sure the agent will be readily available.)

☐ Can you provide at least three names of landlords who are recent clients and sold their investment properties with you, who will serve as references? (Only acceptable answer is "Yes.")

Will the buyer be an investor or a home buyer?

Whether you expect to sell your house to an investor or to someone who will live in the property is very important. The two have very different objectives. A home buyer looking for a place to live will walk in and say, "Can I imagine myself living here?" But a shrewd investor will want to know, "Will I make money renting this property out?" And the situation may be mixed if, for example, you're selling a duplex in which the buyer will live in one part and rent out the other.

USA TODAY Snapshots®

Moving questions

The information that relocating workers and families request most from relocation consultants:

Demographic/ crime data	699 requests
Employers in a specific industry	436
Referrals to doctors/ dentists	393
Recruiters/ Temporary agencies	373

Source: IMPACT Group

By Anne R. Carey and Paul Trap, USA TODAY 2011

Of course, you won't always know who the buyer will be, and you'll want to be prepared in any case. But you may be able to make an educated guess. For example, if you've been the only rental on the block in a desirable neighborhood for the last several years, it's highly likely an interested buyer will consider moving into the place. On the other hand, if you own a condo in a development in which more than half the units are rented, investors may come around looking.

If there's any possibility you'll sell to an investor, part of your sales preparation should involve showing that the property is capable of delivering a healthy return. Your real estate agent, if you work with one, will likely help you prepare a brochure, "pro forma," or similar document that shows prospective buyers the property's potential profitability. This document will include much of the same information you may have had access to when you bought, including the number of units (in your case, probably only one or two) and how much each one rents for each year. This figure—the income—is reduced by the vacancy rate and normal operating expenses.

Your agent will probably encourage you to present these numbers in the best possible light. In fact, the numbers will probably be based on the property's potential, even if you're not realizing that full potential (but make it clear that the numbers are potential, to avoid a charge later that you misled the buyer). For example, even though you've rented your house for $1,000 per month to the same reliable tenant for the last six years, the new owner may actually be able to ask $1,200 per month if it's clear that the market for a property like yours has gone up. Or, perhaps you spent $15,000 replacing the roof last year, which made your expenses unusually high—call this out as an unusual and long-lasting improvement, and note if you can that you don't anticipate significant spending in the next year.

> **CAUTION**
> **It may be time to cut expenses.** Because investors may ask how much you actually spent on maintenance and improvements in the previous year, try to keep these numbers reasonable in the months before you sell. Don't defer needed maintenance—it will cost you more in the long run—but consider holding off on unnecessary improvements.

The savviest investors will want to know what you've actually spent, and will base their own profitability calculations on these numbers. If you get a lower offer as a result, be prepared to justify a higher asking price. For example, you may tell a prospective purchaser, "Because I live far away and didn't have a lot of time to deal with this property, I rented it to a reliable tenant at a below-market rate, even after rents went up in the area. But in this great neighborhood, with low vacancy rates, you could easily find a tenant willing to pay $200 more per month."

If you anticipate selling to someone who plans to live in the house, you'll have a whole different set of objectives. Most important will be making the property physically attractive, as discussed below, under "Preparing the property for sale."

Of course, it's difficult to make a house sparkle if a tenant is still living there. You can't control the tenant's taste in furniture or level of cleanliness. Here are some possible ways to reach your goals without getting resistance from the tenant:

- **Negotiate a move out.** As explained above, if the tenant is on a lease, you may be able to work out an early termination. For example, you could offer to pay moving expenses, pay the tenant a small fee, or reduce the rent for a short period in exchange for moving out more quickly.

- **Pay for a cleaning service.** If you don't want or can't get your tenant to move out, you could instead hire someone to clean the place—maybe once for a thorough cleaning, then regularly to maintain it in good condition. Don't expect the tenant to pay for this. It will still be worth the cost, if it presents your property in the best possible light.

- **Offer to pay for the spruce-ups.** If your tenant has a lot of stuff cluttering the place up, offer to pay for a storage facility, or provide onsite storage if available. You might also want to buy inexpensive items—a new comforter, shower curtain, and so forth—to enhance the appearance of the place.

CAUTION
Be sure to follow state law when showing an occupied property. Most states regulate the reasons you may enter rented property, and how to give notice to your tenants. Check your state's entry laws (find yours in the Landlords section of Nolo.com) and be sure to give adequate notice. Uncooperative or hostile tenants can ruin a showing or open house, so it pays to get your tenants on your side with, for instance, an offer to reduce the rent for the time the property is on the market.

"Staging" Can Bring Faster Sale, Higher Price

Sellers must work harder these days to attract buyers. Yet oddly enough, the trick to making your home stand out is often to make both the interior and exterior look generic, almost bland. And that's where home staging comes in.

"The philosophy is the buyer must be able to picture themselves living in your home," says Fran Freedman, 65, a lawyer in Philadelphia. "The decor should be understated so they can say, 'This would be the perfect place for my...'"

Does it work? When Coldwell Banker Residential Brokerage in Los Altos, California, looked at nearly 2,800 properties in eight U.S. cities in 2004, they found that the staged homes, on average, sold in half the time that the non-staged homes did. The sellers with staged homes ended up with 6.3% more than their asking price, on average, while sellers with non-staged homes sold for 1.6% more.

The cost of hiring a company to stage your home tends to range from $1,800 to $3,800 but can go much higher, depending on the size of the house and the amount of work involved.

Judee von Seldeneck put her staged home in Philadelphia on the market in 2006; it sold in one day, for $700,000.

From moving shrubs to planting flowers, to replacing the knobs on kitchen cabinets and ripping up the carpet on the stairs, every change was made to accentuate the house's best features. There were even pumpkins on the porch to lend a homey, inviting look.

Inside, the stagers "put furniture that looked comfortable but not too heavy, not cluttered," says von Seldeneck, CEO of an executive search firm. The books on shelves, colors of the rug, the furniture—all were "geared more toward younger people."

She spent $8,000 on the job and says, "It was the best money I ever spent."

Short of hiring a company to do the work, there are some simple steps any seller can take to stage a home:

"Staging" Can Bring Faster Sale, Higher Price (cont'd)

- **Cleaning.** The house should be Q-tip clean. Every surface should sparkle; every groove should be dirt-free.
- **Color.** Dark walls make the house look smaller. Walls should be off-white, or have earthy tones if the room has lots of light. Ideally, the carpet would be "real estate beige."
- **Focal point.** To think like a professional stager, stand at the doorway of each room. What features do you want to accentuate? Where's the focal point? (A room should have only one.) Arrange the furniture so the eye is drawn to the focal point.
- **Dining room.** Take out the leaves from your dining table and put no more than four chairs around it. Set the table as if for a meal, and put an appealing centerpiece in the middle.
- **Kitchen.** The exterior of the refrigerator should be bare. Store any appliances out of sight. Hide the trash can, and put the sponge and soap under the sink. You can spruce up an outdated kitchen simply by changing the knobs and hinges.
- **Master bedroom.** Buy a new bedspread, if necessary.
- **Bathroom.** Replace bar soap with liquid. Coordinate all towels using one or two colors. Fold them in thirds and hang them neatly. Clean or replace the shower curtain. Make sure all grout is clean and in good condition.
- **Outside.** Keep the lawn mowed and the edges neat. Trim shrubs, especially around windows. Put flowering plants near the front door. Does the house need painting? Consider painting or staining the front door; it's one of the least expensive ways to spruce up the entry. If there's furniture on the porch, make sure it isn't plastic but rather good wicker or wrought iron. Power wash or stain the deck.

USA TODAY "'Staging' results in faster sale, richer price," by Noelle Knox, October 27, 2006.

Preparing the property for sale

Whether you're moving a tenant out or dealing with a vacant property, you'll want to take some active steps to make things look their best in preparation for sale. You're looking to appeal to the broadest spectrum of buyers so that you can sell quickly at a competitive price. Our advice in Chapter 3 on sprucing up a rental property applies also to preparing a house for sale.

But before you start sprucing up, you may have some deferred maintenance to deal with—repairing dry rot or fixing leaking windows, for example. As much as you may have tried to stay on top of such problems, some may have escaped the tenant's and your notice (or been caused by the tenant).

Leaving minor maintenance matters for the next owner to deal with is usually a mistake. For one thing, in most states, you'll have to disclose problems that you know about, and you'll be in a weaker bargaining position as you and the buyer argue over each necessary change. Ultimately, your house value will go down.

For another, signs of deferred maintenance are a big red flag for potential buyers. They may worry that the property has other hidden problems. If they plan to rent the property out, especially if they plan to keep the same tenants, they may be concerned that your poor main-tenance means the current tenants are unhappy or unlikely to stay. Still, if something major like the roof is old but still functional, you may be best off reducing your price accordingly, or offering a "credit" to the buyer to make the change. This will save you the effort of either taking care of it yourself or negotiating it in the purchase agreement. If a buyer says, "I'm knocking $15,000 off the offer price to replace the roof," you can confidently reply, "Actually, the asking price was set based on com-parable properties, but discounted for the cost of a new roof."

RESOURCE
For more information on all aspects of selling a home, see *Nolo's Essential Guide to Selling Your Home,* by Ilona Bray (Nolo). ●

A Slower Exit: Rent-to-Own Arrangements

Another exit strategy involves selling your investment property to the current tenants. Of course, when you're ready to sell, you can always let them know that the property is going to be on the market and encourage them to put in a bid. But if you know in advance when you want to sell—say, in one to three or even five years from now—you may be able to set up the tenant-buyer scenario at the beginning of the tenancy. Such an arrangement offers both significant advantages and some major risks.

The terms "rent to own" and "rent to buy" are shorthand ways of describing what's legally known as an option contract (to buy the house). Here's how it works: In a contract that's ideally separate from the lease but dependent on the tenant's faithful adherence to the lease terms, the landlord gives the tenant the option to buy the property within a specified period or at a specified date, for a certain price (or manner of arriving at a price; more on that below).

The landlord doesn't exactly give the option away; tenants typically pay for it, normally in an up-front fee to the tune of several thousand dollars. You can also add to your agreement that all or a portion of the tenant's rent payments—most likely a premium added to the fair market rent—up until the time of sale will go toward paying down the principal amount owed on the sale.

Rent-to-own setups are attractive to tenants who are going through short-term hard times and cannot presently buy a home. Perhaps they've been laid off or lost their own home to foreclosure so that they must rent for a while. Or, a medical situation may have temporarily interrupted work and income. These tenants may well be able to buy a home in the near future, as their financial and employment pictures improve, their credit scores go up, and they become eligible for a loan. For continuity's sake (nearness to jobs, school, friends and family), they may be looking for a rental that they can imagine would be a good permanent home for them someday soon.

Advantages and Disadvantages of Rent to Own

Renting to tenants who hope to someday buy their rented home can be a real boon to an owner planning on selling. Because the accompanying leases are at least two years long, you'll avoid the uncertainty and expense of tenant turnover. If the tenant exercises the option and buys the property, you will skip the cost of putting on a regular sale—no fix-up and staging fees and, most importantly, no brokers' commissions. You'll also be blissfully clear of the hassle and stress involved in selling real estate.

Tenants who hope to someday own their rented home will likely be conscientious when it comes to taking care of the property. You can even formally turn over some maintenance responsibilities to them. And because your option contract should specify that they must be "in good standing" with respect to the underlying lease, at the time they exercise the option or even throughout the entire life of the lease, they'll be motivated to pay the rent on time and not cause problems.

Option contracts do, however, have their downsides. Granting an option ties the hands of the landlord in significant ways. Before the option is exercised, you cannot sell to another person or entity (unless that buyer knowingly agrees to buy a property that can be bought out from under him or her by the tenant in the near future, an unlikely prospect). Nor can you readily use the property as collateral for a loan. For example, it may be difficult to get a second mortgage to finance a child's college education—the bank will hesitate because if it has to foreclose and becomes the owner, it will want to sell the home—but the property will be encumbered by the option, which will make it practically unsaleable.

Depending on the laws of your state, you may also have to make disclosures concerning the property and its condition when you and the tenant sign an option contract. These disclosures are no different than the ones that sellers make when involved in a regular house sale, concerning such things as proximity to flood plains and fault lines, the physical condition of the property (mentioning everything from cracked foundations to leaky hot tubs to peeling linoleum), and so on.

Finally, understand that once the tenant properly exercises the option, that contract becomes an irrevocable sales contract. It should be clear on all essential issues. If you want to avoid hassles and the possible disintegration of the sale, you should make the terms of the sale clear right now, in the option contract. Omitting issues like when and in what manner the tenant may exercise the option, the terms of payment, time and place of closing, nature of title to be given, and any adjustments to be made at closing, risks getting into later arguments about these issues—serious arguments that might scuttle the deal. In short, offering a rent-to-own option is not as simple as inserting a lease clause saying, "During the lease term, Tenant will have the option to buy the premises for $XXX." Properly done, it's a sales contract, and will take some work (and professional assistance, from a broker and a real estate lawyer, too). Do not insert an option clause in your lease and think it will work. It won't.

The Option Price

Because you're narrowing your use of the property, as explained above, you can fairly expect to charge the tenant for the option. Ideally, you'll get this fee up front, though some rent-to-own arrangements allow tenants to pay a portion of the option in the form of extra rent each month. Calculating the fee based on 1% of the agreed-upon sale price is common (and we've heard of fees as high as 5%), but don't simply leap at such a figure without doing some further analysis.

The amount you should realistically charge will depend on the value you place on foregoing the rights just explained, and on how much you can reasonably expect a tenant to pay. Add to this sum the value to the tenants to have a house set aside for them, as long as they perform as expected (and assuming they can qualify for a loan). If the house is attractive and likely to draw many buyers, that additional value should be set appropriately high, but if the house isn't really anything special (maybe there are plenty like it on the market), the "set-aside" portion of the option will be less.

Will the option fee be refunded to a tenant who doesn't exercise the option? Most rent-to-buy agreements say no. However, allowing this fee to go toward the tenant's down payment is a common feature of these contracts (although this means that the landlord is effectively not charging for the privilege of giving the tenant the right to buy the house).

> ⓘ **CAUTION**
> **This isn't play money.** A savvy tenant will require you to hold any amounts meant to go toward the down payment in an escrow account, to be released when the sale occurs. Your tenant may also negotiate a term in your option agreement stating that regular rent payments will go straight toward your home mortgage, real estate taxes, and homeowners' insurance, to avoid the possibility that you'll go into foreclosure on the home while the tenant is working toward exercising the option.

Sale Price of the House

When you give a tenant an option to buy, you'll need to either name the house sale price in your option contract or supply an objective way in which that price can be determined later. Naming the price now has the advantage of certainty, but it means that you risk misreading the market. You may specify a sale price that turns out to be less than actual market value at the time of sale, leaving you frustrated that you can't put the house on the open market. Of course, it's also possible that you'll misjudge the other way and end up with a set price that is unrealistically high, given the market value at the time the option is exercised.

Because both owner and tenant are often leery of the risks just explained, they often choose a different approach. You can avoid risk of misjudgment by deferring the price, but you must set up a fail-safe method for arriving at it. For example, your contract might say, "Market value as determined by licensed brokers, one each chosen by landlord and tenant; and if the brokers cannot agree, the price to be determined by a third who will be chosen by the two brokers." That's far better than simply saying, "Fair market value at the time the option is exercised," or "Price to be negotiated at the time," or even "fair market value based on at least two appraisals." All of these leave wide open the possibility that you and the tenant won't be able to agree on a price or a way to mediate your dispute. In such a situation, you will not be able to go to court and get a judge to settle the house price for you. The option will fall apart.

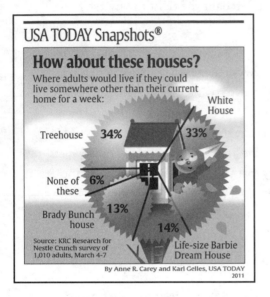

Although providing a clear method for arriving at the fair market value removes the possibility that the deal will fall apart over price disagreements, it has a significant downside: The tenant will have to exercise the option before knowing the price he or she will be expected to pay. The tenant can, of course, do some homework and arrive at a figure that probably should be the ultimate price, but there's no guarantee that this estimate will match the price chosen by the neutral experts. Tenants can end up overextended and feeling cheated in these situations, making for a difficult or impossible sale. If some of the tenants' up-front fee or rent payments were meant to go toward the down payment on the sale, and the sale falls through, your contract may well say that you don't have to return those amounts—but you'll have a doubly angry tenant (or soon to be ex-tenant). The tenant might even start looking for possible grounds upon which to sue you.

When the Tenant Must Exercise the Option

You'll want to give the tenant a specific window of time, or a deadline, by which to tell you that he or she is exercising the option. You may specify that the option be exercised within several months in advance of the end of the underlying lease—this gives you time to begin planning for a sale or a successor tenant. Or, you could set a deadline (like the ending date of the lease), and allow exercise at any time before that, regardless of the amount of time left on the underlying lease (exercise of the option will terminate the lease).

If there's a chance that you will extend the lease, be aware that the option to buy may or may not be extended with it. It all depends on the way judges in your state view the matter, and on what your extension and the original option contract have to say. From the landlord's point of view, it's best to leave nothing to interpretation, and to provide for termination of the option contract when the original lease term ends; then, if you wish, you can specifically extend the option to buy into the renewed lease term (and possibly negotiate better terms, too).

Similarly, it's not clear what might happen to the tenant's option if you allow the tenant to stay on, as a holdover tenant (particularly when the option's exercise period is not specified as a specific date, but rather as the end of the lease term). On the one hand, you might think that because a holdover tenant becomes a month-to-month tenant under the same conditions and terms as existed in the expired lease, the option to buy would extend to the holdover period, too. But some courts view purchase options differently, and won't carry them over to a holdover tenant. The lesson for smart landlords is to keep on top of their leases and never allow a tenant to remain as a holdover in the first place.

Seller Financing and the Tenant's Rent-Paying History

Many lease option sales involve seller financing of the sale—in other words, the tenant will make regular (most likely monthly) mortgage payments to the landlord-turned-seller instead of to a bank or another institutional lender. From a practical point of view, eliminating an institutional lender can save everyone time and save the buyer a considerable amount of money. If the tenant has conscientiously made rent payments, perhaps there's no reason why installment payments shouldn't come straight to you.

If seller financing is something you'll consider, you'll want to decide whether the tenant must have been "squeaky clean" in order to take advantage of the option—that is, whether any prior lease defaults will bar the exercise (current lease violations should give you grounds to refuse to honor the option, as explained below). For instance, you may not want a tenant who has a history of paying rent late to be able to exercise the option, because that tenant will probably have a hard time paying you back on the loan, too. (Be reasonable, though—minor and/ or one-time lease violations won't justify yanking the tenant's option right.) You may also want to insist on certain financial criteria, such as a minimum credit score.

Involve the Mortgage Lender

When tenants expect to use a mortgage lender, it makes sense for them to consult one now, even though it may be years before they take out the loan. The lender may be able to tell them how long it will take, given their current credit situation and expected earnings, to qualify for a loan. Pay attention to that interval—two to five years is typical—and consider allowing the option right and lease to last that long. If you set a shorter period, the tenant may want to exercise the option but be unable to secure a loan.

How Will the Tenant Notify You?

The manner in which you will accept the tenant's decision to exercise the option should be spelled out in advance. While oral notification is enforceable when there's a written option contract, for obvious reasons written notification is preferable. What's more, personal delivery is the best method (certified mail is a good second choice). It's essential to give your tenant a clear template to use when notifying you, like the example below.

Exercise of Option

The undersigned, _____[tenant's name]_____ , Tenant

of the premises located at _____[property address]_____ ,

hereby exercises the purchase option included or referenced in

the____[option contract]____ , dated [date contract was signed] ,

between _____[landlord's name]_____ as Landlord, and

_____[tenant's name]_____ , as Tenant, affecting the

property therein leased and known as

_____[property address]_____ .

Restrictions on the Landlord

Tenants who pay for a valuable option will expect that, should they exercise the option, they will not end up with property that has been encumbered in the meantime with burdens, such as mortgages, mechanics' liens, and so on. (But encumbrances existing at the time the option contract is entered into may come with the property if the option is exercised.) Unless the option contract specifically forbids adding new encumbrances, there's nothing to stop the landlord from adding them (or allowing them to be added). One practical step taken by tenants is to provide for the recording of the purchase option, so that it appears on the property's chain of title. Seeing an option contract may scare off would-be mortgagees. But, it won't stop the filing of a mechanics' lien.

Tenant Improvements and Rent

Many tenants will want the ability to begin improving "their" home, with the value of the improvements credited against the selling price. If you agree, be sure to consider what will happen if the tenant decides not to buy the home—will you reimburse the tenant?

Similarly, tenants may ask you to apply a portion of the rent toward a down payment. As with improvements, you'll need to address what will happen if the tenant does not exercise the option, or if the sale does not go through.

What Happens If You Need to Evict or the Tenant Breaks the Lease?

Your option contract should be very clear that the option will terminate automatically upon termination of the underlying lease. If you need to terminate the lease (if the tenant fails to pay the rent, causes damage, or otherwise gives you solid legal grounds for ending the tenancy), this will extinguish the option. Similarly, a tenant who breaks the lease, even with justification, will lose the option to buy.

To drive this point home, the option contract should specify that the tenant may exercise the option only if in "good standing" with respect to the lease. A tenant who has been terminated or evicted, or one who has left, is obviously not in good standing. Be sure you do not become obligated to return any option fees already paid.

"Right of Refusal" and "Right of Offer"

Instead of entering into a full-blown option contract, some landlords formally agree to give their tenants preferential treatment when and if the property goes on the market. In these situations, the landlord avoids some of the tricky issues mentioned above, but such agreements still have certain drawbacks.

Right of refusal

A "right of refusal" allows the tenant to match or improve on any deal the landlord hammers out with a third-party buyer. After having secured a buyer, the landlord must give the tenant an opportunity to buy the property on the same or better terms. These arrangements are nothing but a headache for a seller, because it means that any potential buyer runs the risk of having the tenant trump the deal. Knowing this, buyers won't bother going through the effort of negotiating with these sellers, and seasoned brokers (on both sides) avoid these situations like the plague.

USA TODAY Snapshots®

Who do we get our financial advice from?

Family members **43%**

Financial advisers **36%**

Source: Sun Life Unretirement Index survey of 1,451 adults 18 to 66.

By Jae Yang and Sam Ward, USA TODAY
2010

Right of offer

A "right of offer" is much milder. The landlord promises to give the tenant the first opportunity to buy the home at the price named by the landlord. If the tenant declines, the home goes on the market. The landlord must not artificially inflate the offering price in order to get rid of the tenant, but must name a commercially reasonable price. As many sellers find out, however, sometimes you don't really know what the house will go for. Selling at your named price might deprive you of a lucrative bidding war (which the tenant could always join at that point, too).

Landlords do not give away rights of first refusal or offer—like options, these rights come at a price.

Get Legal Advice

Think long and hard about whether your interests would be served by giving tenants an option to buy, or even rights of first refusal or offer. If you decide to go ahead, consult an attorney who specializes in real estate law and a tax specialist before signing any contract. Remember, you're dealing with a very expensive investment. And once a tenant exercises an option to buy, it's the same as an irrevocable sales contract. Structuring the option contract (or offer rights) and the attendant sales contract in ways that do not protect your interests could be financially disastrous. ●

Renting Out a Room in Your Home

The exit strategies in Chapters 11 and 12 have focused on getting rid of the rental property, in various ways. But if you can envisage yourself living in the property (or already live there) and renting out a room, this may be a strategy that's right for you.

Most landlords keep their homes and their rental properties separate—they don't share their own homes with lodgers. But in recent years, an increasing number of homeowners have chosen to offer one or more rooms for rent. Often, the motivation is strictly financial (people need the income in order to pay the mortgage). Others simply want the company of another person in the home—whether it's for socializing or to provide the extra security of having someone else around—and the rent money is a bonus.

"Tenants" and "Lodgers": What's the Difference?

A lodger is someone who has a bedroom (and perhaps a bathroom, too) in somebody's home, and enjoys the use of common areas such as the kitchen and living room. Legally, the lodger has "non-exclusive use" of these shared facilities.

Tenants, on the other hand, rent space that is theirs exclusively. The landlord can't offer the space to anyone else, and even the landlord has restricted access to the premises (most states specify the permissible reasons for landlords to enter tenants' rented homes).

The legal difference between lodgers and tenants becomes important in at least two ways. As explained below, homeowners who rent to no more than one lodger may avoid some dictates of the federal antidiscrimination laws. And if you need to evict a lodger, the rules are a bit different, too (see below).

While all landlords want someone who will pay their rent on time, keep their property in good condition, and not cause any legal or practical problems, there are additional things to consider when you plan to share space with a lodger. The lodger must not only have all the good tenant traits discussed in Chapter 4, but must be someone with whom you feel comfortable and secure. This chapter highlights some of the special considerations involved with renting a room in your home—and will help make sure you choose the right kind of lodger to have around. Keep in mind that the focus here is more traditional rental situations, with long-term lodgers, not short-term renters who come through Airbnb or a similar site. See "Is Airbnb or VRBO for You?" in Chapter 1 for more on this subject.

Is Renting a Room to a Lodger for You?

Here are some questions to consider before you start looking for a lodger.

- **Is it legal?** Zoning may be an issue: If your neighborhood is zoned for single-family residences only, operating a "rooming house," even if you have only one roomer, may violate that law. Or, if you own a condo or townhouse in a planned unit development, the homeowners' association rules (CC&Rs) may restrict you from bringing in a lodger.

- **Do you have the space?** A good-sized bedroom (ideally, furnished with a comfortable bed, along with adequate storage and lighting) and separate bath are ideal. You may have to spend some money to fix up your run-down den before you rent it out.

- **How much rent you can collect?** Before you start dreaming of all the money a lodger will bring in, do some homework. Start by checking out comparable rates on Craigslist and local college housing offices. Then subtract the additional costs of having a lodger (such as higher utility and household supplies bills).

- **How do tax deductions fit into your bottom line?** Figuring out the amount of money you'll net from bringing in a lodger involves calculating the tax benefits of renting out a room. Many of the tax deductions available to landlords who rent out entire properties (discussed in Chapter 6) apply to lodger rentals, but you must divide certain expenses between the room you rent out and the part of the house you live in. For example, if you install new wall-to-wall carpet in the entire downstairs of your house, you can deduct only the expenses for the room you are renting out (not the costs associated with installing new carpet outside of the lodger's room).

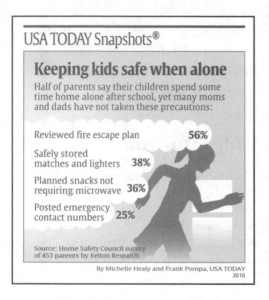

When it comes to expenses for your entire home (such as replacing the roof or installing a security system), you'll need to divide these expenses between the room you rent and the rest of the house—for example, by dividing the expenses based on the number of rooms in your home or the square footage of your house. *Every Landlord's Tax Deduction Guide*, by Stephen Fishman (Nolo), discusses special tax issues involved with renting out a room in your home. Questions to ask yourself include:

- **What is your motivation for bringing in a lodger?** It's one thing to look for a lodger who will be pleasant to have around; it's quite another entirely to expect this person to perform any kind of work or even commit to being at home for specified hours. If you need a caregiver for your elderly parent or child care for your kids, a rent-paying lodger is not the way to go. Instead, consider a caregiver or a nanny. (Finding and working with nannies is covered in Nolo's *Nannies & Au Pairs: Hiring In-Home Child Care*, by Ilona Bray.)

- **Is there a market for the room—and for the type of lodger you want?** If you're in a college town, you may well find plenty of prospects. Then again, if you're a 60-year-old woman, you might not be interested in sharing your house with an 18-year-old. Or perhaps there's a market for your room, but only for seven or eight months of the year.

- **Who is your ideal lodger (and would such a person want to rent a room in your home)?** Sharing your home can be intense (especially if you've never lived with roommates or a large family). You'll want to think long and hard about the kind of person you want to live with, perhaps:

  - Someone who will take care of your dogs when you're on one of your regular business trips or someone who will be gone most weekends?

  - A private, quiet person who pretty much keeps to him- or herself, or an outgoing social type who is happy to share meals and watch TV with you?

  - Someone who eats all meals out or someone who takes over your kitchen three times a day and loves to hold dinner parties?

  - Someone who shares the same values and interests? If you're a vegan or marathon runner, you may not want to live with someone who's grilling steaks every weekend or whose only form of exercise is walking to the car.

- **Do you have children living at home?** If so, you will want to be especially conscientious about choosing a lodger, particularly if the person will be home alone with your children.

- **Are you willing to do the work required to keep the place in good shape?** You may need to make some initial repairs before renting out a room—and be prepared to do so during the lodger's stay. A torn carpet or leaky faucet might not bother you, but they might annoy a lodger.

- **Do you need additional insurance?** Check with your agent to see whether bringing in a lodger will affect your homeowners' insurance (additional costs may at least be tax deductible).

Lodgers and Discrimination

The federal laws that prohibit housing discrimination (discussed in Chapter 4) do not apply to owner-occupied properties of four units or less. Nor do they apply to homeowners who rent out a room in their own home—with one important exception. While you may make decisions that would otherwise expose you to a charge of discrimination, you may not advertise or make statements in a way that indicates a preference (or avoidance) based on a protected group.

In other words, you may decide not to rent to a prospective lodger after meeting this person and learning that he or she is of a certain race, religion, and so on; but if you post an advertisement that reflects your wishes, and if you communicate your preferences to the actual applicant, you're breaking the law. Rather tellingly, this rule is known as "discrimination at the door."

Discrimination at the door does, however, have one exception under federal law. If you have no more than one lodger, you may advertise for a lodger of a specific gender—but that's all. For instance, it's okay to seek "Female lodger wanted," but not okay to say, "Christian lodger wanted."

Various U.S. states have also weighed in on the lodger question, and may have even tighter restrictions.

- **Do you have the personality for this?** If you've been living alone for quite some time, or really value your privacy, or realize you'll have to give up turning the music loud and dancing around the living room, renting out a room may simply not be for you. If certain personality types drive you crazy, you'll want to be sure to weed these people out during the interview process.

Sharing Your Home With More Than One Lodger

If your house is especially large, you may consider bringing in more than one lodger. If so, you'll need to consider how everyone in the house gets along (not just you and the lodger). And as noted above, renting to a lodger may technically violate zoning rules if you live in a single-family-only zone. While it's not too likely that your neighbors will object to one roomer, they may feel differently when multiple people begin parking in their favorite spots, and increasing the noise and activity level of a previously quiet neighborhood.

Basic Steps to Renting Out a Room

Once you've determined that bringing in a lodger makes sense, follow the same basic steps discussed earlier in this book for renting out a room in your home:

- Fix up the room for rent and make other necessary changes in your home.
- Identify your key terms and policies by drafting a rental agreement (a month-to-month contract that can be terminated on short notice). Be sure to cover issues such as kitchen etiquette, quiet times, guests, home business restrictions, shared chores, and so on. California owners can use Nolo's "Renting Out a Room in Your California Home," available as an online form at www.nolo.com.
- Decide the places to advertise for or spread the word about the type of lodgers you want: word-of-mouth, a college housing office, and/or Craigslist are a few possibilities.
- Interview prospects, and give likely candidates a rental application and full disclosure on how the household needs to be run. Be candid and clear here—if you are a neatnik, now's the time to say so. If you don't, you face a future full of silent (or not-so-silent) resentment.

- We'll say it again: Talk more with your prospective lodger about practical issues like pets, noise, drinking, TV preferences, music tastes—everything about your living situation that's important to you.
- Sign a rental agreement.
- Get the lodger moved in.

Checking References and Credit

Landlords who rent apartments or houses have learned to be diligent when checking out prospective tenants (many have learned the hard way). The only way they know whether a prospect will likely be a good tenant (pay the rent, take reasonable care of the property, not cause problems with other tenants, neighbors, or the landlord) is to question former landlords and check the applicant's credit report.

You can and should take some of the same steps when choosing a lodger. Ask for references from former landlords or neighbors or employers. A college transcript of a student renter will tell you loads—good grades and an absence of "incompletes" indicates some degree of seriousness and follow-through.

You won't be able to order a credit report from a credit reporting agency, however, unless you go through the tedious step of establishing your qualifications for handling credit reports (in recent years, Congress has required those who handle these documents to prove to the credit reporting agencies that they have a safe and secure physical setup in their office). Instead, ask applicants to bring a current copy of their report (people can obtain free reports from www.AnnualCreditReport.com or by calling 877-322-8228). If you want to be extra sure that the report has not been doctored, ask the applicant to sit down with you at your computer and order a report on the spot, which you can examine immediately.

Index